HOME RICH

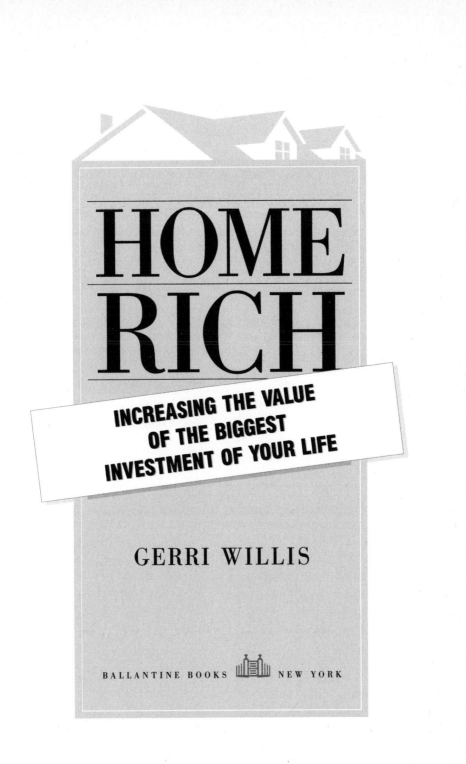

HOME
RICH

INCREASING THE VALUE
OF THE BIGGEST
INVESTMENT OF YOUR LIFE

GERRI WILLIS

BALLANTINE BOOKS   NEW YORK

Published in the United States by Ballantine Books, an imprint of The Random
House Publishing Group, a division of Random House, Inc., New York.

BALLANTINE and colophon are registered trademarks of Random House, Inc.

Library of Congress Cataloging-in-Publication Data
Willis, Gerri.
Home rich : increasing the value of the biggest investment of your life / Gerri Willis.
p.   cm.
Includes index.
ISBN 978-0-345-49044-5 (hardcover : alk. paper)
1. House buying—United States.   2. Home ownership—United States.
3. Dwellings—Remodeling—United States.   4. House selling—United States.
5. Real estate investment—United States.   I. Title.
HD259.W55   2008
643'.120973—dc22   2007032354

Printed in the United States of America on acid-free paper

www.ballantinebooks.com

2   4   6   8   9   7   5   3

Book design by Susan Turner

To my husband, David, without whose patience, support, and slow-braised short ribs this book would never have been written

Preface

A REAL ESTATE EXPERT I KNOW SAYS THAT INVESTING IN REAL ESTATE IS an exercise best left to the professionals. Mere homeowners, he says, should be satisfied with the mortgage deduction and leave it at that. And after seeing the downdraft in home prices over the last couple of years, many folks may be inclined to agree. I am not one of them. My view is this: anything that commands 30 to 35 percent of my income month in and month out had better give me a decent return for my trouble!

If you feel the same way, then *Home Rich* is for you. This book focuses on making your home a solid investment. In the coming pages, you'll learn how to analyze your own financial situation to determine how much house you should buy, whether upgrading makes sense financially, and how to save money when it comes time to sell. I'll introduce you to the single most important number for home owners—no, not home price, but home *equity*—and show you how to grow yours. You'll see firsthand how successful homeowners have transformed their primary home into a lucrative investment and what it takes to cash in that investment when you sell.

This process is far from intuitive and takes extensive planning. While your parents may have been able to rely on inflation to double or triple their initial investment today's homeowners have to be savvier. In fact, the biggest threat to their investment isn't the market, it's the fact that they will stay in it a far shorter time than their parents—just nine years on average. That means that you have to view your home as a medium-term investment rather than a long-term one. But this challenge can be met, and *Home Rich* is your trusted guide as you go through this sometimes difficult process.

While most books focus simply on buying and selling, *Home Rich* takes readers through the whole life cycle of homeownership. After all, even if you buy a terrific house, you'll have to maintain it well over your years of ownership or risk losing the advantage of your savvy initial choice. You'll learn about the critical steps to take in managing and upgrading your home, transforming it into one that will not only attract the next buyer but also be a warm and inviting environment for your family. That's because every successful real estate investment must also be a home as well.

Contents

UPGRADING

SELLING

HOME RICH

1

The Rules

WHEN GREG WAS TRANSFERRED TO WASHINGTON, D.C., HIS WIFE, STACEY, knew immediately she wanted to move to Fairfax County, Virginia. Her family had lived in the area for years and the commute into Washington was a breeze. Unfortunately, the couple had to start their search right in the middle of the spring buyers' frenzy and were competing with other families eager to get into a new home before the school year started. Soon after their search began, they discovered a neighborhood that boasted a pool and tennis club that residents automatically belonged to. And, days later, the couple walked into an open house for a cozy ranch with skylights and new carpeting in every room. The only downside was a strange mildewy odor—but the sellers assured them they had taken care of the problem. The pressure to move quickly was high. Seven other couples at the open house were eager to buy. Greg and Stacey decided they would have to put together a strong offer quickly to compete. They bid the asking price of $669,000. Stacey even wrote a thank-you note to the owners to improve the chances of their bid being accepted. The price tag was a little more than they had anticipated spending, but the

two agreed they could afford their prize if they kept their spending on extras to a minimum. They won the bidding war, but just a month after they moved in, they discovered that the mildewy odor was a symptom of a much bigger water problem: water soaked the basement carpet. They gutted the room down to its studs and installed a new drainage system, as well as a new carpet, wainscoting, and furniture. But that was only a prelude to the problems created a year later by a massive rainstorm.

"At five o'clock on a Sunday morning I heard water running," Stacey recalls. "I went downstairs, and it was like a levee had broken—there was water coming through the wall, up from under the floorboards, everything." Greg and Stacey worked like a bucket brigade emptying the house of water. More renovations ensued.

In the first two years of owning the house, they had to replace several skylights, fix leaky soffits, and excavate the backyard to install French drains. The price tag—a total of nearly $36,000—was sizeable and unexpected. Because the two were stretching to buy the house in the first place, they had little room in their budget to finance the repairs. Greg tapped his retirement fund to pay for the biggest repairs, but the problems left the family strapped. Had the two been in less of a rush and hired an inspector, they would have been spared the setback.

Compare their situation with that of Ted and Barbara. At the time the two decided they had outgrown their Queens, New York, condo, the market couldn't have been more hostile to buyers. Prices were on the rise in Westchester County, where they had decided to move. Attractive homes were drawing multiple bids and bidding wars. If ever there were a time for buyers to hold up and wait, this was it. But the couple came up with a strategy that allowed them to find a home that fit their needs yet didn't break their budget.

They started by investigating neighborhoods. They quickly ruled out the most expensive ones, such as Scarsdale and Bronxville, where competition was the most heated and the potential for overbidding high. And they knew they didn't want to move too far away from their jobs—Ted worked in Queens, while Barbara worked in Manhattan. When Ted's boss suggested they check out his commuter town, Sleepy

Hollow, they liked what they saw. Prices in the town were high but not stratospheric. When they found a quaint bungalow with some maintenance issues, they pounced. Exterior paint was peeling and interior hardwood floors had been badly damaged by renters. The kitchen hadn't been updated in years. Rhododendrons had been allowed to grow nearly to the eaves, and the overall appearance from the outside caused many potential buyers to drive past without even seeing the interior. After confirming the house had no structural issues, the two decided to buy—driven mostly by the idea that the house was well priced for the neighborhood at $475,000. Because the two were able to purchase the house at such an attractive price, they could spend money on upgrades. They had the cramped kitchen stripped out and updated with roomy oak cabinets and stainless-steel appliances. They repainted the house, warming up rooms with rich colors to replace the faded creams and whites. The floors were refinished. The exterior was painted a sophisticated gray-green and the shrubs trimmed or removed altogether. Within a few short months of buying, the house was transformed. "We were enthusiastically welcomed by our neighbors," said Ted. "Most commented they really had never been able to see just how beautiful the house was beneath all those overgrown shrubs. One neighbor even said she would have bought the house long ago had she known what was hidden beneath. That's a great feeling."

After the two had completed the transformation of their home, they set their sights on a real eyesore house in the neighborhood to buy, fix up, and sell—an investment they never would have been able to even consider had they not bought so advantageously in the first place.

Greg and Stacey's failure to investigate the musty odors they smelled during their initial visit ultimately cost them tens of thousands of dollars, stealing any money they might have used for upgrades, while Ted and Barbara's careful investment will likely reap strong returns. Most of the pair's gains will come from sweat equity, but it's no small part of the equation that they also simply bought right, hedging their risks by buying well within their budget and carefully choosing both their neighborhood and their house.

Over the years, Americans have discovered that home ownership is

one of the most reliable methods for building wealth in this country. You
may have seen this firsthand in your own family. Did your grandparents
retire on the proceeds of selling their house? Did Mom and Dad finance
a second home or your education by tapping their home equity? A consumer survey regularly conducted by the Federal Reserve reveals that
the biggest nest egg owned by people entering their retirement years
isn't a 401(k) or IRA, it's their house. And it's little wonder that our
homes are the single most valuable thing we own. A mortgage is an en-
forced savings plan. Unlike investing in your 401(k), for example, you
can't stop paying your mortgage because there's another, more pressing
bill on hand. But it's not just the consistency with which we pay for our
homes that ultimately makes them an attractive investment.

Home values have increased an average of 6.6 percent each year
since 1968, according to the National Association of Realtors. That's less
than the returns on stocks and bonds during the same period. But to
make a true comparison, you need to take into account all the financial
benefits you get from home ownership. The mortgage interest deduction is the fattest tax break most households enjoy. Plus, Uncle Sam also
lets you exclude as much as $500,000 in gains when you sell. The point
isn't that you shouldn't invest in stocks or bonds—you should be well di-
versified, and that means investing in all three: stocks, bonds, and real
estate—but you need to think of your home not just as the place you
live but as an investment you can use to your advantage.

To be sure, real estate can experience negative price appreciation.
Prices can and do go down as well as up. Still, housing returns over the
long haul compare favorably with anything else you're likely to put your
money into, plus there is also a unique advantage to investing in real estate: personal control. For most of us, mutual fund managers or brokers
decide when to buy and sell our stock and bond investments, but with
real estate, you decide when to get into a market or leave it. Likewise,
you decide when to make upgrades to your home and how much to
spend. You determine how much money goes into maintenance. It's
these decisions that will make the difference between a poor investment
and a great one.

We live differently than our parents did—we move more often, we don't buy and hold for decades. For that reason, we have to be much savvier, whether we are buyers or sellers. The stakes in managing your investment intelligently are higher than ever because people stay in their homes an average of just nine years, according to the American Housing Survey for the United States: 2005. In other words, these days homes are more of a medium-term investment than a long-term one. That means if you make a mistake, time isn't on your side. Covering up mistakes becomes difficult because you won't have thirty years of appreciation to make up for a misstep. What's more, the homes you're likely to encounter when you buy may have few, if any, of the features on your wish list. The average home in this country was built thirty years ago, and its architects could hardly anticipate our desires for open floor plans and light-filled rooms, or the fact that many of our homes now accommodate multiple generations. This book will show you how to make smart decisions about your home, from buying it to living in it, changing it, and selling it. *Home Rich* presents a plan you can follow whether the market is rising relentlessly or falling fast. In the end, if you follow the rules of this book and manage your investment wisely, your home will become the best investment you ever make.

To use this book effectively, you can either follow its advice through the entire process of home ownership or dip into it when you need help. It helps, though, to make the right choices from the beginning. Nothing is more important to becoming home rich than choosing the right home to buy in the first place. Price, of course, is critical. Pay too much and you may never get back even your original investment. The condition of the house matters greatly, too. Pick a house with problems and you may be forced to blow your entire renovation budget on repairs you never anticipated. In Chapters 2 through 8, you'll learn the steps to picking the right house: understanding how much house you can afford, choosing a real estate agent to work with, researching the neighborhoods, zeroing in on the best property, and negotiating for that house. And, most important, you'll learn the importance of thinking of a house as an investment even as you shop for a home, getting beyond your ini-

tial, emotional reaction to a property to think about deeper issues, such as its broad appeal, the investments that are likely to pay off, and the health of the neighborhood.

Buying right is important, but it's not the only step in transforming your home into the best investment it can be. The mortgage you choose and the financing that you use at every turn to upgrade and maintain your home are critical. The lending options these days are various and confusing. Thirty-year fixed-rate mortgages are old hat. Bankers have devised all kinds of products to fit every imaginable consumer need. In this book you'll see detailed analysis of mortgages from conventional thirty-year fixed-rate loans to some of the industry's wackier innovations that you'll want to steer clear of, such as interest-only and nothing-down loans. Some of these newer loan products have fallen out of favor but could resurface again to tempt borrowers. In Chapter 9, you'll learn how to navigate this complicated area and when to seek professional advice. Plus, you'll learn how to calculate your equity—what you actually own—and the best ways to grow that investment.

Few of us can afford to buy the home of our dreams. In fact, it can even be difficult just to find a home that works well for our needs. Modifying your home to suit the needs of your family and potential buyers down the road is up to you. We start in Chapter 16 with a discussion of the projects that really pay off and how you can decide which is right for you. From there, you'll learn about small upgrades that make a difference. In Chapter 18, you learn about hiring contractors and what to expect from them. Next, you'll focus on what makes for successful home improvements, the range of design options, and where you can save when accomplishing the most popular upgrades. We'll consider in detail improvements to kitchens and baths for any wallet.

One investment that appeals to buyers more than ever these days is upgrades that reduce your energy bill. In Chapter 13, I'll take you on a tour of the improvements, from insulation to solar panels, that are most likely to make a difference where you live. You'll also learn about other popular green solutions, such as products that produce no or low emissions and architectural salvage.

If it's the exterior of your home you're concerned about, turn to

Chapter 14 to find out about landscaping and garden improvements that can enhance any home's appeal. Whether you live in an urban area with a tiny lot or a sprawling suburban neighborhood, we'll look at solutions that can make your property stand out from the rest. You'll also find a buyer's guide to shrubs and trees for your part of the country. Once again, our focus will be on upgrades with broad appeal that will add to your home's value.

Even if you buy the best-built house in the neighborhood, your investment will still suffer if you don't manage the house over time. Taking care of a home's systems is no easy prospect, but a well-maintained home is something home buyers can sniff out in only a few minutes. Turn to Chapter 15 for details.

Eventually you'll want to sell your castle, and when that time arrives, you'll want to do it with an eye to maximizing your investment gain. Chapters 20 through 23 will guide you through the decision-making process that will get you the best return for your biggest investment. When should you sell on your own? How much should you invest in fixing up the place before putting your home on the market? In Chapter 22, you'll learn the best strategies for selling your biggest asset at the best price.

As you read along, you'll find step-by-step advice on how to make the decisions that will make your home a solid investment. What you won't find is advice for people who want to flip homes—buy and sell them quickly—for a quick gain. That's because this book is no get-rich-quick manual. In fact, I believe that building real wealth results from carefully monitoring and investing in your home over time. You can start by understanding a few essential rules.

KNOW YOUR WALLET

It seems everybody has heard the banker's rule of thumb that you shouldn't spend more than 33 percent of your gross income on housing. But few people seem to abide by it. The ratio of mortgage debt to disposable income has doubled to 18 percent from 8.1 percent in 1980. And while you used to be able to count on lenders to make sure you weren't overspending, the truth is that they aren't taking the rule too se-

riously either. The way bankers these days determine whether you're good for your loan is by using sophisticated new computer programs. Developed by credit bureaus, these programs tell bankers whether you're conscientious about paying your bills on time. The more timely you are with payments, the more likely they are to be willing to lend to you. In other words, if you are a conscientious bill payer, it's up to you to know what to spend. Trouble is, if you make a bad decision—that is, if you choose to overspend—it's a decision that will haunt you for the entire time you own the house and jeopardize your ability to make a solid investment. To get a handle on the numbers, check out Chapter 2 to determine how much you should spend, what loan is right for you, and the costs associated with getting a mortgage. Even if you already have a mortgage, analyzing your budget is critical to making your home a good investment.

PICK A WINNING TEAM OF ADVISORS

Like having children, buying, selling, and managing a home will require backup. You'll need the best real estate agent, lawyer, and mortgage banker (or broker) possible. Many of us will also choose a contractor to make home improvements. And remember, once you identify a team of knowledgeable experts, not only will they help you find a quality home and structure a smart, favorable deal, they will also guide you through the entire process of purchasing and closing on your home. As you begin to decide how to improve and update your abode, these are also the people who will help you figure out the best moves to make. Chapters 4, 5, 18, and 20 provide a detailed guide to getting the perfect home buying, managing, and selling team for you.

LOCATION, LOCATION, LOCATION

That old saying is true. And while it sounds simple, the idea is more complicated than simply targeting your town's most expensive or prestigious neighborhood. Let's face it, most of us can't afford the old-line neighborhoods with the top amenities. For many of us the problem isn't a choice between the most expensive zip code in town and any other, it's

affording any neighborhood at all. In fact, after doing the *Home Rich* analysis, you may find that the expensive neighborhood is ripe for a tumble in prices and you may decide to avoid buying there altogether. The first step in deciding which location is right for you is doing your homework. While the temptation is to search on the Web and to focus your attentions on just the attractiveness of individual properties, in Chapter 7 you'll find out how to analyze neighborhoods' long-term attractiveness on a variety of criteria and to find the one that fits your needs.

PLAY HOUSE DETECTIVE

For some, shopping for a home is like going back to high school. You develop crushes on attractive candidates, but you can't seem to figure out which are the true trophies. Forget sentiment when you shop. Stop searching for a kitchen that resembles your grandmother's and start thinking analytically. After all, you can always remodel to make your kitchen look like Grandma's. You're better off spending your time determining two things: whether the house has "good bones," that is, whether the home's basic design and structure are sound and pleasing to the eye, and whether the fundamental systems of the house—the heating and cooling, plumbing, and electrical systems—are solid. It's up to you to uncover the truth and ferret out the homes that offer the greatest value given their qualities and flaws. Turn to Chapter 8 for tips on vetting homes and uncovering problems while they still belong to someone else. Find out how to hire a professional inspector who can do all the heavy lifting for you. And don't forget that all the skills you develop inspecting potential purchases should be applied to your own home once you buy it. The investigation shouldn't stop once you buy because you'll want to be sure new problems aren't being created on your watch.

BE A LOAN SHARK

Banks have created a myriad of different types of mortgages to satisfy every need—some offering terrific innovations on the thirty-year fixed-rate mortgage, others that are poor substitutes. There's the no-doc loan

and the 3-1, 5-1, or 7-1 ARM. You can pay interest only or—get this—even less than interest. What about a forty-year loan? No matter what your needs, it is critical to choose your financing vehicle wisely, navigating this complex arena to obtain a loan that is ideally suited to your situation. Still, not all innovation has been bad. The Web can help you shop for mortgages, understand the terminology, and even compare terms. Chapters 9 and 11 will show you how to choose the right loan and even survive the closing. Plus, you'll learn how to navigate the world of equity loans and lines of credit if you need to tap the equity you are steadily building.

BEGIN AT THE END

Before you buy, you'll want to think seriously about what improvements you plan to make, what they will cost, and how you'll pay for them. Sounds like a tall order, but unless you have a vision for developing the house in a way to improve its value, chances are you could make poor early decisions that could make it impossible to wring the best possible return out of your house. Starting early can pay big dividends. While the initial analysis that you do won't be conclusive, it should be a fairly reliable guide. In Chapter 8, you'll learn to gauge whether the home you want to buy is the most improved or the least. You'll learn the importance of how long you plan to be in that home. The goal: determining the sorts of upgrades that will make your home outshine neighbors' houses while not burning up too much equity. Using that information plus the details of your situation, you can carve out the best plan for bringing a home to its potential. In Chapter 19, we'll guide you through this analysis, including small-scale improvements that can make a difference.

RENOVATE LIKE A POPULIST, NOT AN ELITIST

When you renovate or restyle a home, it's best to temper your creativity with a little practicality. Ask yourself what it is that the next buyers are most likely to want. Is it a Jacuzzi or simply an updated kitchen? Pool or expanded deck? Sure, you want the ultimate master bedroom with over-the-top master bath fixtures, but spending $250,000 can be a disaster.

Overspending can push your home beyond the reach of the kinds of buyers you will likely attract. The reality is that most money gets spent on kitchens and bathrooms because that's where people spend most of their time, and it's where investment dollars can really shine. Chapter 19 will show you how to choose materials and designs that are sensible and have broad appeal. Plus, you'll learn the importance of making design choices that fit the tastes and predilections of the people most likely to buy a home in your neighborhood.

CRUNCH, CRUNCH, CRUNCH

People everywhere want to know whether home prices are poised to go up or down. Undoubtedly, there are few things more worrying than the idea that the sky-high price you paid for your modest bungalow will become a laughable suggestion when you are ready to sell. Truth is, appreciation is just one part of your return when you sell a house. The other part, and what many people lately have ignored, is their contribution in the form of mortgage payments and renovations. Equity includes all of that plus appreciation. If you've just bought your home in the last few years, chances are you haven't built up much of this good stuff. Equity can serve many purposes: it can be a store of emergency cash in the event that something truly awful happens, or it can be tapped to help improve the value of your property. Of course you eventually have to pay it back. But the key to doing the latter well is analyzing your local market trends and then spending that money judiciously. Go to Chapter 12 to find out how to manage your equity over time and Chapters 3 and 22 to learn about tracking price trends.

GET LUXURY FOR LESS

These days, luxury doesn't simply mean more space. Let's face it, those sprawling McMansions once may have seemed like exclusive retreats. But now with energy prices on the rise, they're criticized as expensive Sheetrock palaces. The real way to boost your luxury quotient is with high-end finishes and carefully chosen design elements. The idea of extending taste and style throughout your home is a trend that is hard to

ignore. Think of it as luxury living without the mansion. As a smart
homeowner focused on the value of your home, you're better off con-
centrating on features and fit rather than square footage. Chapter 17
shows you how to increase the elegance of the interior of your home
without incurring a high price tag. Chapter 14 will help you find the
luxury finishes that won't break the bank for your garden and yard.

PRIORITIZE YOUR IMPROVEMENTS

It's all well and good to add an outdoor Jacuzzi to the deck off your master bedroom, but you might be better off making simpler improvements
first, such as updating the baths and kitchens. Understanding the improvements that will add the most value to your home is key while
keeping in mind how long you plan to live there and when exactly you
plan to sell. The tendency is to become obsessed with the renovation
that gets the most ink in home design magazines, such as the outdoor
kitchen with all the bells and whistles. You're far better off evaluating
your specific property and what would make it more appealing to potential buyers. See Chapter 19 to get details on picking the right renovation.

CONSIDER GOING GREEN

Forget Earth shoes and composting. While getting off the grid is a worthy goal, the truth is that for homeowners who've bought an older
house, the price of producing enough energy to make their home self-
sustaining is too high to be cost-effective, especially in the short run.
Those photovoltaic solar panels and thermosiphon water heating systems are pricey. However, you can do your bit for the universe and see a
return on your investment by picking up on some green trends. Go to
Chapter 13 for tips on going green.

CASH IN WITH CARE

Getting the most for your carefully managed investment requires you to
be smart about how you put your home on the market and manage the
selling process. If, like most of us, you own your home for just nine years,

you could own five to six homes over your lifetime. That means you'll want to manage your home carefully. Selling with an eye toward getting the best return on your investment is handled in Chapters 20 to 23.

To be sure, buying and managing a home is a complicated process. But it doesn't have to be impossible, and it certainly should have a financial reward. *Home Rich* is here to help you achieve those goals and enjoy your investment at the same time. Good luck as you start your journey.

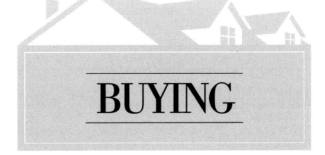

BUYING

2

How Much House Can You Afford?

SPENDING THE RIGHT AMOUNT FOR YOUR HOUSE IS CRITICAL TO MAK-
ing a good investment. If you agree to spend more than you can afford,
you set yourself up for all kinds of problems, from picking a mortgage
that is too risky to scaling back on regular maintenance. And in a market where prices are falling, you risk financial disaster if you spend more
than you ought. Imagine: if you stretch to buy that $400,000 castle and
it falls in value by 15 percent, your investment is now worth $340,000.
If you have just $40,000 in equity, you'd have to put cash down if you
were forced to sell because you'd still owe the bank $20,000. (Here's the
math: your original debt of $400,000 minus the sale price of $340,000
is $60,000 you owe the bank, minus your $40,000 equity is $20,000.)
And that doesn't even cover sales commissions. Owing more than a
house is worth, commonly called being upside down in your mortgage,
is a worst-case scenario, but one easily avoided if you do the research you
need to make sure you can afford the house you want to buy.

Finding the magic number, however, requires some homework. First
off, you'll want to understand the rules of thumb that set spending
guidelines. Spend no more than 28 to 33 percent of your gross income

on housing—that's called the housing expense ratio by lenders. Another way to look at it is this: you won't want to spend more than 36 to 38 percent of your income on overall debt—called your total obligation ratio. Now, you're probably wondering why there is a range in each case of two to three percentage points. The difference is this: buyers qualifying for what the government calls "conforming loans," that is, loans for less than $417,000, must meet the 28 percent limit for housing expenses and 36 percent for total obligations. If your loan is bigger, a so-called jumbo loan, you'll be allowed to stretch a little further, spending 33 percent of your income on housing and 38 percent on total debt. Below, you'll calculate how much house you can afford using both the total obligation ratio and the housing expense ratio. For safety, go with the calculation that provides the most conservative budget.

Here's how to put these rules of thumb to work. To begin figuring out how much you can borrow, start with getting a handle on your income. Calculate your gross monthly salary, which you can do based on pay stubs. Next, you'll want to come up with a cold, hard estimate of any additional income you can expect to earn each and every year. This is trickier than it sounds, particularly for salespeople who work on commission or others who have volatile income for any reason. What lenders are looking for are verifiable estimates of additional income. For that reason, you'll want to use an additional-income figure that you've actually been able to earn and have receipts for during the past two years.

Below, you'll calculate your income for the purposes of buying a house. Next, you'll calculate your monthly carrying costs, and finally, you'll determine exactly how much how you can afford.

Step 1: Determining Income

1. Gross monthly salary _____
2. Bonuses, commissions _____
3. Divide line 2 by 12 _____
4. Add lines 1 and 3 _____

This equals your true monthly income, what bankers call your "qualifying income."

Next, you'll figure out how much house you can afford using the housing ratio. This calculation will help you determine how much of your income you can afford to pay for housing. In order to get a realistic sense of this cost, you'll need to include property taxes, utilities, insurance, and maintenance costs. To get an estimate of property taxes, contact the local tax assessor's office in the town you're planning to buy in for an average. You'll also need to estimate your utilities costs on a monthly basis. Fortunately, the federal government does it for you at www.fns.usda.gov/FSP/rules/Memo/SUAAlpha.htm. An estimate of homeowner's insurance is even easier. The national average is $56 per month, but you can find state-by-state estimates by clicking on the "Media" link at the Insurance Information Institute's website at www.iii.org. Getting a sense of maintenance costs will require a bit of chicken-and-egg calculation. In other words, you need to know the value of your house before you know maintenance costs, which typically run 1 to 2 percent of your home's value. For a home value of $224,900, that would mean maintenance costs of $2,249 to $4,498 annually, or $374 to $562 a month. To find values appropriate to where you want to live, ask your local Realtors organization for the area's median value.

Step 2: Your Home-Operating Costs

5. Monthly property taxes _____
6. Monthly utilities costs _____
7. Monthly homeowner's insurance costs _____
8. Monthly maintenance costs _____
9. Total _____

The number on line 9 gives you a more realistic idea of your monthly carrying costs for owning a home. Next, you'll calculate the portion of your monthly income that should be spent for housing and how well it fits your budget.

Step 3: Your Monthly House Budget

10. Multiply your monthly income
    (see line 4 from step 1) by 0.28 _____

11. Subtract line 9 from line 10 _____

If you have a number of long-term obligations such as college debt or alimony, you will want to incorporate it into your calculations. Go back to step 1 and grab your qualifying monthly income number. Next, consider your other monthly obligations.

Step 4: Adding Long-Term Obligations

12. Multiply your monthly income
    (line 4 from step 1) by 0.36 _____

13. Monthly credit card debt _____

14. Monthly car payments _____

15. Monthly student loan payments or school tuition _____

16. Child support or alimony _____

17. Monthly life insurance payments _____

18. Monthly payments for any other loan or note _____

19. Total _____

Now you have a firm idea of your monthly long-term obligations. The next step is to calculate how much you can spend each month for housing given your total debt.

Step 5: Your Bottom Line

20. Add your monthly carrying costs for the home from line 9,
    step 2 from the previous statement and your long-term debt
    from step 4 above _____

21. Subtract line 20 from the figure you calculated in line 12,
    which is the maximum you should be paying each month for
    all of your debt. This is how much you should have available
    for your monthly mortgage _____

If this number is negative, then you'll need to rethink your budget by paying off a long-term obligation or delaying a home purchase until your income rises.

Finally, compare line 11 (this is how much you can afford to spend for your mortgage each month given your income and the additional costs of owning a home beyond the mortgage) and line 20 (how much you can afford to spend on your mortgage each month given all your debt). To be conservative, budget the smaller of the two figures for your mortgage each month. Of course, you'll also want to take into consideration how much you have to put down as a down payment. In recent years, lenders have allowed credit-worthy buyers to put little or nothing down. But you'd be well advised to put some of your money into your investment. This will give you immediate equity in the house and a safety net if something goes wrong. What's more, if you put down less than 20 percent, you'll have to pay your lender for private mortgage insurance until your equity hits 20 percent. And putting down a healthy amount at closing will also reduce your monthly mortgage costs. Use step 6 to calculate the impact of your down payment on your monthly mortgage.

Step 6: The Down Payment

1. Enter your maximum budget from line 21 on previous worksheet _____

2. Divide line 1 by 0.80 if you're putting down 20 percent, 0.90 if you are putting down 10 percent. If you're only putting down 5 percent, divide by 0.95. This is your monthly mortgage obligation, including your down payment _____

Now that you know how much you can afford to spend each month on housing given your debt and your down payment, you'll want to know how big a loan you can qualify for given the interest rate you are likely to pay. For that, check out the HSH Autoqual Table.

Match the maximum monthly payment you can afford at the bottom of the columns with the term you plan to pay off your loan, either fifteen or thirty years. Locate the interest rate you are likely to pay on the left (you can get current rates offered by banks in your area at www.hsh.com). Where these three items come together is the amount you can borrow. Remember, though, this is an upper ceiling on spending. You can spend less. In fact, you probably should. Spending less will give you wiggle room if the unexpected happens, such as illness in the family or the loss of a job.

HSH® AUTOQUAL TABLE™

Rate %	15 Year	30 Year	15 Year	30 Year	15 Year	30 Year	15 Year	30 Year	15 Year	30 Year
4.000	101.4	157.1	135.2	209.4	169.0	261.8	202.8	314.2	236.6	366.6
4.125	100.5	154.8	134.1	206.3	167.6	257.9	201.1	309.5	234.6	361.1
4.250	99.7	152.5	132.9	203.3	166.2	254.1	199.4	304.9	232.6	355.7
4.375	98.8	150.2	131.8	200.3	164.8	250.4	197.7	300.4	230.7	350.5
4.500	98.0	148.0	130.7	197.4	163.4	246.7	196.1	296.0	228.8	345.4
4.625	97.2	145.9	129.6	194.5	162.0	243.1	194.5	291.7	226.9	340.4
4.750	96.4	143.8	128.6	191.7	160.7	239.6	192.8	287.6	225.0	335.5
4.875	95.6	141.7	127.5	188.9	159.4	236.2	191.3	283.4	223.1	330.7
5.000	94.8	139.7	126.5	186.2	158.0	232.8	189.6	279.4	221.2	325.9
5.125	94.0	137.7	125.4	183.6	156.7	229.5	188.1	275.4	219.4	321.4
5.250	93.2	135.8	124.3	181.0	155.4	226.3	186.5	271.6	217.6	316.9
5.375	92.5	133.9	123.3	178.5	154.2	223.2	185.0	267.8	215.9	312.5
5.500	91.7	132.0	122.3	176.1	152.9	220.1	183.5	264.1	214.1	308.2
5.625	91.0	130.2	121.3	173.7	151.7	217.1	182.0	260.5	212.5	304.0
5.750	90.3	128.5	120.4	171.3	150.5	214.1	180.6	257.0	210.7	299.8
5.875	89.5	126.7	119.4	169.0	149.3	211.3	179.1	253.5	209.0	295.8
6.000	88.8	125.0	118.5	166.7	148.1	208.4	177.7	250.1	207.3	291.8
6.125	88.1	123.4	117.5	164.5	146.9	205.7	176.3	246.8	205.7	288.0
6.250	87.4	121.8	116.6	162.4	145.7	203.0	174.9	243.6	204.1	284.2
6.375	86.7	120.2	115.7	160.2	144.6	200.3	173.5	240.4	202.4	280.6
6.500	86.0	118.6	114.7	158.2	143.4	197.7	172.1	237.3	200.8	276.8
6.625	85.4	117.1	113.8	156.1	142.3	195.2	170.8	234.2	199.3	273.3
6.750	84.7	115.6	113.0	154.1	141.2	192.7	169.5	231.2	197.7	269.8
6.875	84.0	114.1	112.1	152.2	140.1	190.2	168.1	228.3	196.2	266.3

Rate %	15 Year	30 Year	15 Year	30 Year	15 Year	30 Year	15 Year	30 Year	15 Year	30 Year
7.000	83.4	112.7	111.2	150.3	139.0	187.8	166.8	225.4	194.6	263.0
7.125	82.7	111.3	110.3	148.4	137.9	185.5	165.5	222.6	193.1	259.7
7.250	82.1	109.9	109.5	146.5	136.9	183.2	164.3	219.8	191.7	256.5
7.375	81.5	108.5	108.7	144.7	135.8	180.9	163.0	217.1	190.2	253.3
7.500	80.9	107.2	107.8	143.0	134.8	178.7	161.8	214.5	188.7	250.2
7.625	80.2	105.9	107.0	141.2	133.8	176.6	160.5	211.9	187.3	247.2
7.750	79.6	104.6	106.2	139.5	132.7	174.4	159.3	209.3	185.9	244.2
7.875	79.0	103.4	105.4	137.9	131.7	172.3	158.1	206.8	184.5	241.3
8.000	78.4	102.2	104.6	136.2	130.8	170.3	156.9	204.4	183.1	238.4
8.125	77.8	101.0	103.8	134.6	129.8	168.3	155.7	202.0	181.7	235.6
8.250	77.3	99.8	103.0	133.1	128.8	166.3	154.6	199.6	180.3	232.9
8.375	76.7	98.6	102.3	131.5	127.8	164.4	153.5	197.3	179.0	230.2
8.500	76.1	97.5	101.5	130.0	126.9	162.5	152.3	195.0	177.7	227.5
8.625	75.5	96.4	100.7	128.5	125.9	160.7	151.1	192.8	176.3	224.9
8.750	75.0	95.3	100.0	127.1	125.0	158.8	150.0	190.6	175.0	222.4
8.875	74.4	94.2	99.3	125.6	124.1	157.1	148.9	188.5	173.8	219.9
9.000	73.9	93.2	98.5	124.2	123.2	155.3	147.8	186.4	172.5	217.4
9.125	73.4	92.1	97.8	122.9	122.3	153.6	146.8	184.3	171.2	215.0
9.250	72.8	91.1	97.1	121.5	121.4	151.9	145.7	182.3	170.0	212.7
9.375	72.3	90.1	96.4	120.2	120.5	150.2	144.6	180.3	168.8	210.3
9.500	71.8	89.1	95.7	118.9	119.7	148.6	143.6	178.3	167.5	208.1
9.625	71.3	88.2	95.0	117.6	118.8	147.0	142.6	176.4	166.3	205.8
9.750	70.7	87.2	94.3	116.3	117.9	145.4	141.4	174.5	165.1	203.6
9.875	70.2	86.3	93.7	115.1	117.5	143.9	140.5	172.7	164.0	201.5
10.000	69.7	85.4	93.0	113.9	116.3	142.4	139.5	170.9	162.8	199.4
10.125	69.2	84.5	92.3	112.7	115.4	140.9	138.5	169.1	161.6	197.3
10.250	68.8	83.6	91.7	111.5	114.6	139.4	137.6	167.3	160.5	195.2
10.375	68.3	82.8	91.1	110.4	113.8	138.0	136.6	165.6	159.4	193.2
10.500	67.8	81.9	90.4	109.3	113.0	136.6	135.6	163.9	158.3	191.3
10.625	67.3	81.1	89.8	108.2	112.2	135.2	134.7	162.3	157.2	189.3
10.750	66.9	80.3	89.2	107.1	111.5	133.9	133.8	160.6	156.1	187.4
10.875	66.4	79.5	88.5	106.0	110.7	132.5	132.8	159.0	155.0	185.5
11.000	65.9	78.7	87.9	105.0	109.9	131.2	131.9	157.5	153.9	183.7
11.125	65.5	77.9	87.3	103.9	109.2	129.9	131.0	155.9	152.9	181.9
11.250	65.0	77.2	86.7	102.9	108.4	128.6	130.1	154.4	151.8	180.1

11.375	64.6	76.4	86.1	101.9	107.7	127.4	129.2	152.9	150.8	178.4
11.500	64.2	75.7	85.6	100.9	107.0	126.2	128.4	151.4	149.8	176.7
11.625	63.7	75.0	85.0	100.0	106.2	125.0	127.5	150.0	148.7	175.0
11.750	63.3	74.3	84.4	99.0	105.5	123.8	126.6	147.2	147.7	173.3
11.875	62.9	73.6	83.8	98.1	104.8	122.6	125.8	147.2	146.7	171.7

| P & I | $750/Month | | $1000/Month | | $1250/Month | | $1500/Month | | $1750/Month | |

Rate %	15 Year	30 Year	15 Year	30 Year	15 Year	30 Year	15 Year	30 Year	15 Year	30 Year
4.000	270.4	418.9	304.2	471.3	338.0	523.6	371.8	576.0	405.6	628.4
4.125	268.1	412.7	301.6	464.3	335.1	515.8	368.6	567.4	402.2	619.0
4.250	265.9	406.6	299.1	457.4	332.3	508.2	365.6	559.0	398.8	609.8
4.375	263.6	400.6	296.6	450.6	329.5	500.7	362.5	550.8	395.5	600.9
4.500	261.4	394.7	294.1	444.1	326.8	493.4	359.5	542.7	392.2	592.1
4.625	259.3	389.0	291.7	437.6	324.1	486.2	356.5	534.9	388.9	583.5
4.750	257.1	383.4	289.3	431.3	321.4	479.2	353.5	527.2	385.7	575.1
4.875	255.0	277.9	286.9	425.2	318.8	472.4	350.6	519.6	382.5	566.9
5.000	252.9	372.5	284.5	419.1	316.1	465.7	347.7	512.2	379.3	558.8
5.125	250.8	367.3	282.1	413.2	313.5	459.1	344.9	505.0	376.2	550.9
5.250	248.7	362.1	279.8	407.4	310.9	452.7	342.0	498.0	373.1	543.2
5.375	246.7	357.1	277.6	401.8	308.4	446.4	339.3	491.0	370.1	535.7
5.500	244.7	352.2	275.3	396.2	305.9	440.3	336.5	484.3	367.1	528.3
5.625	242.7	347.4	273.1	390.8	303.4	434.2	333.8	477.7	364.1	521.1
5.750	240.8	342.7	271.8	385.5	301.0	428.3	331.1	471.2	361.2	514.0
5.875	238.9	338.1	268.7	380.3	298.6	422.6	328.5	464.8	358.3	507.1
6.000	237.0	333.5	266.6	375.2	296.2	416.9	325.8	458.6	355.5	500.3
6.125	235.1	329.1	264.5	370.3	293.9	411.4	323.2	452.5	352.6	493.7
6.250	233.2	324.8	262.4	365.4	291.5	406.0	320.7	446.6	349.8	487.2
6.375	231.4	320.5	260.3	360.6	289.2	400.7	318.1	440.7	347.1	480.8
6.500	229.5	316.4	258.2	355.9	286.9	395.5	315.6	435.0	344.3	474.6
6.625	227.7	312.3	256.2	351.3	284.7	390.4	313.2	429.4	341.6	468.5
6.750	226.0	309.9	254.2	346.9	282.5	385.4	310.7	423.9	339.0	462.5
6.875	224.2	304.4	252.2	342.5	280.3	380.5	308.3	418.6	336.3	456.6
7.000	222.5	300.6	250.3	338.1	278.1	375.7	305.9	413.3	333.7	450.9
7.125	220.7	296.8	248.3	333.9	275.9	371.0	303.5	408.1	331.1	445.2
7.250	219.0	293.1	256.4	329.9	273.8	366.4	301.2	403.1	328.6	439.7
7.375	217.4	289.5	244.5	325.7	271.7	361.9	298.9	398.1	326.1	434.3

Rate %	15 Year	30 Year	15 Year	30 Year	15 Year	30 Year	15 Year	30 Year	15 Year	30 Year
7.500	215.7	286.0	242.7	321.7	269.6	357.5	296.6	393.2	323.6	429.0
7.625	214.1	282.5	240.8	317.8	267.6	353.2	294.3	388.5	321.1	423.8
7.750	212.4	279.1	239.0	314.0	265.5	348.9	292.1	383.8	318.7	418.7
7.875	210.8	275.8	237.2	310.3	263.5	344.7	289.9	379.2	316.3	413.7
8.000	209.2	272.5	235.4	306.6	261.6	340.7	287.7	374.7	313.9	408.8
8.125	207.7	269.3	233.6	303.0	259.6	336.7	285.6	370.3	311.5	404.0
8.250	206.1	266.2	231.9	299.4	257.6	332.7	283.4	366.0	309.2	399.3
8.375	204.6	263.1	230.1	296.0	255.7	328.9	281.3	361.8	306.9	394.6
8.500	203.0	260.1	228.4	292.6	253.8	325.1	279.2	357.6	304.6	390.1
8.625	201.5	257.1	226.7	289.2	251.9	321.4	277.1	353.5	302.3	385.7
8.750	200.1	254.2	225.1	286.0	250.1	317.7	275.1	349.5	300.1	381.3
8.875	198.6	251.3	223.4	282.7	248.3	314.2	273.1	345.6	297.9	377.0
9.000	197.1	248.5	221.8	279.6	246.4	310.7	271.1	341.7	295.7	372.8
9.125	195.7	245.8	220.2	276.5	244.6	307.2	269.1	337.9	293.6	368.7
9.250	194.3	243.1	218.6	273.4	242.9	303.8	267.1	334.2	291.4	364.6
9.375	192.9	240.4	217.0	270.5	241.1	300.5	265.2	330.6	289.3	360.6
9.500	191.5	237.8	215.4	267.5	239.1	297.3	263.3	327.0	287.2	356.7
9.625	190.1	235.2	213.9	264.7	237.6	294.1	261.4	323.5	285.2	352.9
9.750	188.7	232.7	212.3	261.8	235.9	290.9	259.5	320.0	283.1	349.1
9.875	187.4	230.3	210.8	259.1	234.3	287.9	257.7	316.6	281.1	345.4
10.000	186.1	227.9	209.3	256.3	232.6	284.8	255.9	313.3	279.1	341.8
10.125	184.7	225.5	207.8	253.7	230.9	281.9	254.0	310.0	277.1	338.2
10.250	183.4	223.1	206.4	251.0	229.3	278.9	252.3	306.8	275.2	334.7
10.375	182.2	220.8	204.9	248.5	227.7	276.1	250.5	303.7	273.3	331.3
10.500	180.9	218.6	203.5	245.9	226.1	273.3	248.7	300.6	271.3	327.9
10.625	179.6	216.4	202.1	243.4	224.5	270.5	247.0	297.5	269.5	324.6
10.750	178.4	214.2	200.7	241.0	223.0	267.8	245.3	294.5	267.6	321.3
10.875	177.1	212.1	199.3	238.6	221.4	265.1	243.6	291.6	265.7	318.1
P & I	$2000/Month		$2250/Month		$2500/Month		$2750/Month		$3000/Month	

Source: HSH Associates, http://www.hsh.com © 2006

3

Assessing the Market

THE HEALTH OF THE LOCAL REAL ESTATE MARKET WILL BE A CRITICAL factor in determining just how far your housing budget will go and how you'll negotiate for a house. As part of the research you conduct before even hiring a real estate pro, you'll want to know whether homes in your targeted market are selling fast at record prices or languishing for weeks looking for buyers. Just a little legwork now can help you get a feel for both prices and housing stock. At this point it's fine to have several neighborhoods or even more than one town under consideration. The steps you take now to assess the market will help you narrow your search.

START YOUR RESEARCH ON THE WEB

These days, real estate agents are no longer the sole gatekeepers of information about housing and housing prices. Start your research on the Web, which is chock-full of tools to help home shoppers. To see how far your money will go in a neighborhood across town or across the country, go to http://hpci.coldwellbanker.com. The site's Home Price Com-

parison Index will tell you the equivalent value of houses in three hundred cities. For example, a $650,000 property in Montclair, New Jersey, would sell for about $457,000 in Charlotte, North Carolina, or $419,000 in Bozeman, Montana.

To drill down, go to www.zillow.com, where you'll actually be able to see neighborhoods that have drawn your interest. The site uses mapping technology to give users a look at individual neighborhoods and houses from satellite photos. Better yet, you can instantly find home values based on public records without having to talk to a real estate agent. Not every state is covered, and while the site is no substitute for a professional appraisal, it is handy for a quick idea of values in neighborhoods that have drawn your attention. Next, point your browser to the websites of the biggest real estate brokerages in town. If there is a particular brokerage that is active in the neighborhood you're interested in, go there first. If you're unsure, try www.realtor.com, which brings together listings from Realtors all over the country. Look at listings that match your budget. Do these homes have what you're looking for in terms of the numbers of bedrooms, baths? What about overall size? Location is critical, too. At first glance, you'll simply want to know whether you can afford to buy what you need in the neighborhoods you've targeted. If not, you'll need to broaden your search.

EVALUATE YOUR STANDING AS A BUYER

As you begin to get a feel for the community and how far your money will go, you'll also want to get a sense of the strength of the real estate market. You'll want to know whether the town or city you're looking in is experiencing a buyer's or seller's market, and the prospects for price appreciation. Remember, the market is in a constant state of flux. Inventory supply and demand determine whether buyers or sellers have the advantage. Keep in mind that trends emerging in one part of a market may not play out in others. When the San Francisco market slowed in 2000, for example, owners of high-end homes were forced to take steep price cuts of 20 percent and more, while prices of entry-level homes continued to rise.

A good place to start finding this kind of specific information is on county board of Realtors websites, some of which publish quarterly reports on home sales including median prices and the number of homes sold. By viewing reports from several quarters, you'll get a sense of whether sales and prices are picking up or leveling off. (Beware the seasonal changes in the market, however. Winter is traditionally slow, while sales typically spike in spring). If this information is not published for the county you are interested in buying in, you may need to contact a real estate agent. Next, to evaluate the market's health, use the benchmarks the pros use—price per square foot and days on market. The way to do this is to return to the websites of the major real estate brokerages in the towns you are investigating. Search the sites for listings of homes that fit your parameters, including locations, number of bedrooms, baths, and overall size. Divide the offer price by the number of square feet for each home that fits your criteria. Take an average of all the houses. This will give you a rule of thumb—a price per square foot—that you'll be able to use as a guide to determine how fairly priced the properties you consider are. You'll know which homes are overpriced and which are underpriced.

Next, you'll want to consider how long it takes homes to sell in your market. The pros call this statistic "days on market." When a boom is getting ready to cool and prices are poised to fall, the first thing that happens is that homes sit on the market for longer than usual. Conversely, if a market is picking up, the length of time houses sit on the market shortens. As a general rule of thumb, when houses turn over in just a month, it's considered a seller's market, particularly when the seller gets the price he or she asked for. However, the typical days on market statistics vary by region, so you'll want to get details from your local Realtors association. Any agent active in the market will have a sense of the number and should be willing to share it with you.

One fact to keep in mind as you do your research is this: much of the sale price data lags what is going on in the market. That is because once a seller accepts an offer; it can be three months before the paperwork is filed at the county courthouse. That means getting up-to-date

information on prices is difficult. If you're in a market in transition where you want to know what prices houses are selling for right now, you'll have to cultivate a relationship with a real estate agent, who is more likely to be privy to such insider info or at least know whether the sellers were able to get their asking price. And don't be afraid to ask neighbors who have recently sold or just put their homes on the market whether they are getting offers at their asking price. They can be a good source of information as well.

TAP LOCAL SOURCES

As part of your research, you'll want to think big picture too. Watch the websites of the local newspapers to find out changes in the local economy. Scan for headlines about corporate expansions. An influx of workers means more demand for housing and, possibly, higher prices. Large layoffs can reverberate negatively throughout the real estate market. For example, months after the major Detroit automakers started laying off white-collar workers in 2006, the number of homes foreclosed on spiked. Few things are more important to maintaining housing prices than job growth, but keeping up with the headlines will also allow you to monitor issues that could be important to home values, such as redevelopment plans, tax hikes, or new highway construction.

4

Picking a Real Estate Agent

BUYING A HOUSE IS A STRESSFUL ENDEAVOR, AND WITH SO MUCH ON THE line—your wealth, your happiness, even your security—you may decide to have a professional at your side. A top-notch real estate agent can save you both time and money; the poor ones can cost you. Take the case of an Annapolis, Maryland, home buyer named Carol. Her agent helped her find a home she loved—one with plenty of upgrades, including a pool, something Carol thought she'd never be able to afford. The price, just $350,000, and the location of the house a stone's throw from Chesapeake Bay were irresistible. Carol had just one worry—the deck around the pool was narrow, possibly too narrow. She worried that it violated local building codes. The fact that the owner, a builder, had installed it himself did little to reassure Carol that the pool was built correctly. Even so, the total package was hard to pass up. She bid on the house and signed a contract, making her offer contingent on the seller providing the proper permits for her to inspect. "My mother was a broker, and I remember her telling me about homes that had been built without the proper permits and later had to be torn down," she said.

As Carol's agent began getting the paperwork together for the sale, she assured Carol that she had double-checked the permits with the county and that everything seemed in order. As the closing date neared, however, Carol still hadn't been sent copies of the permits. Frustrated, she called the county offices herself and found that as she suspected, the work had been done without the proper permits. She learned that if she bought the house, landscaping would have to be removed, walls would have to come down, and the swimming pool would have to be filled in, at a total estimated cost of $130,000. Naturally, Carol used her contingency clause as an out and didn't buy the home, but she felt duped by her agent. "I felt like there was collusion between my agent and the listing agent—they worked for the same company," says Carol, who went on to find a new agent to land a home.

Carol's example is extreme. Few experienced agents would make a gaffe as serious as Carol's did, but picking a reliable and knowledgeable agent in the first place not only helps you land on the best choice in the least possible amount of time but also can prevent you from making a terrible mistake. Making a good choice when looking for an agent can be tricky because requirements for entry into the profession can be lax. In some states, getting a real estate license can take little more than a week's worth of training.

THE AGENT'S RESPONSIBILITIES

At a minimum, you'll want someone with experience in the neighborhood you're conducting your search in. Remember, your agent will serve as your face to sellers, voicing your offer and negotiating on your behalf. Agents are obligated to pass on any pertinent information about a deal, including any offers from rivals and details about the sellers that they may have gleaned, including their timetables—all information that can be critical to successfully negotiating your deal. As your representative in the deal, they are obligated to be loyal to your interests, obey your wishes, and maintain confidentiality.

Good agents think ahead, anticipating problems and making sure they understand clients' desires. One agent in Anacortes, Washington,

grills her buyers not only on the features and amenities they desire in a home but also about the reason they want them. Do they want a waterfront property so they can walk down the beach or just for the view? There are few sandy beach properties in Anacortes, so if long walks on the beach are in her clients' plans, she'll expand her search to other communities. The agent has a familiarity with recent sales in the market and can quickly tell that a house priced at $210 a square foot is overpriced in a neighborhood where the last three homes sold for an average of $187 a square foot. She is also sure to present her buyer's offers in person. That way, she says, she can explain the offer and, why, more often than not, it's her final. Her approach has worked. Her best success was getting owners of a house in the San Juan Islands to knock $700,000 off the $3.5 million asking price. This is the kind of agent you'll want—one that thinks ahead and is thorough and detail-oriented.

Most real estate agents work on commission. Sellers pay them that commission, which currently averages just above 5 percent. That commission is split between the seller's listing broker and the selling agent. That means the more sales they close, the more money they make. It's in their best interests to work quickly and make decisions fast. And that benefits you. A good agent is a quick study of your needs and directs you to properties that fit those parameters. They have broad knowledge of a community, including school district boundaries and the average number of days a home sits on the market, but should also have a sense of the smaller details, such as quirky homeowner association rules that place a limit on the number of pets you can own. A good agent will steer you clear of homes that are too unusual to command a healthy resale price.

The best agents go the extra yard, like one Columbia, South Carolina, broker who is so fastidious that he doesn't take a seller's word on the square footage of the house. Instead, his team goes in and measures the house themselves. Moreover, he asks sellers to give him a CLUE (Comprehensive Loss Underwriting Exchange) report, which details insurance claims made against a property, an indicator that insurance rates might skyrocket. His habit of performing a closing-day walk-through scored benefits for one buyer when he spied mops and buckets piled in

the corner of the kitchen. The mess concealed the fact that a leak the previous day had soaked the floor, buckling the hardwood. Before the buyers agreed to close, he arranged for the sellers to put $5,000 in an escrow account to cover the cost of replacing the floor.

As you begin your search, you'll need to understand some real estate lingo. First off, there are two basic types of real estate pros, agents and brokers. Real estate agents are sales associates, professionals who can buy and sell real estate under the supervision of brokers. Brokers have to meet higher standards and generally run the local sales office; they usually buy and sell properties as well. Both agents and brokers may be Realtors, which is a trademarked designation of the National Association of Realtors. Realtors agree to abide by a code of ethics and can take advantage of seminars and educational opportunities that aren't available to nonmembers. Realtors who specialize in residential real estate can earn a Certified Residential Specialist designation, which means they have additional training in all aspects of home selling and buying.

BEWARE CONFLICTS OF INTEREST

As a buyer, however, you may have less leverage with agents than you realize because of the way agents are paid. Bottom line: the seller is paying the commission that will be split between the agent representing the seller, called the listing agent, and the agent representing you as the buyer. Understand that the agent's loyalty may lie with the seller, especially if you drive by a house you immediately fall in love with and call the agent's name on the For Sale sign in the front yard. If you do that, you're talking to the seller's representative, who is obligated to do everything he or she can to get the best possible price.

The fact that agents are working on commission cuts two ways: while it focuses them on getting the deal done fast, it is also an incentive to get you to pay top dollar for a house. And agents may also get fees for recommending anyone from a mortgage broker to a home inspector. If you get a referral for a service from the agent, ask if the agent is getting any sort of compensation. The problem with these fees isn't that they are illegal; they're not. The problem is that they typically aren't communi-

cated to you, and you end up choosing the house or professional because you think it's the best available when it's simply the choice that gives your agent the biggest paycheck.

The biggest conflict of interest facing agents is dual agency, or when a single agent represents both buyer and seller. There is also another form of dual agency called "designated agency," when the buyer's and seller's agents both work for the same company. One California court case illuminates the problem with this kind of conflict. The buyer filed a suit against his agent's brokerage after he paid $3.2 million for a four-bedroom home in Palo Alto, some $1 million over the asking price. The buyer claimed he originally bid $2.8 million but was forced—unfairly— to bid up because of dual agency. This kind of arrangement is most typical in small markets where there are few agents. But it poses problems for the buyer because the agent who should be the buyer's advocate is also representing (or the agent's agency is also representing) the seller who is paying the commission. That means that pressure is high to boost the buyer's bid. Phantom rival bidders have been known to emerge to encourage buyers to sweeten their offer. In other cases, critical information is never communicated to the buyer. Take the Portsmouth, New Hampshire, couple who went to see a condo on the market and was shown the "great view" from the living room windows. Unfortunately, the listing agent "forgot" to tell them that that view was about to be blocked off by a new development planned for the empty lot next door to the building.

One way to get around this problem is to use an exclusive buyer's agent, a sales pro who only represents buyers. You decide how much to pay a buyer's agent, and you can opt to pay a flat fee rather than a percentage of the home's value. Hiring a buyer's broker helps you avoid the typical conflicts of interest, since your agent won't be splitting his or her commission with the seller's agent. You can find exclusive buyer's agents at the website of the National Association of Exclusive Buyer Agents (www.naeba.org). Keep in mind that the "buyer's agent" designation is sometimes being used by agents who do split fees. For that reason, you'll want to detail your expectations in the contract you sign with the agent.

INTERVIEWING CANDIDATES

Now, if this has you worried about working with any agent at all, don't despair—there are lots of talented pros out there. To develop a list of prospects, start by talking to friends and neighbors for recommendations. Good agents get great word of mouth. Drive through the neighborhood you're interested in buying in and look to see if there is one agent that dominates the For Sale signs. Agents often work in their own neighborhood, which means they will have lots of detailed information simply from having lived in the area. As you troll the websites of the major brokerages, watch for the names of agents that pop up over and over again on the properties that most appeal to you. Once you've whittled your list down to three to five agents, you'll want to sit down and interview them. Here are the questions you'll want to ask as you interview prospective agents:

1. *How experienced are you in the market I'm looking in, and do you work full time?* There are more agents than ever before—some 2.5 million—and many have recently joined the ranks of sales professionals. You'll want to use an agent who isn't using your search as a training manual. Also be on alert for part-timers. Over the years, the industry has attracted people who moonlight as agents, while their true expertise is in another field. Avoid those as well.

2. *Are you an expert in the sorts of properties or neighborhoods I am interested in?* Agents often develop an expertise in a specific type of home—say, conventional house or condo—or in a particular part of town. You want someone who has the good sense not to try to be everything to everybody.

3. *Are you a member of the National Association of Realtors?* Agents who are members of the National Association of Realtors are the only agents allowed to call themselves Realtors (the word is trademarked). They are bound to follow a code of ethics that requires them to pass along to you any pertinent information about a

property. If a Realtor believes a seller's information about a property is flawed, he or she is obligated to look into it on behalf of the buyer. The information flows both ways. For example, if your credit history is spotty, a Realtor is obligated to alert the seller. If you have a problem with a Realtor, you can take the case to arbitration for resolution.

4. *How many clients have you worked with this year?* An agent who juggles too many customers often leaves important details to underlings who may be too junior to follow up efficiently. This may require reading between the lines. If the candidate doesn't respond to your phone calls in a timely manner, that's a clue to look elsewhere.

5. *Will you review new listings throughout the week and call me right away about ones that fit my parameters?* Some agents are a little slow off the mark. In a red-hot market, hours can matter—another buyer might beat you to the home of your dreams.

6. *What's your sense of the market I am interested in?* Since you've already assessed the market yourself, you'll have some idea of whether the agent is really familiar with the neighborhood or merely putting on a good show.

7. *How do you communicate with clients?* If you are conducting your search long distance, this will be particularly important. An agent who is accustomed to staying in touch by e-mail may be a poor fit for the buyer who requires a daily telephone conversation.

8. *Can you give me references from five recent clients?* You'll want to call them and ask about their satisfaction with the agent.

After interviewing your candidates and evaluating your research, you should pretty quickly come to a conclusion about which agent best suits your needs. Don't stop there, though. Before you make your final decision, make sure he or she is licensed by the state by calling the real estate

commission. The Association of Real Estate License Law Officials maintains a state-by-state list of licensing agencies on its website at www.arello.com.

MANAGING YOUR AGENT

Getting a top-notch effort from your agent requires some work on your part. One of the most common stumbling blocks to a good relationship with your agent is that home buyers fail to communicate clearly. Couples send mixed messages to agents about everything from the style of house they prefer to the neighborhood they want to live in. To get the best results, sit down with your partner before you begin your search to determine the basics of what you are looking for. Now that you've got a shopping list, you can narrow down the number of candidates you actually go out and see. Share the list with your agent so the agent has details about what you are looking for. Have your agent send you all the listings in your price range in your target neighborhoods, but don't spin your wheels visiting the brick split-level when you've got your sights set on a Cape Cod. Choose one partner to communicate with the agent. That way you'll be less likely to send mixed messages. For more information on communicating with your agent, see Chapter 8.

5

Choosing a Mortgage Lender

EVEN AS YOU SHOP FOR A HOUSE, YOU'LL WANT TO GET YOUR FINANCING lined up. That process starts with choosing a mortgage lender that offers competitive rates and that you feel comfortable dealing with. Now, you may ask, "Why would I start looking for a mortgage before I've found the home I want to purchase?" The answer is simple: having your financing lined up early gives you a competitive edge over other buyers. Sellers consider buyers who have gone to the trouble of lining up their financing as more serious and view their offer more favorably. Besides, you have no idea if the first home you look at will be the one you end up making an offer on.

There is no shortage of places to get mortgages these days. Television commercials tout no-closing-cost loans, and mortgage spam fills e-mail in-boxes with impossibly low interest rate offers. It seems like mortgage lenders are everywhere. But picking the right lender—one that is reliable, sensitive to your needs, and capable of negotiation—is critical to getting the right loan and best deal.

The lending business has changed a lot in the past few years. The

good news is that if you are getting into the market for the first time ever or just the first time in a long time, the fundamentals are the same—and straightforward. At its simplest, a mortgage is a loan that makes up the difference between the down payment you're making on your home and the purchase price. So if you're buying a $250,000 house and putting down 20 percent, or $50,000, your mortgage covers the difference, or $200,000. Unlike other types of loans, mortgages use real estate as collateral. That means if you fail to make your monthly payments, the bank has the right to take your house from you. A mortgage has a term, or length, of fifteen, thirty, or even forty years, although many people refinance—swap out of their loans—long before their term ends.

But other things about the business of mortgages *have* changed. One of those changes—the fact that mortgage lending has become incredibly competitive—works in your favor. So many players are in the field that you can play one against another, which I'll show you how to do later in this chapter. Other changes are less than friendly to consumers. The number of loan products has grown dramatically, and while some are good innovations, others should be ignored completely (see Chapter 9 for details). Bottom line: the less complicated your loan, the better the terms you are likely to get.

SURVEYING THE PLAYERS

Finding a lender is like tracking down a real estate broker or contractor. Start by asking friends and family members for recommendations. A respected real estate agent is another place to turn for suggestions. You'd do well to take a look at all your options, from Internet players and your company or union's credit union to your local mom-and-pop savings and loan. The more offers you can compare, the better chance you have of finding the best deal possible. Whether it's a credit union or a bank, the place to get started is where you have your checking account right now. Go to that institution's website and find the rates it touts to customers. Next, head to www.hsh.com and www.bankrate.com. Both of these sites will provide you with rates being offered in your area. Although these rates aren't necessarily ones you can qualify for, you'll

quickly get a sense of which institutions are most aggressively courting borrowers by offering the lowest rates. That will give you a baseline of comparison.

Next, get online with a website that brings a number of lenders to the table, such as www.lendingtree.com or www.eloan.com. These sites act as lead generators for banks, and some sell their own loans as well, so you'll want to be careful just how much personal information you part with. By spending a little time filling out forms, you can fairly quickly come up with mortgage offers to see whether they offer more attractive deals. And don't worry, if you conduct your mortgage search efficiently, inquiries into your credit report won't impact your credit score.

HOW LENDERS EVALUATE YOU

Like many other businesses, mortgage lending is now run by software programs. Forget the old green-eyeshade-sporting accountants crunching numbers late into the night. These days whether or not you get a loan will come down to whether an automated underwriting program deems you worthy. These programs consider income, how long you have been in your job, and, most important, your credit score to determine just how much of a lending risk you are. While the debt ratios we described in Chapter 2 are important to you in determining how much *you* should decide to spend, lenders base most of their decision on how much they will lend you on how well you've handled credit in the past. That means if you have a credit score of 700 or higher, you'll be given wide latitude in borrowing and offered published rates. However, if your score is less than 650, you'll find you are offered rates well above the advertised ones. The differences are big, as you can see in the table that follows. A person with a FICO credit score of 760 or better will pay $227 less per month for a $216,000 thirty-year fixed-rate mortgage than a person with a FICO score of 620, for a savings of $2,724 a year. This is also a good time to check your credit reports to make sure they don't contain errors that drag your credit score down.

If your FICO score is	Your interest rate is	And your monthly payment is*
760–850	5.86%	$1,276
700–759	6.09%	$1,307
680–699	6.26%	$1,332
660–679	6.48%	$1,362
640–659	6.91%	$1,423
620–639	7.45%	$1,503

*Loan amount in all cases is $300,000.
Source: FICO, as of July 2007

You can look at your credit reports for free at www.annualcredit report.com, or at www.myfico.com you can purchase your credit score.

A HOME LOAN IN YOUR BACK POCKET

As you search for a house to buy, you'll quickly learn that it's not always the buyer offering the biggest price whose offer is accepted. Sellers want to see that you're serious about your offer and that you've done your homework before starting your search. For that reason, you'll want to have in hand as you shop evidence that will prove you can get a loan. There are two ways of doing that: getting prequalified or preapproved for your loan.

A lender can typically prequalify a borrower for a loan with a few pieces of information, including income and employment status in order to conduct a simple credit check. Getting a prequalification letter is painless and fast: you provide the financial info, the lender provides the letter. For that reason, sellers and their agents don't take it very seriously. A loan preapproval, however, is a better negotiating tool. A preapproval typically takes more time and is a deeper look at your financial picture. A lender will verify income, assets, and credit score to qualify you for a loan—not just take your word for it. If you're preapproved, you'll en-hance your negotiating position with sellers, because you'll take off the

table the question of whether you can get a loan—you've already demonstrated you can get one. Getting preapproved doesn't mean you have to go with that lender for the home you are making the offer on. In fact, once your offer is accepted, you'll want to get at least three lenders to compete for your business, pitting them against each other to get the best-priced deal. Use the terms of your preapproved loan as a basis of comparison to the other offers.

WINNOWING THE FIELD

Narrowing your sights to a handful of potential lenders is the next step. Who is offering the best rates, and whom do you feel comfortable with? Well-known national lenders such as Washington Mutual and Wells Fargo, for example, target borrowers who want home loans. Large national banks can offer some of the best deals for the simplest sorts of loans because their sheer size can command the best rates. But you'd be doing yourself a disservice not to broaden your search. Online lenders are eager to grab market share, and others, such as credit unions, may be motivated by more than just profit in determining their rates. Regional thrifts shouldn't be ignored. When vetting small players, check with your local Better Business Bureau and state attorney general's office to make sure they are legitimate.

ONLINE OR CONVENTIONAL LENDER?

If you spend any time at all looking at mortgage websites, you'll pretty quickly come across claims that the rates available in the virtual world beat those offered by conventional lenders hands down because they don't have to operate expensive branch networks. That's not necessarily the case. Offers made to you will depend on your credit score. Brick-and-mortar lenders have their own advantages in the market. They may have well-known brand names or reputations as solid lenders in local communities, either of which may allow them to offer better terms. What's more, some websites aren't the disinterested listers of mortgage rates they may claim to be, but rather electronic advertising circulars that solicit payment from lenders who want to list their rates on the site. That

means their listings are neither complete nor fact-checked. Other mortgage lending websites use their status as a "store for lenders" to cloak their real intent—pushing their own loans. Not all online mortgage marketplaces are trying to pull the wool over your eyes, so start by using their information as a point of comparison. Then if you find a virtual-world offer that you like, you may be able to take the negotiation on terms off-line, if you prefer to do so.

SHOULD YOU USE A MORTGAGE BROKER?

In recent years, mortgage brokers have become a popular alternative for busy consumers who don't want to roll up their shirtsleeves and research loans on their own. Mortgage brokers act as an intermediary between you and the lender, and originate about two-thirds of mortgages annually. A good broker is your guide through the loan process, ensuring that you are qualified for the loan and arranging for the property appraisal. A bad one may put you in a loan you can't afford. The broker should provide an estimate of closing costs. He or she should be able to draw mortgages from various sources, including some you wouldn't be able to find on your own, and match you with the appropriate loan. Brokers are best used by people who have unusual credit backgrounds, such as a poor record of paying debt, being self-employed and having difficulty proving earnings, or having paychecks that vary greatly because of bonuses. People in any of those situations will need help in finding lenders on their own. Mortgage brokers are attractive because they can tap a variety of lending sources and not just limit themselves to a single bank.

Be sure to vet your mortgage broker the way you would any other professional. Not all states require that a mortgage broker be licensed or even registered with the state. Remember, there is a lot riding on your decision. Robert learned this the hard way. As the closing date for his purchase approached, he found that his mortgage broker was increasingly hard to reach. He thought he had qualified for a thirty-year loan that had a fixed rate of 7.5 percent and covered some of the closing costs. Instead, at closing he was presented with two loans, one that covered 80 percent of the price and another that covered the remaining 20

percent, and the interest rate was far higher than what Robert had been promised, 8.99 percent. To top it off, the loan included a prepayment penalty that assessed a 5 percent fee if more than 10 percent of the loan was paid off in less than sixty months.

"In addition to a completely different loan and higher interest rates, we now have to carry the loan for a minimum of five years. We called [the broker] at the closing table and were unable to reach him," says Robert. He immediately postponed the closing. When he finally reached the broker, he says all he got were excuses. "He told me that interest rates had gone up and that's why ours was higher. He never locked in the initial rate, and he forgot to mention the rider," says Richard. "Unfortunately, we did not have time to work with another lender or we would have lost our earnest money deposit, so we went with what we were offered."

To avoid Robert's fate, do your homework. First step: ask for referrals from friends and family. Then shop around. You'll want to get a rate quote from at least three brokers. Do this on the same day so the comparison is accurate. You'll need to ask the brokers about their fees, how long their company has been in business, and also how much experience this particular broker has under his or her belt. Go to the Better Business Bureau and ensure that this particular company doesn't have any blotches on its record.

Make sure you understand how the broker is being paid. Is it a straight administrative fee? Typically brokers are paid more for selling complicated loans. That means you could end up paying for complicated features you don't need. Watch out for yield spread premiums (YSPs), a rebate that a lender will often pass along to a broker for a higher-interest-rate loan. Ask for an explanation of any fees you don't understand. A mortgage lender earns an origination fee, while a broker is paid a commission on the loan. Finally, get everything in writing, signed and on company letterhead, especially the lock-in rate for your loan.

6

Avoiding Mortgage Fraud

AS YOU SEARCH FOR THAT BEST LOAN, YOU'LL WANT TO TAKE GREAT
care in avoiding mortgage fraud, the fastest-growing white-collar crime
in the country. The crooks are increasingly difficult to spot because they
pose as legitimate mortgage brokers and bankers. The FBI says that organized fraud groups have infiltrated the mortgage brokerage business
and lenders report losses in the billions. Con artists often prey on consumers with less-than-perfect credit, the elderly, or minorities. As with
many illegal schemes, the crooks change their cons over time to avoid
detection.

Often the schemes rely on the greed of victims or their embarrassment over poor credit or foreclosure worries. One Kansas City con artist
and his cronies purchased run-down properties, secured fraudulent appraisals, and took out mortgages in the names of "straw purchasers," who
were told that they were doing a favor for a real estate investor who had
maxed out his credit. In return, they were promised $1,500 or $2,000.
Another of his schemes was nearly undetectable to victims until it was
too late. He targeted senior citizens who owned their homes outright

and made up fake deeds, forging the owner's signature and notarizing them himself—a process that gave him ownership of the properties. Such a scam is easy to execute. Not only is it cheap and simple if you understand the laws, but county courthouse officials are ill-prepared to spot such scams. Other scams are designed to rip off the bank. In California's Bay Area, agents at one real estate brokerage inflated property prices by as much as $50,000 to $150,000. The sellers then returned the cash after the deal closed. Called a "cash-back" deal, this scheme can ruin people caught up in it by sticking them with a mortgage that is too big for them to handle. It also inflates values throughout the town or neighborhood where it occurs, hurting homeowners who weren't even duped by the crooks.

According to the FBI, common fraud schemes include:

1. *Fictitious or stolen identity.* A false name is used on a mortgage application. The applicant's name, personal information, and credit history are used without the person's knowledge. For someone whose identity is stolen, the problems are many. It may take years for you to realize that someone has taken out a mortgage in your name.

2. *Foreclosure fraud schemes.* The con artist targets homeowners who are at risk of defaulting on their mortgage or losing their home in foreclosure. They convince the homeowners that they can save their home in exchange for a transfer of the deed and up-front fees. The con artist profits by remortgaging the property or pocketing the fees. The owner loses his home.

3. *Property flipping.* A property is purchased, appraised at a higher value, and then quickly sold. The appraisal that established the higher price is fraudulent; the scheme may also include doctored loan documents or inflating the buyer's income. You'll want to see the appraisal that the mortgage company has gotten from its appraiser, and double-check that the square footage is accurate. Better yet, spring for your own independent appraisal. The mortgage

company will still likely use its own appraiser, but at least then you have an independent voice that can second the mortgage company's findings or raise a red flag.

4. *Equity skimming.* An investor uses false income documents and credit reports to obtain a mortgage in the straw purchaser's name. After the closing of the deal, the straw buyer signs the property over to the investor in a quitclaim deed that relinquishes all rights to the property. The investor fails to make mortgage payments and rents the property until the house is foreclosed on.

5. *Silent second.* The buyer of the property borrows the down payment from the seller by using a second mortgage that is not disclosed to lenders. The lender believes the borrower has invested his or her own money in the down payment, and may agree to lend more than the borrower's income would normally qualify for.

6. *Mortgage elimination schemes.* These involve companies that promise to eliminate your entire mortgage debt by using a supposed loophole in federal lending laws. It sounds too good to be true, and it is. But enough folks out there have fallen for such lines to attract the attention of the FBI and consumer protection groups. The thrust behind mortgage elimination is that the loan itself is invalid due to an interesting interpretation of banking laws and therefore homeowners can get that loan wiped out without losing their house. The reality? Homeowners pay hefty up-front fees to these companies who tout their mortgage elimination prowess through a series of steps, and then their homes often end up in foreclosure.

Although complicated, most mortgage frauds fall into one of two camps: those in which borrowers play along, knowingly or unknowingly, in order to buy a house, and those in which scam artists try to bilk banks or owners out of money. At the heart of these schemes, typically,

is some type of misstatement, misrepresentation, or omission of fact that an underwriter or a lender relies on to make a loan. For that reason, buyers should be wary of any real estate professional, whether an agent, lender, or mortgage broker, who asks them to lie on an application, sign documents that are incomplete, or leave some areas blank. Hire your own appraiser to determine the value of a piece of property before you buy it; don't rely on referrals from high-pressure salespeople. Review the title history of the property you are buying to determine whether the property has been repeatedly flipped—sold multiple times within a short period—to falsely boost its value. Verify property values by looking at recent comparable sales in the area, as well as tax assessments. Make sure the name on your application matches the name on your identification.

Often it's not fraud but rather bad judgment that lands home buyers in trouble. For instance, securing a no-income-documentation loan when you don't have the income to qualify for a standard mortgage will only leave you scrambling for payments. Oftentimes the broker or lender encourages such behavior, however innocent it may seem at the time. The best way you can protect yourself is to shop around and never exaggerate financial information on a mortgage application no matter what the broker or lender is suggesting that you do.

7

Narrowing Your Search

LOCATION IS PROBABLY THE MOST CRITICAL ISSUE DETERMINING HOME values. Let's face it—while you can fix the shortcomings of many homes by adding a bath or upgrading the kitchen, there's not much you can do to shore up a dangerous neighborhood or improve the school district. What's more, a good neighborhood will appreciate at a steadier rate than other areas, holding its value better in weak markets and appreciating more in heady times.

EVALUATING THE NEIGHBORHOOD'S LOCATION

For most of us, several things go into making a good neighborhood. It should be close to things that are important to you, such as work, good schools, or big parks, and it has to offer the services you'll need as you go about your day-to-day activities, such as convenient grocery stores and doctors. Naturally, curb appeal—meaning, for example, the attractiveness of street lighting, sidewalks, and fixtures, how well the home styles blend together, and the relative repair of the street—factors into many buyers' decision-making process as well. It's easy enough to get distracted by the

pictures of homes on realty websites and ignore bigger issues, such as whether the neighborhood is in transition or whether it's constant, how safe the neighborhood is, and whether it's about to be bypassed by a new state highway construction project. All these issues will be important variables in home value when you buy and when you sell.

To narrow your search, point your browser to two websites with reams of information about individual towns and neighborhoods. *Money* magazine's annual Best Places to Live list is available free on the Web at http://money.cnn.com and has write-ups on one hundred towns that the magazine's editors believe stand out from the competition. You'll quickly find detailed information from cultural attractions in these locations to weather statistics, and it has quirky lists that you won't find anywhere else, including locations with the highest population of singles or skinny residents. For a site teeming with data, check out www.home fair.com. This site will help you evaluate how well you'll fit into a new neighborhood. You'll learn the median age of residents, average household size, and average education level attained by residents. And there are critical issues relevant to home values, such as the proportion of owners versus renters (a higher proportion of owners signals more neighborhood stability) and the number of vacant homes (always a negative). Curious about how long it takes residents to commute to work? Homefair has the answer.

As you do this research, consider how close the neighborhood is to major transportation arteries and public transportation. Is the commuter train station nearby? Better yet, is it walkable? Are highways that connect you to the region easily accessible? Where are the major shopping hubs? Is there a decent grocery nearby? What about your doctor and other services such as drugstores and dry cleaners? If you're unsure how well situated the neighborhood you like is, go to http://local.yahoo.com and find out the proximity of the services you'll need.

GETTING THE SKINNY ON SCHOOL DISTRICTS

Good schools are always key to home values. Although fewer and fewer households are made up of the traditional family unit of two parents and

two children, it pays to buy in neighborhoods with top-notch schools. One Ohio homeowner found this out the hard way. Donna chose her neighborhood, Norwood, located inside the Cincinnati, Ohio, city limits, largely because of its affordable prices. Schools weren't great, but the couple planned to send their kids to private school anyway. Norwood was close to downtown and near upscale neighborhoods such as Hyde Park and Mount Lookout. While many of the town's industrial employers had moved out in the 1980s, town officials were attempting a comeback. A new open-air shopping mall had been built in 1999. The number of young families who seemed to be moving in and spending money encouraged Donna and her husband. "There was new landscaping," she recalls. "You could tell people had done work." The couple bought a five-bedroom home in 2001 for $165,000, half the price of an average home in Hyde Park. But the value has barely inched up since. As it turned out, the poor schools and weak economic base were signals that home prices had little chance of rebounding. Far from being the city's next hot neighborhood, which Donna had hoped, Norwood continues to languish.

Getting good information on schools is easy. Web resources for home buyers include www.schoolmatch.com, where you'll find test scores and student-teacher ratios. School system reports will cost you $34. Another good school website is www.schoolmatters.com, which allows you to compare student performance by district and even to sort the data for better-performing schools. This service is free. If you already know the school district you want to buy in, check with the local school board to make sure you understand the boundaries of the district. Some have this information online.

If you're new to the area and not sure what district to target, contact the high schools directly in the towns that have drawn your interest. They'll provide free (yes, free) self-evaluations that describe students' performance on SAT tests, the number of advanced placement courses offered, and other data that should help you evaluate their performance. While many parents focus on just one number—the teacher-to-student ratio—there are other factors you'll want to weigh. Be sure to ask about

dropout rates. While high schools eagerly offer graduation rates, few dropouts ever make it that far. Check out school budgets, zeroing in especially on the amount of the budget that goes to instruction.

ESTIMATING NEIGHBORHOOD SECURITY

Safety matters too, and it will be important when you resell. Dangerous neighborhoods get bad word of mouth with Realtors and are difficult to sell in. Crime statistics are available on the Web. Point your browser to www.homefair.com, where you can determine your risk for violent and property crimes ranging from rape to larceny by zip code. This is particularly useful for buyers who may be attracted to some of the emerging neighborhoods that became popular between 2000 and 2005, such as Red Hook in Brooklyn, New York, and the South End in Boston. Neighborhoods that reclaim former industrial areas can be dangerous, and you'll definitely want to assess your safety. The Web is also a good resource to find out whether the neighborhood you're targeting is home to sex offenders. The website www.klaaskids.org/pg-legmeg2.htm provides links to other sites that specialize in providing information on sex offenders by state, and www.registeredoffenderslist.org provides a free estimate of the number of sex offenders by neighborhood. Another resource is your local sheriff's office and police department. But let logic be your guide. If the neighborhood is located on top of an interstate exchange, you could be headed for trouble. Burglars like to hit homes near freeways for quick getaways. And it may be only partly an urban legend that sneakers hanging from utility lines signals drug dealing in the neighborhood.

PROPERTY TAXES

You're not done yet. One step you won't want to forget is checking in with city hall. Local governments matter greatly to homeowners. It's here that you'll learn about property tax levels. Property taxes are on the rise across the country. Between 2001 and 2005, annual property tax collections soared 35 percent to $352 billion, according to Census Bureau estimates. Notice of higher tax rates is typically made in the fall of each

year, and with a little elbow grease you can find out whether higher
taxes are in the offing. There are two key factors to understand: the
home's assessed value and your millage rate, the amount of money you
owe per thousand dollars of property value. Towns and cities that wish to
raise taxes can either decide to reassess properties (and therefore raise
your assessed value) or boost your millage rate. Either way, before you
buy in a neighborhood, you'll want to know if a tax hike is on the hori-
zon. City hall is also where you'll hear about initiatives to seize property
using eminent domain powers, which could squash a neighborhood's
home values, or plans to build a new interstate exchange, which could
send values skyrocketing. Once you've done your research online, you'll
want to visit the neighborhoods with the highest appeal at different
times of day and week. Visit during the morning or afternoon rush hour
to find out which streets become busy shortcuts. And don't forget to
visit on the weekends to find out whether parents are confident enough
to allow their children to play outside on their own. The more time you
spend on the ground, the better sense you'll get of the neighborhood
and whether it's right for you.

8

Finding the Right House

IT IS FAR TOO COMMON FOR COUPLES TO GO OUT SEARCHING FOR THE
right house, spending hours on the search for just the right property—
and ultimately spinning their wheels. Your ideal home, a cozy bungalow,
is your partner's idea of a cramped and airless nightmare. The reality is
that few couples actually sit down and discuss what they want to buy. Do
they want a quaint Cape Cod? An edgy contemporary? You'll encounter
far less frustration if you sit down with your partner and create a list of
what your dream house actually includes. That may take some doing,
particularly if you are a first-time buyer. One shortcut: talk about what
you like and don't like in your parents' house or the homes of friends. As
you start to talk about the features of places the two of you have spent
time in, you'll get a sense of whether you will only be happy on a cul-
de-sac or in a traditional colonial. Now that you've got a shopping list,
you can narrow down the number of candidates you actually go out and
see. Have your agent send you all the listings in your price range in your
target neighborhoods, but don't waste time visiting the brick split-level
when you've got your sights set on a Cape Cod.

As you develop your list and attend your first open houses, remember: it's not just *your* house you're buying. Not only do you have to find a house that appeals to your family, it will also need to be appealing to other buyers when you sell. As you search it's all too tempting to think of what it would be like to live in the house. Wouldn't it be delightful to wake up in that sumptuous, roomy master bedroom on the second floor? Isn't it convenient that the kitchen opens into the family room? Remember, though, that you'll ultimately want to sell this house, and when you do, the long, uphill driveway that seemed grand when you bought the place may worry buyers who see its potential as an icy slalom course for their cars in the winter. Shop for the home with the broadest appeal—that means no surprises in terms of materials or design. And stay away from the most expensive home on the block. That beautiful house on the hill can easily turn into a white elephant if the market goes south, plus it means that you have no room to make upgrades to update the house and to bolster its value.

Joe and Sandi profited from doing just that, having perfected the art of picking a house with broad appeal and managing it for the next buyer. When they were building their first home in a small town in northern Pennsylvania, the couple didn't have children and weren't planning any for a while. Still, they selected a neighborhood in a good school district. To appeal to commuters, they chose a site a couple of miles from the highway. They found a quarter-acre lot bordered in the back by property that was owned by the Pennsylvania Gas and Water Company and couldn't be developed, adding further to its appeal to potential buyers.

"The quarter acre was bigger than either of us grew up on," Sandi recalls. "But we knew this would appeal to families with kids. We knew we should have a yard, because the family could put up a jungle gym or whatever in there."

The pair considered building a three-bedroom bi-level house. "But the builder told us we would get more for resale with four bedrooms than with three bedrooms," Sandi says. When the couple, who are fond of vibrant colors, decorated their house, they toned down their selec-

tions, opting for a more neutral palette. "We didn't want to get too crazy because we knew that wouldn't appeal to everybody. Our eye is always toward resale. The more people we can appeal to, the better."

That planning paid off. The couple sold their house for twice what they paid for it. They have made similar moves in and out of three subsequent homes, piling on the profits each time. They've made manageable changes, such as finishing the basement to increase the square footage without major construction or installing wainscoting to make the house more visually appealing. But their first rule is to buy right, right from the start.

While they are happy in their current home, the two continue to stay on top of what's going on in the real estate market around them. "Realtors send us stuff all the time. When houses are going up, I pull the sheets to see what they're selling for. We pay attention to what's selling in what price range and why," Sandi says. "We feel that real estate is an investment. Most purchases you lose money on, but an investment in homes you can recover later in life."

THE HUNT

Like any pursuit, house hunting develops a momentum of its own. Before you know it, you grow so accustomed to spending your Saturday and Sunday afternoons looking at houses on the market that you forget what life was like before the search. And you can easily enter a sort of pack mentality when faced with others looking at the same house. You're better off being disciplined about what you're looking for and succumbing to emotion as little as possible. Carry your checklist with you and take notes on which homes meet your specific needs.

As you consider making an offer on a home, you'll want to think about more than just its curb appeal. This is where your team comes in. Make sure that before you close on a house you have your inspector investigate the entire house, all its major systems as well as its structural soundness. Ask the seller for a written disclosure attesting to the condition of the property, which is simply a detailed checklist disclosing any defects in the house. The owners don't have to fix the problems, but

once you know they exist you can bring them up to negotiate a lower price.

You'd be well advised to examine the home yourself from room to room, roof to basement, inside and out. Have your inspector test for radon, lead paint, and carbon monoxide emissions. Turn on all the lights, then turn on the air-conditioning. If the lights dim, tell your inspector so he or she can give special attention to the wiring and fuses. Have an exterminator investigate for rodents, which can escape a regular inspector's eye. Don't forget a septic test if the house is not on a sewer line.

It's not just older homes that have problems. New-home builders are notorious for taking shortcuts. Often the builder you negotiate with isn't even the one constructing the home, turning instead to subcontractors some of whom might cut corners and trim costs. They might use particleboard instead of wood, plastic pipes instead of copper, prefabricated sections instead of those constructed on site. (Some of these choices can be fine options, but you need to know when you're getting the less expensive choice.) Remember, builders are practiced at making the model home look enticing. High-end furnishings and appliances add panache to even the most mundane new home, while mirrors make tiny rooms look bigger. Inspect the size of the furniture, too. Sometimes models are furnished with smaller-scaled furniture to make rooms appear larger.

You should also consider bringing your contractor with you to eyeball the possibilities for upgrades as well as costs. This is the beginning-at-the-end thinking we described in Chapter 1. If you find a cute ranch that would be perfect except for its undersized kitchen, now is the time to get a sense of just what a bigger kitchen might cost and whether it's even possible to add another five hundred square feet to the home's footprint. A contractor you've already developed a relationship with will be happy to take an hour and help you land his or her next project.

Bottom line: anything that needs fixing that your sellers haven't taken care of will ultimately come out of your pocket, compromising your ability to reinvest and build your home's value.

GETTING A GOOD HOME INSPECTOR

The bottom line if you are buying a house: get a home inspection. During the housing boom, buyers often gave up their right to have a house inspected, but that's a mistake. A good inspector sees things you probably won't. Is that effervescence on the basement walls a sign of water damage or nothing to worry about? Does the house need a major electrical upgrade? Is the roof safe or on the verge of needing replacement? These are questions that you'll need a pro to sort out. But be aware that home inspection is still a largely unregulated profession. In fact, in twenty states there aren't any licensing requirements at all, meaning that virtually anyone, from a moonlighting plumber to a part-time construction worker, can call him- or herself a home inspector. Thirty other states have legislation in place that regulates home inspectors, though the hoops they have to jump through vary greatly.

Start with professional organizations to find an inspector. The American Society of Home Inspectors (ASHI) requires that its fully accredited members pass a written examination and have a minimum of 250 home inspections under their belt. To further stave off any conflicts of interest, the organization's code of ethics prohibits inspectors from doing any contracting work on the home within one year of the inspection.

A home inspection should follow the standards of procedure laid out by ASHI. Typically it is a three-hour process in which the inspector examines the structural and mechanical condition of the house. The inspector will look at the heating, cooling, electrical, and plumbing systems as well as the foundation. A good overview of what is covered can be found at www.ashi.org, where you'll also find a virtual house inspection tool that details common house problems. Just as important as what is covered is what is not. The inspection does not cover mold, and the inspector is not required to look for termites. However, the inspector will tell you about any wood damage he or she sees, though there's no requirement to determine the cause of that damage. An inspection is

a must before buying a home. Smart sellers also get an inspection before they put their homes on the market in order to get a heads-up about any looming problems. As a buyer, you will want to be present at the home inspection. That's because a good inspector will give you a lesson in maintenance of the house as well as a tour of its workings. He or she can show you water shutoff valves, describe the workings of the furnace as well as the routine maintenance it requires, plus tell you whether that electrical box is adequate or below standard.

Tom Kraeutler, a former New Jersey home inspector and the current co-host of *The Money Pit*, a radio show about home improvement, saw it all during his twenty-odd years on the job. A good inspector, he says, can be a great resource; however, he is well aware of the conflicts of interests that home inspectors face. For starters, home inspectors rely on agents for business. "Most agents want to get the deal closed. In the eyes of agents, you are only as good as your last home inspection," says Kraeutler.

While inspecting a house in northern New Jersey, Kraeutler found himself up against an agent who wanted to see the deal go through no matter what. The house was vacant and part of an estate sale. The young couple and their agent trailed him on the day of the inspection, but it quickly became clear to Kraeutler that the agent wasn't acting in the buyers' best interests. "The agent had an answer to everything. The window frames were rotted, and she told the buyers, 'Well, you're handy.' I told the buyers that the house had major electrical problems, and the agent said, 'All homes need a little work.' " But then Kraeutler came to the attic. He pulled down the stairs and heard a loud screech, a sound that he initially assumed was just the rusty staircase. But he wasn't prepared for what lurked in the attic: "It was entirely covered in bats, and there was bat guano everywhere." Six months later he performed another inspection for the same couple, who by then were working with a new agent.

To make sure your inspector isn't under the thumb of real estate agents, interview buyers the inspector has worked with before. Find someone you like and give that person repeat business yourself. Make

sure you attend the inspection and ask as many questions as you can. Another option that works: bring along to the inspection a friend with experience in construction to ask serious questions. Sometimes a little competition can prompt an inspector to divulge information you may need.

9

Choosing the Right Mortgage

WHILE MORTGAGE LENDERS ADVERTISE A LOAN FOR ANY BUDGET, THE explosion of loan types has made the process of getting a mortgage infinitely more confusing. Even the way in which lenders make money off mortgage loans has changed—with big implications for borrowers. Years ago, lenders made their money by taking in deposits (savings accounts and CDs) and paying interest on them at one rate and lending that money back out at a higher rate (mortgages). Not anymore. In recent years, many lenders have opted to sell their mortgages to investors. That means the bank may hold your loan for only a short period of time. In the end, it's the investors that have to worry about whether you're good for the loan. And that very big change in the way banks lend money to homeowners has altered the rules. These days the burden is on you to make sure you have the right loan and the right terms. Do you want a thirty-year fixed-rate loan? An adjustable? What about the offers for a no-closing-cost loan? In this chapter, I'll make sense of it all, showing you how to choose the best mortgage for your situation.

THE IMPORTANCE OF INTEREST RATES

As much as the lending business has changed, one thing remains the same: the importance of interest rates. Just as car dealers try to get you to focus solely on your monthly payment rather than the total purchase price of a car on the auto lot, some mortgage lenders and brokers will make you think that getting the best mortgage is as simple as seeking out the lowest monthly mortgage payment. It's not. The single most important criterion in shopping for your loan is the interest rate you'll be charged for borrowing the money. To understand the impact of rates, imagine if you were financing $200,000 in mortgage debt when rates were at their highest levels in recent memory—an astonishing 18.45 percent in October 1981 for a conventional thirty-year fixed mortgage. Had you paid that rate of interest, you would have faced a monthly mortgage payment of $3,087. Mortgage rates hit their low of 5.23 percent in June 2003 for conventional loans. A $200,000 mortgage financed at that rate would have cost you just $1,101 monthly, or a little more than a third of the 1981 mortgage. Clearly, big differences in mortgage rates can hit your wallet hard, but even small differences in rates can squeeze your monthly budget.

If you were buying a median-priced home with a down payment of $18,000 at an interest rate of 6 percent, in the simplest terms, your transaction would look like this:

Home price	Down payment	Rate of interest	Monthly payment
$218,000	$18,000	6.0%	$1,199

Now, here is the scary part: if you kept that loan for thirty years and never refinanced or sold the house, you would pay total interest of $231,676—more than the original value of the house. Even a slightly lower rate cuts your costs significantly. Imagine you keep the total home price and down payment the same but lowered the interest rate:

Home price	Down payment	Rate of interest	Monthy payment
$218,000	$18,000	5.75%	$1,167

Lowering your mortgage rate by a quarter of a percentage point cuts your monthly mortgage costs by $32 and your annual mortgage tab by $384. Over the life of the loan, you would pay total interest of $220,172, or $11,504 less than the loan made at 6 percent.

To run your own calculation, go to www.bankrate.com, and click on "Mortgage Payment Calculator." You can get an idea of mortgage rates in your area at www.bankrate.com or www.hsh.com. As a rule of thumb, mortgage rates have hovered around 8 percent over the past couple of decades.

FIGURING OUT THE RIGHT LOAN FOR YOU

One of the dirty little secrets of mortgage lending is this: brokers and bankers historically have not had any obligation to tell you whether the loan they are selling you is affordable for your wallet. While stockbrokers have an obligation (called suitability) to refuse to put you into an investment that isn't appropriate for your portfolio, lenders faced no such requirement. For that reason, as you shop for a mortgage, it's important that you determine which type of loan suits your needs before you hit the mortgage broker's office or sit down with a loan officer. The sad fact is that some lenders and brokers put borrowers into loans they can ill afford or that set them up for problems down the road. You can avoid this if you figure out ahead of time what type of loan you want. Even though loan types have proliferated in the last few years, many of the new innovations are poor choices for most of us whose primary goal is building equity. Two mortgage types merit consideration by most borrowers: fixed-rate mortgages and adjustable-rate loans.

FIXED-RATE MORTGAGES These loans are the plain vanilla choice of the mortgage world and a solid option for most home buyers when rates are reasonable. A fixed-rate mortgage is pretty straightforward. It offers a fixed annual percentage rate for the life of the loan, which is typically fifteen or thirty years. In mid-2006, interest rates on fixed-rate mortgages were about a third of a percentage point higher than a mortgage that carried an adjustable rate, but the difference between the two (sometimes called the

"spread") can vary. The longer the term on a fixed-rate loan, the higher the interest rate. The average fifteen-year loan carries a rate of about 0.33 percentage point lower than a thirty-year mortgage on average.

Fixed-rate loans go in and out of favor with the home-buying public, of course. When interest rates were dropping in the early 2000s, demand for mortgages with fixed rates fell while buyers dived into the super-low rates of adjustable-rate mortgages. In mid-2006, as interest rates were creeping up, the allure of a low rate that doesn't change came back into vogue. In fact, the very banks that had recommended the super-low-rate adjustables started encouraging buyers of those mortgages to get a fixed-rate loan. You get it: fixed- and adjustable-rate loans are like fashion— sometimes they are in and sometimes they are out. You'll want to avoid the trends and choose the lowest-cost loan that suits your needs.

If you are buying a home that you plan on being in for more than ten years and if you believe that rates are likely to be headed higher, then a fixed-rate loan is a safe bet.

How long to extend those payments will largely depend on what your wallet can handle. Consider two $300,000 loans, one with a fifteen-year term and the other with a thirty-year term:

15-YEAR LOAN TERM		30-YEAR LOAN TERM	
Fixed rate	Monthly payment	Fixed rate	Monthly payment
6.19%	$2,562	6.63%	$1,922

As you can see, the longer-term loan has a lower monthly payment because you are stretching your debt over a longer period of time. Of course, your lender charges you more since you're locking that rate for a longer period of time. While the fifteen-year payment is $640 higher a month, the interest rate is lower and your mortgage debt will be history in just fifteen years rather than thirty years.

There are options beyond thirty years. Here's how a forty-year loan for $300,000 compares:

40-YEAR LOAN TERM

Fixed rate	Monthly payment
6.88%	$1,838

As you can see, extending the loan an additional ten years buys you some savings. The monthly payment is $84 per month cheaper than the mortgage payment for the thirty-year fixed-rate loan. However, there is a steep cost to those small savings. You'll pay an additional $190,444 in interest over the life of the loan. In short, more of each of your payments goes to interest rather than building equity—not a good scenario.

Bottom line: a fixed-rate loan is a good product for buyers who are committed to their town or neighborhood. For example, if you prefer to stay near extended family, or maybe you're committed to having your children remain in the same school district from kindergarten through high school graduation, a thirty-year fixed-rate loan will eliminate the uncertainty of any change in your mortgage payment for the life of your loan. What's more, a fixed-rate loan is one of the most straightforward for lenders to process. Costs should be low, and the ability to build equity is high.

ADJUSTABLE-RATE MORTGAGE Adjustable-rate mortgages, or ARMs, start out with a fixed-rate period in which the interest rate is lower than what would be found on a fifteen- or thirty-year mortgage. That fixed-interest-rate period can last anywhere from one month to ten years. Now, here's the catch. When the fixed-rate period ends, the interest rate adjusts, and so do the monthly payments. The rate typically adjusts annually, but in some cases it can change every single month.

For example, let's say you wanted to take out a three-year adjustable-rate mortgage for $145,000. The initial rate of 6.0 percent is locked for three years, and after that the rate could adjust once a year, every year. In that first thirty-six months, the payments may seem well within reach, but if the rate goes up just one percentage point, you're in for an ugly surprise.

Loan amount	Initial interest rate	Original monthly payment
$145,000	6.0%	$869

If rates rise 1 percent:

Loan amount	New interest rate	New monthly payment
$139,493	7.0%	$959

If rates rise 5 percent, the pain is even deeper:

Loan amount	New interest rate	New monthly payment
$139,493	11.0%	$1,349

That's a difference of $90 a month with a 1 percent increase in interest rates or a $480-a-month increase if rates go up 5 percent. If you're considering an ARM, ask your lender to show you exactly how much in mortgage payments you'd be on the hook for before and after adjustments.

How does the lender determine what your new reset rate is? Your rates are tied to one of several market rates:

1. *London Interbank Offered Rate* (also called LIBOR) is the interest rate international banks pay each other. If your loan is linked to LIBOR, it will move quickly. That means if you're in a rising rate environment, you'll get the full impact of that quickly. Conversely, if rates are falling, you'll enjoy the benefit of lower costs.

2. *11th District Cost of Funds Index* (COFI) is the interest rate that banks in the western part of the United States charge each other. This is a slow-moving index.

3. *Weekly constant maturity yield* on the one-year Treasury bill. That is the yield that debt securities issued by federal government pay. Another fast-moving index.

Simply put, your interest rate will change with the market. If rates are on the rise, your mortgage will become more expensive. Conversely, if rates are falling, so will your monthly payment.

The good news is that there are limits or "caps" on how much rates on ARMs can adjust. There are both caps on the periodic changes—that is, the annual or monthly adjustments—and caps on how much rates can adjust over the life of the loan. The periodic caps for annual adjustments are typically 2 percent up or down. Common lifetime caps are 5 to 6 percentage points from the initial interest rate. Be sure to check these caps before you borrow. If the loan has no lifetime cap, don't buy the product. Get your lender to work out the worst-case scenarios so you can see exactly how bad things could get under the terms of the loan.

To be sure, these loans need to be used with care and are best chosen by people who know for certain that they will be selling their home or refinancing *before* the rate adjustments. For example, if your company rotates managers every three years or your personal expectation is that you'll stay in a particular area only until the kids reach school age, then you have an opportunity to lock in a mortgage rate that matches your time commitment—and one that will be lower than conventional fixed rates. Typically, borrowers can lock in an initial loan rate that lasts three months, a year, three years, five years, seven years, or even ten years. Be careful here, though—it can be difficult to see into the future. Employer commitments can change, and so can your own.

Watch out for super-short initial interest rate locks. Some unscrupulous lenders have offered initial rate locks of 0 percent, but those locks typically last only three months or less. There's no point to picking one of these loans. Fees make up for whatever advantage you gain during that initial period.

Also, watch out for ARM fees. If you choose an adjustable rate mortgage, scour the documents to see whether your lender is planning to charge you a prepayment penalty, this is a fee that can amount up to six months of mortgage payments. It's assessed if you decide to refinance your loan. Prepayment penalties lock borrowers into toxic loans by making it too expensive to get out of the loans.

LOANS TO SCRUTINIZE In recent years, mortgage lenders have come up with literally hundreds of variations on the thirty-year fixed-rate loan. Some of these were originally offered to people with special situations—those whose income was difficult to document or others whose income streams were uneven. Over time, some of these variations were offered to bigger groups of people, many of whom simply couldn't afford them. To be sure, the bells and whistles offered in many of these loans simply are not worth the price. For that reason, many of the loans you'll see described in the next page or two have fallen out of favor. However, you could see some of them resurface, so for that reason it's worth understanding how they work; in case an over-eager lender decides to pitch you one in the coming years, you'll know the downsides.

INTEREST-ONLY MORTGAGES Mortgage brokers touted these loans to buyers who were having a hard time affording the house of their dreams. And it's true that getting an interest-only mortgage resulted in super-low payments. That's because instead of paying down some of that principal in the early years, usually the first five or ten years of the loan, borrowers had the option of paying only enough to cover the interest due on the loan. That meant they weren't building any wealth, nor were they boosting their ownership position. Interest-only mortgages simply aren't for anyone serious about building an investment. While borrowers may have had good intentions to pour that additional money saved on the payment into another investment, maybe stocks or bonds, the sad truth is that managing that kind of tradeoff is tough even for professional real estate investors. And if you think the jump in payments is big when an ARM resets, wait until you see what happens to your interest-only mortgage when its rate resets. Here's why: if you take out an interest-only mortgage and opt to pay only interest for an initial five-year period, after that five years are up, you still owe the entire loan balance except now the payments are amortized over twenty-five years.

Check out this comparison of two loans, one an interest-only loan and the other a conventional thirty-year mortgage after five years (when the interest-only lock resets):

30-YEAR FIXED-RATE LOAN

Initial loan balance	Interest rate	Initial mortgage payment
$350,000	6.0%	$2,098

AFTER FIVE YEARS

Loan balance	Interest rate	Mortgage payment
$325,690	6.0%	$2,098

INTEREST-ONLY LOAN

Initial loan balance	Interest rate	Initial mortgage payment
$350,000	6.0%	$1,750

AFTER FIVE YEARS

Loan balance	Interest rate	Mortgage payment
$350,000	6.0%	$2,255

So here you can see the downsides of the interest-only loan. After five years of making payments, you have no stake in your house—own no portion of it. Worse, your monthly payments rocket $505 higher. And now you only have twenty-five years to pay off that loan. Plus here's the real nightmare scenario: what if you have to sell the house and prices in your area have fallen? In our example, you'd still be on the hook for your $350,000 loan, but your house might not draw any offers that high. You would have to pay the difference between whatever the market would bear—say, $320,000—and your loan balance, or $30,000.

It was easy enough for borrowers to get talked into one of these loans. After all, a mortgage broker might whisper, "Wouldn't it be nice to have an insurance policy so that if you want to pay only interest for one month, you can?" The problem with that logic is that it's tough to maintain discipline in paying down your mortgage when so many other things compete for your dollars. You'll be sorely tempted to pay interest

only when the credit card bill comes due or for any other of a myriad of reasons. The fact is there are better, cheaper ways of getting an insurance policy, such as taking out a home equity line of credit (HELOC). With a HELOC you'll continue to pay your mortgage in full each month while tapping your equity. To be sure, you'll pay interest on your line of credit, but at least you can deduct that interest (in most cases) from your taxes.

LOANS FOR THE CASH-STRAPPED No money? No problem. If you believed mortgage lenders, there was a loan for every borrower, even the ones who didn't have any skin to put into the game. While standard practice is to put 20 percent of the purchase price down to secure the investment, lenders have in recent years eased credit standards to allow home buyers to buy with a very small down payment or even without one at all. Nothing-down loans were exactly what they sound like: the lender financed the entire purchase price in a single loan. Combination loans or piggyback loans achieve the same effect but involve two mortgages, a first and a second.

But home buyers interested in building equity struggled with these mortgages. They had no equity to tap in the event of disaster, say, to fix the roof or pay hospital bills. Plus, the loan was more expensive than the plain-vanilla mortgages like a thirty-year fixed-rate loan. Remember, lenders require that borrowers who do not put down 20 percent pay private mortgage insurance (PMI) to cover them in case the borrower defaults. The costs aren't small—as much as hundreds of dollars every year.

STATED-INCOME LOANS Lenders require a lot of documentation of your financial situation, especially your income, before they agree to give you a mortgage loan. But if you work for yourself or most of your income comes in the form of bonuses, you may have a difficult time proving your earnings. So-called stated-income mortgages were for people in just that predicament. Instead of turning over the usual W-2 tax form to your lender, though, you would have had to prove your annual earnings using tax returns and bank statements. There are several types of no-

documentation loans, but the one you're most likely to use (unless you are incredibly wealthy) is the stated-income mortgage. Bartenders and small-business owners across the country opt for these kinds of loans. The bad news is that you'll pay more for this type of loan—as much as half a percent more in mortgage interest.

This loan came to be known as the "liar's loan," because it was often used by borrowers who inflated their income. Although lenders have become reluctant to underwrite these loans, they could come back into favor for people who are self-employed. Be sure to document your income as responsibly as you can, if you apply for one of these mortgages. Remember, it's your responsibility, not your lender's, to know whether you're spending too much for housing. And be prepared to pay a higher rate of interest than that levied fixed-rate-loan borrowers.

NO-CLOSING-COST LOANS Closing costs are a burden, and lenders eager to remove any barrier to borrowers sometimes advertise a no-closing-cost loan. Don't believe it. You still pay the fees, but instead of paying your closing costs up front, you pay them over thirty years. Your lender simply rolls that debt into your principal loan amount or charges you a higher interest rate.

SUBMITTING THE PAPERWORK

Once you have found the lenders you like (as described in Chapter 5) and gotten a sense of how much interest you're likely to be charged as well as the type of loan you want, you'll need to submit your paperwork for a loan. It's best to apply with several lenders so that you have the luxury of choosing from several offers. This is a time-consuming affair, a real financial strip search. To speed things up, you'll want to bring together the following documents:

1. W-2s for the past three years
2. Pay stubs for the past two months
3. Two years of federal tax returns
4. Two months of bank statements

5. Investment account statements

6. Any current mortgage statements

7. Purchase contract for the home

8. Divorce decrees

9. Receipts for deposits on the home

COMPARING OFFERS

Once you have several offers from online lenders or other sources, you'll want to compare these offers. Each lender should quote you an interest rate for your loan, closing costs, and any points associated with that loan. A point is a way of "buying down" the interest rate on your loan. One point translates into 1 percent of the total loan amount. In order to fairly compare offers, you will need to get quotes from different lenders on the same day. Mortgage rates change continuously, and even a day's delay can mean that you're comparing apples to oranges. Set aside time to devote to this process.

Making comparisons is easier said than done. If you only had to compare interest rates, it would be a piece of cake. In reality, the lender terms you'll compare will be far more complicated. When you line up your offers side by side, look for APR, or the annual percentage rate— this is simply your total annual cost for the loan, which includes not just the interest rate but other costs as well. You can use the APR to make an apples-to-apples comparison between banks. The lower the number, the less interest you'll pay. Where you'll likely see a difference among the quotes is in the origination and administrative fees as well as in the discount points that we described earlier. If you're only planning to stay in a home a short period of time, then paying the points up front isn't worth it. The longer you plan to have your mortgage, the more it makes sense to pay points up front, because you'll benefit from the loan's lower rate for a long time.

One area where borrowers can make up some ground is administrative fees. Watch out for application and processing fees. These are the pesky charges you'll encounter when you apply for a mortgage. Bankers

know that not all applications turn into loans, and so these cover the company's costs for processing your information. But this is where lenders sometimes boost their payout. These fees will be detailed in a document called the good-faith estimate, which lenders are required to give you three days after you apply for the loan. Question charges you think are excessive. (See Chapter 11 for more on monitoring these.) Ultimately, you'll want to choose the lender with the lowest interest rate and the best terms.

10

Negotiating the Deal

NEGOTIATING THE PRICE ON A HOUSE—LIKELY THE BIGGEST INVEST-
ment of your life—can be intimidating. Problem is, no one simple strategy always works. For example, in hot markets, it's not unheard of for
sellers to price their property lower than what it should sell for. Listing a
home for $399,000, say, instead of the $415,000 that the location commands sparks interest and excitement, drawing more buyers to an open
house than might otherwise come. Sometimes, agents will hold an open
house for only a short period of time, forcing all interested buyers to
cram into the house at the same time, making it appear that demand for
the property is high. Buyers feel pressured to buy today for fear of being
priced out tomorrow. Their bids come in higher and higher. In the end,
having sparked a bidding war, sellers might walk off with $5,000 to
$15,000 more than they would've gotten to begin with. You want to
avoid those bidding wars, and you'd best be advised to slow down. Most
people want to rush negotiations, but remember this is when you have
the most leverage over the seller, who needs you at the negotiating table.
For you, there could always be a better home around the corner.

The first step—choosing your initial offering bid—is the most important. Set it too high and you can't go back. If you set it too low, you could lose out on a gem. This is where your research comes in handy. First check out the comparables—those price-per-square-foot numbers we talked about in Chapter 3—and apply that to the total square footage of the house. That's a great starting point for a bid. Next, try to determine how long the house has been on the market. The longer the sellers have been holding on to the home, the antsier they will be to sell. Plus, their real estate agent will be motivated to make a deal if she or he has been marketing the house for months. Agent contracts typically specify a time frame. Most last only ninety days. As time goes by, pressure increases for the agent to generate a sale before the seller decides to move on to another agent.

Ask whether sellers in the area are giving any concessions. Are sellers paying points on buyers' loans? Throwing in furniture? This is critical to understanding how much leverage you have. If the house has been on the market awhile and sellers are loading buyers with goodies such as free groceries for a month, you'll want to bid below what you estimate the house is worth. In any market, you'll want to understand the rules for bidding. In some areas, negotiations can continue with a number of bidders until the seller asks for everyone's highest and best offer. At that point, the best offer gets the house.

If you're thinking about launching a lowball offer, you should understand that it's most likely to be successful when the market is slowing down after a big run-up or when prices are tumbling. In such markets, people who have locked in incredible gains may be willing to lose some profit in order to sell their house. Be prepared to deal with large-scale repairs, since sellers who accept lowball offers often do so because full-price buyers aren't willing to accept their "as-is" condition. Remember, if you are going to bottom-fish, be prepared by having more than one property you are interested in. Most sellers are reluctant to accept bids well below their asking price.

But that brings up a point that many newbie buyers miss. The quality of your offer isn't expressed simply by the size of your offer. You'll

also be evaluated on the soundness of your offer. Sellers want every assurance that you can close on the house and that your offer is real. For
that reason, they tend to favor offers in which buyers are making significant down payments. At the very least, you'll want to be prequalified or,
preferably, preapproved for your loan. For details on how to get prequalified and the advantages of being prequalifed, see Chapter 5.

Flexibility can be another way to get your offer chosen. Often buyers are under some sort of time pressure to sell. Maybe they are retiring
and have already bought their dream home at the beach. Rather than
foot two mortgages, they may want to sell quickly. Or maybe the kids
need to get started in the new school district before the new school year
gets under way. Either way, if you can move quickly, that can make your
offer even more appealing.

As you go through a negotiation, it's all too easy to get caught up in
the emotion of the moment. This leads to bidding wars and bloated
mortgages—exactly the kind of thing you'll want to avoid. Keep your
wits and establish a friendly relationship with the owners. Sometimes
writing a letter about why you like the house can tip the balance when
two offers are similar. If the market is cooling, you'll find yourself with
more leverage than the buyer. Even so, you may need to convince the
seller that the price set for their castle is too high. To do that, you should
consider having an appraiser make an estimate of the value of the house.
This takes the burden off you to prove your point and brings in another
voice for sellers to consider. If you are in a market that is well past its
peak, you'll want to consider asking for concessions. Ask whether the
seller will pay your mortgage points if you offer the asking price. Will
they throw in the Wolf range? Or give you a free month's worth of groceries? At the end of the day, your successful negotiation will be only as
good as your research, and that means looking for the little clues along
the way. Note whether the master bedroom closet is half empty. That
could signal a divorce. Multiple For Sale signs in the garage could mean
the seller has had a difficult time unloading the home.

Remember, if a deal is keeping you up nights, then it's not for you.
By this point, you should have a solid enough understanding of what

you can afford and what the market will bear to feel comfortable with any offer you are making. And always keep in mind the appeal of the house as it is today and as you'd like to see it—whether that appeal makes sense for you and the future families that will own it.

GET THE BEST ADVICE

It may seem as if the attorney handling your sale or purchase is really secondary, a paper pusher in a business that is pretty straightforward. But that's not the case. An attorney can be a key ally who watches your back and doesn't let little details that can cost you thousands of dollars slide by. Not all states require that an attorney handle the closing process. In some states, a title agent does the paperwork. Either one will help you navigate the details, do title searches, prepare deeds, and work with the agent to coordinate the closing with the lender. A good real estate lawyer or title agent can be an important member of your team, closely reviewing closing documents and watching out for red flags that can turn into a nightmare.

Mike, a Nassau County, New York, homeowner, knows firsthand what can happen if an attorney isn't thorough. He arrived at his newly purchased home one afternoon only to find the builder of the home next door to his property tearing down part of his back deck. With his daughter in his arms, Mike called the police and grabbed a camera to document the destruction. "The builder of the new home had called us after we moved in, and told me that they would have to come out and cut down our deck. I assumed it was a mistake," he says.

Turns out that the deck was on his neighbor's property, a fact that the title company missed because it relied on an old survey. A mention that an old survey was used was in the closing documents, but his attorney completely missed it. And after the builder was done taking down part of the deck, what was left wasn't even safe to walk on. "He cut down half of it and sort of left it dangling. We were lucky that it wasn't our kitchen or bedroom," he says, noting that there is a larger issue than the immediate damage. "The damage has reduced the value of the home."

Mike spent $4,500 just to shore up the deck, but more work re-

mains, and the title company offered only $3,000 for the mistake. His lawyer has been less forthcoming, and he plans on taking her to small claims court. When he confronted her with the problem, she wasn't willing to accept any part of the blame. "No one is willing to point the finger," Mike says. He admits that he didn't choose the best lawyer for the job. In fact, the attorney wasn't even a real estate lawyer, but rather one whom Mike and his wife had used to work on their wills. Says Mike: "She told us that from time to time she had done real estate deals."

Solicit names of good attorneys or title agents from friends and family. Don't hire a friend or family member. Work with an attorney who is experienced in real estate closings. They don't have to be real-estate-only lawyers, but you shouldn't hire the family lawyer whose expertise is really trusts and wills. Also be aware of the conflicts that an attorney and title agent can have. Attorneys often refer business to title agencies, an arrangement that some states are cracking down on. In the summer of 2005, the California Department of Insurance settled a lawsuit with several large title companies that resulted in refunds to consumers of $25.3 million. The lawsuit alleged that these title companies were paying illegal kickbacks to lenders, home builders, and real estate agents in order to get business referrals.

APPRAISAL PITFALLS

Appraisals are designed to ensure that homeowners are not overextending themselves when purchasing a property. It also gives the lender an insurance policy. If you were to default on your loan, the bank would have to foreclose on the house and sell it. For that reason, your lender has to make sure the house is correctly valued and it isn't lending more than the property's worth. For the most part, appraisals confirm the agreed-upon purchase price. But there are times it comes in higher or lower than that number. If your property appraises lower than the agreed-upon sales price, it can kill the deal because the buyer will have to pony up more money out of pocket to cover what the mortgage doesn't. If the house appraises higher, then congratulations to the buyer, who has just earned some quick appreciation.

Since the lender is the one hiring the appraiser, buyers don't have too much say in the selection process. However, you can make it known that you are a smart consumer. Ask for a copy of the appraisal report and request that the lender use an appraiser with the right credentials. An appraiser should at a minimum be licensed by the state. An indicator that an appraiser is a solid pro is certification from the Appraisal Institute, such as the SRA designation, which means that the appraiser has at least two years of experience under his or her belt and two hundred hours of in-classroom training.

Appraisals are required by the lender but paid for by the buyer and generally run $350 to $750. In arriving at an estimate of a home's value, an appraiser uses comparable sales data (typically at least three similar properties that have sold within the past six months) and takes into account the condition of the home, location, and recent improvements that have been made to a property, such as a kitchen remodel.

Buyers should be on the lookout for problem appraisals in hot markets because identifying recent sales can be a problem. In fast-moving markets, homes that sold two months ago might not reflect the going rates of properties that sold just a few weeks ago. In these types of markets when prices are constantly on the rise, appraisals can come in below the market value of a property, disappointing both lenders and agents eager to see a property estimate meet a sales price. In fact, the Appraisal Institute, the professional membership organization for the industry, identified pressure on appraisers as the number one problem in the industry. It is lobbying Congress to pass legislation that would bar such pressure. Donald Kelly, vice president of public affairs at the Appraisal Institute, attributes this stepped-up bullying to increasing home prices and "plain old lender greed. When parties that have an interest in the transaction going forward are in a position to influence the appraisal, that leads to problems." Loan officers on commission have a vested interest in seeing the deal close, even though it is certainly in the best interest of the lender in the long run not to have the appraisal value inflated.

Kelly receives a steady stream of faxes and even copies of voice mails that detail the demands lenders are placing on appraisers. "A loan officer

might tell an appraiser that the contract price for a property is $325,000 and if they can't support that price they should stop the appraisal. Others are even more aggressive and have told appraisers that couldn't support a property's value with local data to use data from another area," he says. "A lot of good appraisers get out of the business and consumers end up with inexperienced appraisers. Someone with two years in the business trying to establish themselves will be rolled right over by the lender."

Real estate agents can influence the process by suggesting that home buyers go to a specific mortgage company because it uses appraisers who turn out estimates that fit in with the sale process of a home. Facing a rash of inflated property values, banks are making changes. To fight against mortgage fraud, Fannie Mae started requiring its lenders to use a new form that requires more documentation of sources for comparable sales data. Banks are hiring more in-house appraisers. Bottom line for buyers: the appraisal process isn't something to ignore. Demand qualified, independent appraisers be used in your purchase.

11

Surviving the Closing

COMPLETING THE PURCHASE OF YOUR HOUSE, CALLED THE CLOSING OR settlement, can be a tedious or even harrowing two to three hours. This is when you, the buyer, sign the lender agreement for the mortgage and pay your closing costs. You'll also sign the documents to transfer title of the property.

When Karen and Len bought a house near Chesapeake Bay, they took their real estate broker's recommendation for a loan officer. Karen says she initially wanted a straight thirty-year fixed mortgage for the entire cost of the house, but the mortgage lender suggested splitting the financing into two parts, called a piggyback loan. The first mortgage of $270,000 would cover 80 percent of the purchase price and carry a fixed rate of 5.85 percent, while the other 20 percent would be financed by a home equity line of credit. The couple liked the idea, especially when their loan officer told them they could lock in the rate on the second mortgage after three months. They applied for the loan. But just forty-eight hours before the closing, the loan officer called to tell them that instead of a fixed-rate loan, they would have to go with an interest-only

mortgage plus pay one point to keep the interest rate of 5.85 percent. "We were moving out of a rental and had given notice to our landlord, plus there is the pressure from the seller and earnest money and time invested. We were stuck," says Karen. At the closing, Karen admits, they made a critical mistake. Overwhelmed by the sheer amount of paperwork and documents to sign, they neglected to double-check the interest rates on the loans. "The paperwork is incredible. You don't have time to read through everything. Plus, in Maryland you have to have an attorney at the closing, and I thought he would point this stuff out to me," she explains. "I could not stop kicking myself for this mistake."

When the first statement arrived, the rate on the second mortgage, the HELOC, was three-quarters of a percentage point higher than the couple expected. Turns out they had signed the document that laid out the higher interest rate. To top it off, when they went to lock in the rate on the second mortgage at the three-month mark, they were told that the loan had been sold and the rate couldn't be locked in. "Essentially, until the sale closed, no one could touch the loan," she said. After months of calls, the bank finally agreed to buy back the loan and allow the couple to lock in the rate of 7.72 percent.

THE PROCESS

Clearly, you don't want to find yourself in a situation like Karen and Len's. Preparation is essential to avoiding any surprises. The day before the closing, gather all the paperwork that you've gotten throughout the process. It's a good idea to have on hand your good-faith estimate of closing costs from the bank, the contract of sale, and the proof of title search and insurance if your attorney or title agent has told you it's your responsibility to bring it. Also gather your home appraisal and inspection reports. You might want to have these on hand at closing.

Most important: make sure your lender gives you a HUD-1 settlement statement before you sit down at the closing table. The HUD-1 is the final list of closing costs; it itemizes the services that are being provided to you. Your best strategy is to get this the day before and carefully compare it to the good-faith estimate of settlement costs your lender

was required to give you when you completed your loan application. Making this comparison is the only way to know whether the lender is trying to change the terms of your loan at the last minute or load up your deal with junk fees. See "The Fees" on page 86, for more details.

A day before the closing, you may have the opportunity to walk through the house one more time. Take advantage of this offer. This way, you'll be sure to know whether the owners have actually moved out and whether the property is still in the same condition as when you agreed to buy it. If there is a problem, you have the right to delay the closing.

Although procedures vary greatly state by state, most closings will include your attorney or title agent, a representative of the title company, the home seller, the seller's real estate agent, the buyer (that's you), and your lender. The closing agent—your lender or a representative of the title company—typically runs the meeting. As the buyer, you'll be signing essentially two sets of documents. One set will deal with the mortgage, the other with transferring title of the house. In addition, you'll also pay your closing costs, if you have not rolled them into your mortgage amount, and any real estate taxes or insurance premiums you pay will go into an escrow account to ensure that the taxes and insurance are paid on time.

THE HUD-1 FORM

This settlement statement is intimidating, with as many as fourteen hundred different lines of information written in a language that can be difficult to decipher. We've included a copy of the form at the end of this chapter so you can inspect one. The first page of the form summarizes your costs and any adjustments that may need to be paid, such as county taxes, homeowner association fees, or fuel oil. Section 100 will detail the price you're paying for the home as well as the cost of any personal property you may be buying from the seller.

At line 200, you'll see any adjustments that are being made for items the seller owes, such as taxes. The seller pays you for these at the closing table. Line 303 details the amount of cash you'll need to bring to the closing table.

Information on fees starts at line 900, with lender fees and insurance premiums. Also included are title charges starting at line 1,100, government record and transfer charges at 1,200, and additional settlement charges 1,300.

OTHER DOCUMENTS

The number of documents you'll be required to sign or look over during the closing is huge. Be on the lookout for the following, in addition to the HUD-1:

- *Final Truth in Lending Act statement.* Outlines the cost of your loan, your rate of interest, and any modifications made between application and closing.

- *Mortgage note.* Your promise to pay your mortgage and details of the loan.

- *Mortgage or deed of trust.* Gives your lender a claim against the home if you fail to pay your mortgage.

THE FEES

Every year, Americans spend $110 billion buying and selling houses—and that doesn't include the price of the homes themselves. The Internet may have cut the cost of everything from clothes to gardening tools, but when it comes to buying a home, the costs continue to rise. In fact, by some estimates, we could save as much as 23 percent on the closing alone if only we contested fees and found alternative vendors for some services.

Your lender estimated the closing fees you'd be paying in your good-faith estimate. It's your responsibility to compare those estimates with what you are asked to pay at the closing, which is detailed in the HUD-1 form.

It's easiest to break the fees into three camps: set fees, often going to third parties (such as an appraisal fee); fees that are going to the lender and fattening its profit; and prepaid fees such as one year of property taxes. Fees going to third parties shouldn't be different from the good-

faith estimate provided. If they are markedly different, ask questions. Pre-paid fees can change from the estimate. After all, a lender might not know the exact property taxes for the house at the time it quoted you the closing costs.

Broker or lender fees have various names, such as "origination fee," "lending fee," "administrative fee," and "discount points." If these weren't on the good-faith estimate but show up on the HUD-1 document, speak up at the closing. Also, if you see something called a "yield spread premium," raise your voice. A yield spread premium is a fee that the bro-ker is being paid by the lender for putting you in a higher-interest-rate loan, often to cover some of the closing costs. So if the loan has a yield spread premium but you aren't getting any compensation for closing costs, ask some tough questions. Document preparation fees, which can cost $150 to $250, are typically junk fees and should be contested. Com-mitment fees, processing fees, and underwriting fees should be closely examined.

Other prepaid items include taxes that you will have to pay up front, flood insurance premiums, government fees, one year of property taxes, and tax stamps. Prepaid insurance and taxes are typically paid into an es-crow account to protect the lender from borrowers who fail to make their payments. The lender makes the insurance and tax payments on your behalf. The government limits how much in insurance premiums and taxes they can collect up front to two months of monthly insurance and tax costs. Third-party fees include the cost of an appraiser and a pest inspection.

Closing costs can range anywhere from 2 to 4 percent of the total loan amount. Some undoubtedly will change from the good-faith esti-mate. But remember, closing costs are negotiable. Depending on the market, you may even be able to have the home seller pick up some of those costs.

PROTECTING YOURSELF

As Karen and Len's experience shows, lenders and mortgage brokers can promise anything, but when it comes to the closing, they may deliver

something far different. The key to protecting yourself is to be totally honest with your lender about your financial situation. Don't misrepresent your income or credit. It's embarrassing to have had financial problems, but if you've filed for bankruptcy or faced collection agencies for late payment of debt, you need to come clean to your lender. Likewise, if you're self-employed, claim only the income that you can actually prove with receipts. Karen and Len could have saved themselves a lot of heartache by carefully reading their lender's letter of commitment, which spells out in much more detail than the good-faith estimate what the terms of the loan will be. The letter is more accurate because it's written after the lender has done most of its due diligence. Remember, a lender is well within its rights to change the terms of your loan if it discovers during the underwriting process that you failed to share important financial information.

When it comes to a rate lock, make sure you understand how long you are locking it in for and when the rate lock expires. Get the offer in writing from your lender stating the details, what the rate is, whether it is locked until closing, and at what point the rate will float.

BE YOUR OWN ADVOCATE

If you get to the closing table and find that the terms of your loan have changed dramatically or new fees have cropped up, complain right away. You may think you have no leverage at this point, but the opposite is true. From the seller's point of view, the worst thing that can happen is that you walk away on closing day.

You should know that federal law makes it illegal for anybody to get a fee for recommending settlement services. For example, your mortgage lender can't pay your real estate agent $250 for referring you to the lender. That's a kickback government regulators do not allow. Also, settlement fees must go to the person who provides the service. Under federal law, your lender can't add to an appraiser's fee, for example, and keep the difference.

A. **Settlement Statement**

U.S. Department of Housing
and Urban Development

OMB Approval No. 2502-0265
(expires 11/30/2009)

B. Type of Loan

1. ☐ FHA 2. ☐ FmHA 3. ☐ Conv. Unins.	6. File Number:	7. Loan Number:	8. Mortgage Insurance Case Number:
4. ☐ VA 5. ☐ Conv. Ins.			

C. Note: This form is furnished to give you a statement of actual settlement costs. Amounts paid to and by the settlement agent are shown. Items marked "(p.o.c.)" were paid outside the closing; they are shown here for informational purposes and are not included in the totals.

D. Name & Address of Borrower:	E. Name & Address of Seller:	F. Name & Address of Lender:

G. Property Location:	H. Settlement Agent:	
	Place of Settlement:	I. Settlement Date:

J. Summary of Borrower's Transaction		**K. Summary of Seller's Transaction**	
100. Gross Amount Due From Borrower		**400. Gross Amount Due To Seller**	
101. Contract sales price		401. Contract sales price	
102. Personal property		402. Personal property	
103. Settlement charges to borrower (line 1400)		403.	
104.		404.	
105.		405.	
Adjustments for items paid by seller in advance		**Adjustments for items paid by seller in advance**	
106. City/town taxes to		406. City/town taxes to	
107. County taxes to		407. County taxes to	
108. Assessments to		408. Assessments to	
109.		409.	
110.		410.	
111.		411.	
112.		412.	
120. Gross Amount Due From Borrower		**420. Gross Amount Due To Seller**	
200. Amounts Paid By Or In Behalf Of Borrower		**500. Reductions In Amount Due To Seller**	
201. Deposit or earnest money		501. Excess deposit (see instructions)	
202. Principal amount of new loan(s)		502. Settlement charges to seller (line 1400)	
203. Existing loan(s) taken subject to		503. Existing loan(s) taken subject to	
204.		504. Payoff of first mortgage loan	
205.		505. Payoff of second mortgage loan	
206.		506.	
207.		507.	
208.		508.	
209.		509.	
Adjustments for items unpaid by seller		**Adjustments for items unpaid by seller**	
210. City/town taxes to		510. City/town taxes to	
211. County taxes to		511. County taxes to	
212. Assessments to		512. Assessments to	
213.		513.	
214.		514.	
215.		515.	
216.		516.	
217.		517.	
218.		518.	
219.		519.	
220. Total Paid By/For Borrower		**520. Total Reduction Amount Due Seller**	
300. Cash At Settlement From/To Borrower		**600. Cash At Settlement To/From Seller**	
301. Gross Amount due from borrower (line 120)		601. Gross amount due to seller (line 420)	
302. Less amounts paid by/for borrower (line 220)	(	602. Less reductions in amt. due seller (line 520)	( )
303. Cash ☐ From ☐ To Borrower		**603. Cash** ☐ To ☐ From Seller	

Section 5 of the Real Estate Settlement Procedures Act (RESPA) requires the following: • HUD must develop a Special Information Booklet to help persons borrowing money to finance the purchase of residential real estate to better understand the nature and costs of real estate settlement services; • Each lender must provide the booklet to all applicants from whom it receives or for whom it prepares a written application to borrow money to finance the purchase of residential real estate; • Lenders must prepare and distribute with the Booklet a Good Faith Estimate of the settlement costs that the borrower is likely to incur in connection with the settlement. These disclosures are manadatory.

Section 4(a) of RESPA mandates that HUD develop and prescribe this standard form to be used at the time of loan settlement to provide full disclosure of all charges imposed upon the borrower and seller. These are third party disclosures that are designed to provide the borrower with pertinent information during the settlement process in order to be a better shopper.

The Public Reporting Burden for this collection of information is estimated to average one hour per response, including the time for reviewing instructions, searching existing data sources, gathering and maintaining the data needed, and completing and reviewing the collection of information.

This agency may not collect this information, and you are not required to complete this form, unless it displays a currently valid OMB control number.

The information requested does not lend itself to confidentiality.

L. Settlement Charges

	Paid From Borrowers Funds at Settlement	Paid From Seller's Funds at Settlement
700. Total Sales/Broker's Commission based on price $ @ % =		
Division of Commission (line 700) as follows:		
701. $ to		
702. $ to		
703. Commission paid at Settlement		
704.		
800. Items Payable In Connection With Loan		
801. Loan Origination Fee %		
802. Loan Discount %		
803. Appraisal Fee to		
804. Credit Report to		
805. Lender's Inspection Fee		
806. Mortgage Insurance Application Fee to		
807. Assumption Fee		
808.		
809.		
810.		
811.		
900. Items Required By Lender To Be Paid In Advance		
901. Interest from to @$ /day		
902. Mortgage Insurance Premium for months to		
903. Hazard Insurance Premium for years to		
904. years to		
905.		
1000. Reserves Deposited With Lender		
1001. Hazard insurance months@$ per month		
1002. Mortgage insurance months@$ per month		
1003. City property taxes months@$ per month		
1004. County property taxes months@$ per month		
1005. Annual assessments months@$ per month		
1006. months@$ per month		
1007. months@$ per month		
1008. months@$ per month		
1100. Title Charges		
1101. Settlement or closing fee to		
1102. Abstract or title search to		
1103. Title examination to		
1104. Title insurance binder to		
1105. Document preparation to		
1106. Notary fees to		
1107. Attorney's fees to		
(includes above items numbers:)		
1108. Title insurance to		
(includes above items numbers:)		
1109. Lender's coverage $		
1110. Owner's coverage $		
1111.		
1112.		
1113.		
1200. Government Recording and Transfer Charges		
1201. Recording fees: Deed $; Mortgage $; Releases $		
1202. City/county tax/stamps: Deed $; Mortgage $		
1203. State tax/stamps: Deed $; Mortgage $		
1204.		
1205.		
1300. Additional Settlement Charges		
1301. Survey to		
1302. Pest inspection to		
1303.		
1304.		
1305.		
1400. Total Settlement Charges (enter on lines 103, Section J and 502, Section K)		

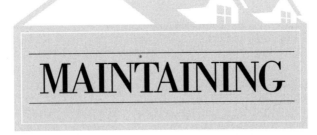

MAINTAINING

12

Managing Your Equity

TO TRULY BECOME HOME RICH, YOU HAVE TO RECOGNIZE THAT THE real bottom line isn't your house's bricks and mortar; in all likelihood, that belongs to your lender. What you own—your true wealth—is your equity. And that equity needs one thing: managing.

Home equity sounds complicated initially, but it's pretty straightforward. Put simply, it's whatever payments toward principal you have made plus any appreciation from gains the market has given you or that you earned yourself with home improvements. Say you bought a $500,000 house three years ago and put $100,000 down and took out a $400,000 loan. Well, right off the bat you have $100,000 in equity. Fast-forward three years. Your $400,000 thirty-year mortgage secured with a 6.5 percent fixed interest rate has you making monthly payments of $2,528. Over those thirty-six months, you've built up another $14,331 of equity. To top it off, home prices have appreciated a handsome 15 percent, so the house would sell for $575,000, a full $75,000 more than you paid for it. Total equity from your down payment, payments on principal and appreciation after three years: $189,331. Not too shabby.

Equity is important because it gives you both options and protection. Tapping your equity with a home equity loan or line of credit, for example, can fund a bathroom renovation, or a home equity loan can pay off credit card debt. Keep in mind that you will want to pay it back. But most important, equity keeps you from losing your shirt. When it comes time to sell the house, the equity you've built up ensures that you will be able to pay off the mortgage with the proceeds from the sale, even if the market takes a dip. Of course, becoming home rich isn't just about scraping by. Your house should return a healthy profit whether you plan to live in it thirteen years or thirty.

While equity is straightforward, managing it is far from simple. In this chapter, I'll guide you through the many facets of home equity, from tracking how much you have to adjusting your financing and payments to help you accumulate more of this good stuff. Of course, there are plenty of wrong turns out there that can derail you on your path to racking up equity. I'll advise you on what to watch out for and how to handle your single biggest investment, your home, in a changing interest-rate environment.

CALCULATING YOUR EQUITY

FIGURING OUT YOUR PRINCIPAL PAYMENTS You know precisely how much your mortgage payments are, but your payments toward principal are just a portion of that total. Most of your monthly payments in the early years are earmarked to pay interest costs of the loan. That proportion changes over time until the last years of your loan, when most of your payment goes directly to principal. For example, on a thirty-year fixed-rate loan of $300,000 and a rate of 6.4 percent, just $276.52 of your first mortgage payment of $1,876.52 goes to paying down principal. The rest, or $1,600.00, goes to paying your interest costs. It's not until the nineteenth year of your mortgage that the situation reverses—more of your monthly payment goes to principal than interest. To determine just how much of your payments have been going to principal, go to www.bankrate.com and navigate to "Mortgage Payment Calculator." By entering the terms of your loan, including rate of interest, amount financed, and term of repayment, the calculator will show you the portion of your monthly mortgage payment going to principal for each month.

Add up those payments for however long you've had the loan. You can also check your monthly statement from your lender.

DETERMINING APPRECIATION AND DEPRECIATION Appreciation can make a huge difference in your wealth. If you live in an area where prices improve at a slow rate, which is typical in much of the Midwest, for example, then your wealth from your home will also grow slowly. Or you could have the opposite situation, like Dana in Las Vegas. She knew that her five-bedroom house in Las Vegas had grown in price in the four years since she and her husband purchased it, but she was shocked at just how much the value had gone up. She got estimates from both an appraiser and a few local Realtors who pulled "comps," or a competitive market analysis, which looked at recent home sales in her neighborhood. "It's quite astonishing that you can make $250,000 in four years," says Dana, who says the house had a market value of $525,000. Having enjoyed such a price run, Dana decided to leverage that gain to build even more value in her eleven-year-old house. She refinanced her mortgage at the end of 2005, taking out $10,000 in equity to fund small improvements, including replastering the ceiling and replacing all the windows. She hasn't sold yet, but she expects to pocket a handsome return when the time comes.

Just as appreciation can be a tremendous boon to your wealth, so depreciation can be a drag on your bottom line. Furthermore, declining values can make it difficult or impossible to refinance, or pull equity, out of your home for other purposes. And, naturally, this can make it tough to sell. Thomas and his partner, Josh, had spent hours improving their quaint New Jersey bungalow, investing a total of $60,000. But when Josh unexpectedly received a dream job offer on the West Coast, the two were stuck. Prices had fallen 8 percent in one year in their neighborhood. There was no way they could recoup their investment in the house. They finally decided to rent their home until the market corrected, but the decision was painful. Had prices not corrected, they would have been able to sell and collect a tidy profit.

Figuring out what gains you've achieved through appreciation can be as simple as calling up an appraiser and paying the $300 or so for a formal appraisal. You could also estimate those gains on your own for free. If you

worked with a real estate agent, call the agent and ask for appreciation rates for your area. Ask him or her how much prices have gone up for your town or county in each year since you've owned the home.

A typical calculation for a home whose owners have held the house for four years might look like this:

Home purchase price	$350,000
Year one appreciation, 3%	$10,500
Year two appreciation, 3%	$10,815
Year three appreciation, 5%	$18,565
Year four depreciation, 2%	($7,797)
Current home value	$382,083

One note here: a calculation like this will help you understand part of the power of home ownership as an investment. Notice just how quickly the value of your home grows. That's because your appreciation gains are calculated on the total value of the home, not just on the value of your equity. In other words, you may not own the whole thing yet, but you get the benefits of having control of such a large asset. Notice, too, that prices can move up or down—appreciate or depreciate—and you'll need to factor both into your analysis.

CALCULATING CONTRIBUTION FROM UPGRADES The increased value will also stem from the upgrades you've made to your abode. Whether you've gutted and replaced the kitchen or added a master suite, you've improved your investment and boosted your equity. That's the good news. What most people don't realize, however, is that the return on your investment isn't 100 percent. In other words, you won't get back $1 for every $1 you spend. Your returns depend on just how popular the renovation is. On the next page, you'll see the typical returns for popular projects. They are based on actual returns on actual projects. Go to www.remodeling.hw.net for more details, including returns for projects organized by where the homeowners are located.

RETURNS ON RENOVATIONS
2006 National Averages

	Project	Job Cost	Resale Value	% Cost Recouped
MID-RANGE	Attic bedroom remodel	$44,073	$35,228	79.9%
	Basement remodel	$56,724	$44,685	78.8%
	Bathroom addition	$28,918	$21,670	74.9%
	Bathroom remodel	$12,918	$10,970	84.9%
	Deck addition	$14,728	$11,307	76.8%
	Family room addition	$74,890	$53,519	71.5%
	Home office remodel	$20,057	$12,707	63.4%
	Major kitchen remodel	$54,241	$43,603	80.4%
	Master suite addition	$94,331	$68,458	72.6%
	Minor kitchen remodel	$17,928	$15,278	85.2%
MID-RANGE	Roofing replacement	$14,276	$10,553	73.9%
	Siding replacement (vinyl)	$9,134	$7,963	87.2%
	Sunroom addition	$49,551	$32,854	66.3%
	Two-story addition	$105,297	$87,654	83.2%
	Window replacement (wood)	$11,040	$9,416	85.3%
	Window replacement (vinyl)	$10,160	$8,500	83.7%
UPSCALE	Bathroom addition	$60,535	$44,041	72.8%
	Bathroom remodel	$38,165	$29,529	77.4%
	Major kitchen remodel	$107,973	$81,896	75.9%
	Master suite addition	$176,268	$128,096	72.7%
	Roofing replacement	$24,693	$18,012	72.9%
	Siding replacement (fiber cement)	$13,149	$11,573	88.0%
	Siding replacement (foam-backed vinyl)	$11,139	$9,258	83.1%
	Window replacement (wood)	$16,910	$13,952	82.5%
	Window replacement (vinyl)	$13,120	$11,109	84.7%

Source: www.remodeling.hw.net

To determine your return, simply multiply the percentage of cost recouped by the cost of your upgrade.

PUTTING IT ALL TOGETHER Now you have all the elements you need to calculate how much equity you have in your home. Getting the final number is simple—just add your principal payments, your down payment, any appreciation, and any contribution from upgrades. This is the wealth you've accumulated in your home—and what you'll want to nurture, grow, and protect. You'll be able to tap it in the event of emergency—to pay for a new roof if your old one collapses, or to pay medical bills if someone in your family gets sick. It will likely be the source of some of the money you might use for upgrades to the house and what you'll use to pay the commission of the real estate agent who sells your house.

SMART MOVES TO GROW EQUITY

CHOOSE THE RIGHT MORTGAGE Few decisions are more important than using the right mortgage. When Allison and Andy decided to buy their home, the young couple had only $12,000 in savings to put down and plenty of college debt. They knew they would have to stretch to buy a home in suburban Portland, where prices had been rising consistently. When they found the three-bedroom home of their dreams priced at $320,000, they decided to take the leap, using some creative financing to qualify for a loan. By opting for an adjustable-rate mortgage that allowed them to pay interest only for most of the debt and then simultaneously taking out a second mortgage—a home equity line of credit—to cover the balance, they just managed to qualify for their loan. Problem is, rates rose dramatically, pushing their monthly payments $155 higher for the home equity line of credit. Worse, they knew that in just two short years, the interest on their first mortgage would reset higher as well. Allison worried that they were making no headway on their loan since they were making interest-only payments. The burden of their $1,800 monthly mortgage payment seemed heavier each month. Fortunately, Allison's parents stepped in and gave them some financial help until they could refinance into a thirty-year fixed-rate mortgage. Had they encountered a real financial emergency, they could have faced foreclosure.

As you shop for a mortgage loan, you'll want to make sure both that it's affordable and that it helps you build equity month to month. Reevaluate your loan as market conditions change to make sure that you con-

tinue to build equity and keep your financing costs as low as possible. Allison and Andy exposed themselves to mortgage costs that could rise dramatically. Both their first and second mortgages had adjustable-rate features. Using an interest-only feature further weakened their position by preventing them from building equity. Ultimately, they stretched too far to buy their dream home. The best solution would have been to buy a smaller home or to delay home buying to build a larger down payment.

For most of us, a plain vanilla fixed-rate mortgage or a no-frills adjustable-rate mortgage in which the initial fixed-rate period corresponds with the amount of time you plan to stay in the home makes the most sense for building equity quickly.

REFINANCE YOUR LOAN The rate of interest you pay on a loan is critical to building wealth. That's because the more you pay in interest, the less you have available for paying principal. Even a point and a half difference can mean a lot to your monthly payment. If you have a thirty-year fixed-rate loan for $150,000 financed at 8.5 percent, you could cut your monthly payments by $155 if you refinanced your loan at 7 percent. For that reason, you'll want to keep a sharp eye on mortgage rates at all times. An easy way to do that is to bookmark websites such as www.bankrate.com and www.hsh.com. Both allow you to monitor rates in your part of the country. A refinance helps you to make the most of those falling rates by getting a cheaper mortgage or rolling a thirty-year mortgage and a high-rate second mortgage into one low-rate loan.

It used to be that for a refinance to make sense there had to be a two-percentage-point difference between the rate you could get and the rate you currently have. But automation of loans has made it possible to get a good deal when the spread is smaller. A good rule of thumb to follow: you'll want to consider refinancing your mortgage into a new one when rates drop one percentage point below your loan's rate.

However, refinancing is not without its costs, and for that reason, it may not be for everyone. For example, if you have a thirty-year loan and are ten years into the loan, you probably won't want to consider refinancing into another thirty-year loan because you would end up paying enormous interest costs on the remainder of your loan balance. A person

in that situation may well want to consider refinancing into a fifteen-year loan if the higher monthly payments are affordable.

Here is a list of the typical costs you'll face for refinancing:

Application fee	$275		**Title insurance**	$400
Credit check	$45		**Appraisal fee**	$300
Attorney fees	$675		**Inspection fee**	$250
Lender attorney fees	$450		**Document fee**	$200
Title search fees	$200		**TOTAL**	$2,795

These costs are estimates. You may face higher or lower costs. For example, attorney fees can range from $350 to $1,100. As you can see, these costs are similar to the costs for closing a loan. You may also have to pay local taxes and transfer fees that could add up to additional thousands of dollars. What's more, you could opt to pay points, to buy your rate down further. (One point equals 1 percent of your loan amount.)

Sometimes the best refinance deals are only available through your existing lender. Ask for a "loan modification." Although these are less widely available now than they have been in the past, a loan modification is a great deal because it cuts your costs by adjusting your existing mortgage rather than requiring you to get a new one. Costs are about $200. If a loan modification isn't possible, ask whether your lender will make available a "streamlined" mortgage. Sometimes lenders will cut the costs of refinance for existing loan customers, because they can eliminate some of the paperwork associated with mortgage loans. This is another low-cost refinance that is cheaper because the paperwork is minimized. Appraisal and application fees may be waived. Major lenders typically offer streamlined mortgages. To qualify for these inexpensive options, however, you'll have to have good credit and a history of paying your bills on time. A third option is to ask your existing lender for a "no-cost refi," in which the costs are rolled into the amount being financed or your interest rate is raised to recoup the costs. You'll still pay the costs, but over thirty years, instead of up front.

If none of these programs are available to you check out which of the major lenders are working aggressively in your area at www.hsh.com by offering the most competitive interest rates. Contact several of the most aggressive large lenders, such as Washington Mutual and Wells Fargo, for offers. Inspect each offer with care. Lenders will find a way to make a refinance offer to almost any borrower. For that reason, if you have less-than-perfect credit, you'll want to pay particular attention to the terms being offered. Make sure the interest rate offers a clear improvement over what you already have. With each offer, be sure to get a clear explanation of the fees they will charge you to process your refinance.

Remember, while the monthly savings on your mortgage can be impressive, you'll also have the extra burden of the refinance costs, which can run into the thousands, plus your home mortgage deduction will drop because you'll be paying less in interest. To determine how much you'll lose in tax savings, multiply your savings by your federal tax rate. For example, if you stand to save $400 each month and are in the 33 percent tax bracket, you'll lose tax savings of $132 monthly, for a net savings of $268 a month.

To determine how long it will take you to break even if you refinance, follow this simple formula: add up the refinance fees and divide the total by your after-tax monthly savings on the refinance. The result? The number of months until you break even. For example, using the figures above, if our refinance fees were $6,300, then our break-even point would be twenty-three months or nearly two years. Remember, if your break-even period is longer than the amount of time you plan to be in the house, you'll want to forgo the refinance.

REFINANCE YOUR HOME EQUITY LINE OF CREDIT Because home equity lines of credit have variable rates of interest, they can become expensive quickly. For that reason, if you have a large HELOC debt and mortgage rates generally aren't above their long-term averages of 8 percent, you may want to consider refinancing both loans into one. To know whether it makes sense, you'll need to calculate a blended rate of interest.

Let's say you have total mortgage debt of $300,000, $200,000 of

which is a first mortgage financed at a rate of 6.5 percent. The remainder is a home equity line of credit with an outstanding balance of $100,000 at 8.0 percent. Divide your first mortgage amount ($200,000) by the total ($300,000) and multiply by the interest rate (6.5 percent) for a total of 4.33 percent. Next divide the outstanding HELOC balance ($100,000) by the total debt ($300,000) and multiply by your rate (8.0 percent) for a total of 2.67. Add the two rates together (7.0 percent). That is the rate you'll have to beat to make sure the deal is worth your while.

PAY IT DOWN FASTER Another way to build equity is simply to pay down your mortgage loan faster. With your actual interest costs totaling hundreds of thousands of dollars over the life of the loan, it's no wonder that plenty of people advocate paying down your mortgage as quickly as possible. After all, if you have a thirty-year fixed-rate mortgage for $250,000 at 7 percent, you'll end up paying total interest of $348,772 by the end of your mortgage term. In reality, you'll want to consider several issues before throwing every last nickel at your mortgage. First off, determine whether or not your current mortgage has a prepayment penalty; such fees can run into thousands of dollars. Remember also that to the degree you pay down your mortgage, you'll also cut into your mortgage interest deduction.

A good way to prepay is to add an additional mortgage payment a year. By adding just one additional payment, you'll significantly cut into the loan balance. This is most easily done by adding a twelfth of a payment to each regular monthly mortgage payment or by adding an extra payment during one of the months with five weeks. Lenders offer biweekly plans that require you to pay half of your monthly mortgage payment every two weeks so that you end up making that extra payment, but in reality fees for those programs are such that you probably come out ahead just doing it on your own.

Remember, you don't want to allocate every nickel to your mortgage at the expense of your retirement savings and an emergency savings plan.

GET RID OF PRIVATE MORTGAGE INSURANCE If you put less than 20 percent down when you bought your house, you may be paying private mort-

gage insurance, a policy that reimburses lenders if you default on your mortgage. Most lenders require PMI until your loan-to-value ratio drops below 80 percent. Simply put, the loan-to-value ratio is the ratio of your loan size to the appraised value of your house. For example, you may have a loan of $250,000 on a home with a value of $275,000, a 90 percent loan-to-value ratio, calculated by dividing $250,000 by $275,000. As you make payments your loan size falls; appreciation can also boost your value. After a few years of this, you probably don't technically have to have private mortgage insurance. The problem with PMI is that lenders may fail to cancel it, and homeowners sometimes forget they are paying it. Most homeowners are eligible to get rid of PMI and stop paying their mortgage premiums once their equity reaches 20 percent. For example, if you had a $300,000 home you purchased with a down payment of just 10 percent or $30,000 two years ago, your calculation might look something like this:

Down payment	Sum of principal payments for two years	Appreciation of 5 percent for two years	Total equity gain
$30,000	$6,238	$30,750	$66,988

In this case, you have more than enough equity built up to make a case for dropping the mortgage insurance. The next step is to call your lender's customer service department and ask the proper procedure for getting PMI removed. In all likelihood, they will require a formal written request from you as well as an appraisal of the value of the home made by a professional appraiser. Make all your payments in a timely fashion during this period, since your lender will weigh how conscientious you are about your bill paying in making the decision to drop its requirement for private mortgage insurance.

EQUITY MANEUVERS TO BE WARY OF While shopping to refinance, you may be offered a cash-out option. Simply put, this means that you'll refinance your mortgage for more than you currently owe and take the difference

out. This tends to be popular when home values have risen dramatically, and, it's easy to see why. When the appraisal comes in much higher than you bought your home for, it may feel like found money. That's how it seemed to Sue and Joe, a couple who originally paid a modest sum, just $106,000, for their Littleton, Colorado, home. Home values in their part of the country soared in a short time, and a month after they bought their house, they had it appraised again. Its value had jumped to $125,000. Ultimately the home's value spiked to a high of $330,000. As the value rose, the two decided they wanted to tap some of those gains to pay off credit cards and car loans. So the two refinanced, taking out a mortgage for $297,000. Even though the value of their house was rising, their income wasn't. When their monthly mortgage payments soared to $2,356, the two could no longer keep up. They missed two payments, ultimately defaulted on their mortgage, and were forced to pack up and leave.

It's difficult for most people not to succumb to the temptation in such a situation to take advantage of market gains and use their mortgage like a piggy bank. But the best course of action is to use the funds judiciously, earmarking them for purchases that would increase the value of your investment or as a last-gasp emergency fund. Don't use equity from a cash-out refinance or home equity loan or line of credit to pay for anything you wouldn't want to finance over thirty years. It's hard to make an argument for paying for vacations or electronics over such a long period, even if the interest rate is lower than those on credit cards.

While a cash-out refinance can be used to achieve a better investment if you use the extra funds judiciously, other products such as option ARMs and interest-only loans are equity busters. Turn back to Chapter 9 for a refresher on choosing the right mortgage.

PROTECTING YOUR INVESTMENT

Protecting your investment is critical. If you have a mortgage, your lender will require you to have a homeowner's insurance policy. Even if you don't have a mortgage, you should get insurance. The unexpected can happen: a tree falls on the house, a sewer backs up, a burglar breaks

in and steals your jewelry. The only way to keep from raiding your equity each time something unfortunate happens is to have financial backup in the form of a homeowner's insurance policy.

Buying coverage is trickier than it seems. Nearly two-thirds of homes are insured for less than their full value. That's right—if the worst happened, such as a storm blowing the house over, most people wouldn't be able to rebuild, or at least not rebuild a home like the one they currently have. A quick way to find out the replacement value of your house (for a fee) is to point your browser to www.accucoverage.com.

Given the rash of hurricanes, mudslides, and twisters over the last few years, underwriters have been angling to limit their risk for some catastrophes. In the spring of 2006, some major underwriters stopped writing new homeowner's policies as far north as New York State because of worries that a hurricane could hit that area. If you live in an area prone to disaster (think Florida, California, and the Carolina coast), you'd do well to use an independent insurance agent who can help you shop for the best possible coverage. Independent agents represent many companies, not just one, and experienced agents can guide you to the underwriters that are best for your specific issues, whether it's a sloping lawn that floods or a location fifty feet from ocean spray. If your greater concern is price, seek out direct insurers, such as Geico, that don't pay for a big sales force.

When shopping for a homeowner's policy, you'll be offered the choice of cash value or replacement cost coverage. The two are exactly what they sound like. Cash value coverage means that your insurer will pay the current value of your belongings. So if you paid $4,000 for your flat-panel TV but the market value of it today is $1,000, your cash value policy will pay out $1,000. A better alternative is a replacement value policy that guarantees you'll be paid whatever it costs to replace your stuff. One Virginia couple found that out the hard way when their home was destoyed by fire. Their policy covered little more than the assessed value of the home—far less than what they needed to rebuild. A two-year legal battle ensued, and while the insurer finally paid an additional

$25,000 over what it initially agreed to pay, the family was still on the hook for the $200,000 it cost them to rebuild.

Where these policies get really tricky is in the details. More and more, policies are written with exclusions for specific problems. For example, many insurers are starting to write policies that exclude wind damage in the event of a hurricane, and they already exclude coverage for damage from flooding. Bottom line? Some insurers are walking away from any hurricane coverage at all. If you live in an area where hurricane water damage is common, get a flood insurance policy. Flood insurance is underwritten by the federal government but sold by insurance agents. The policies may not cover all your damage—coverage limits are typically $250,000 for the structure and $100,000 for contents—but it's far better than having no coverage at all. And don't substitute your agent's advice for your own when it comes to flood insurance. One Mississippi couple took their agent's advice not to buy flood insurance coverage and reaped horrible results: their home was destroyed by the storm surge from Hurricane Katrina, and their insurer sought to pay them just thousands. Federal flood insurance coverage would have made them whole.

Meanwhile, construction and materials costs are rising too. To get the clearest idea of just how much coverage you need, ask a contractor what it would cost to rebuild. To be safe, make sure your policy has an inflation guard so that its value will be adjusted for rising prices.

If you collect anything of value—say, rare baseball cards or African art—you'll want to make sure your homeowner's policy has a rider or endorsement that provides for coverage if something happens to your valuables. You'll pay about 1 to 4 percent of the item's value. If you keep valuables in a safe deposit box at your bank branch, you'll still need insurance, though it will likely cost less. Other special circumstances to make sure you're covered for include sewer and drain backups. Most policies don't cover it, but you can ask for a rider that will add the coverage. Plus, if you do live in an area where cataclysmic weather is common, you'll also want to consider buying a rider to cover what it will cost to meet new building codes that may not have been in place when your house was built. You'll also want to look into liability coverage that

protects you from lawsuits. A policy that gives you $1 million worth of coverage is probably about right. That will likely mean that you'll need to buy an umbrella policy in addition to the maximum limits on your coverage.

Insurers keep track of your claims using CLUE, the Comprehensive Loss Underwriting Exchange database. When you are searching for a policy, check out the claims that insurers see by getting your CLUE report for free at www.choicetrust.com. Challenge mistakes and submit updates to make sure you're not overpaying for your policy.

13

Going Green

THESE DAYS GREEN PRODUCTS AND STRATEGIES ARE BECOMING ESSEN-
tial to combating rising energy costs. And it's not just higher heating-oil
costs that consumers have to worry about. For years now, the national energy grid has struggled to keep up with demand in peak usage months,
especially during the summer. As a result, the number of blackouts and
brownouts has quadrupled since 1995. Electricity prices are spiking as
well, and that means pain for homeowners, particularly those living on
fixed incomes or in expansive homes whose vaulted ceilings and impressive two-story entryways are now viewed suspiciously as energy hogs.
The good news: new green technology is helping consumers save money
on their bills by boosting energy efficiency. Of course, that's not the only
promise of sustainable design. It can also cut household waste and minimize use of harmful substances and nonrenewable resources.

FORGET YOUR OLD ASSUMPTIONS

If it's been a while since you heard about green building initiatives, you
may assume that such homes resemble the rural Texas home that

Rhonda and Bradley built back in 1986. Rhonda and her son and daughter had developed severe chemical sensitivities from the indoor air pollution in their suburban Chicago home, and she was determined that their new home would be as close as possible to outdoor living. In place of enclosed bedrooms were screened-in porches, where the family slept all year round, "except when the rain was horizontal," says Rhonda. Ceiling fans kept the house cool on all but the hottest nights of the year. Closets and storage cabinets were also kept on the screened-in porches, away from the home's few enclosed rooms, to keep down the indoor pollution. And they built the house with only one bathroom, in part to reduce the risk of mold, but also "because my daughter was a preteen at the time and I figured she'd have to talk to us if she had to wait to get in the bathroom."

The house was a haven for the family—the children recovered from their chemical sensitivities. The home was even featured as a case study in a 1999 book on healthy homes. But when Rhonda and Bradley decided to sell the house in 2004, they realized that everything that made their home perfect for them made it a problem to sell. "The Realtors didn't think anyone would pay a premium for all the special things that were particular to our lives," says Rhonda. Potential buyers couldn't fathom living without air-conditioning in Texas, or getting by with just one bathroom. After months on the market, they finally sold their house for $210,000—some $40,000 less than they had hoped to get for it. "Our home gave us back our health, so even if we got nothing for it, it would have been a worthwhile investment, but it was not our best investment in a financial sense," says Rhonda. "Almost everyone who saw the house was very impressed but just couldn't imagine living that way."

When we think of green homes, we tend to picture something weird and unlivable, such as geodesic domes, composting toilets, off-the-grid solar power systems—certainly not the kind of home that can generate buyer interest or even a higher selling price. But the past decade has seen major changes in what constitutes a green home. These days, you don't have to choose between being healthy and having a home that is a

good investment as well. Previously cumbersome alternative energy sources have gotten more compact and less expensive. And, contrary to popular belief, green building doesn't necessarily cost the homeowner any more than any other kind of remodeling with an eye toward future resale. In fact, according to a recent study, six out of ten homeowners say they would consider integrating green design practices into a future home improvement project. And it's no wonder. Current technologies can shave heating and cooling bills by 30 percent. "Those of us who have been working in sustainable design for more than a decade, we just can't believe what a tipping point there's been in the last twelve months in consumers' interest," says Lyn Falk, president of Solterra Studios, a green design/build firm in Cedarburg, Wisconsin. "People sit up and pay attention when you talk about the bottom line—their wallet or their health. Green building is about both, so it's rising in popularity and importance."

SAVING ENERGY: INSULATION, APPLIANCES, AND HVAC

When it comes to saving energy, the good news is that you can do as much or as little as your budget will allow. Start with the simple stuff— such as buying a programmable thermostat—that will help you whittle down your energy bill without your even noticing. In fact, if you do nothing more than install a programmable thermostat, seal leaky air ducts, choose energy-efficient appliances as you replace older models, and replace incandescent lightbulbs with compact fluorescent bulbs (CFLs last ten times longer and use 66 percent less energy), you will ultimately cut your energy bill by 30 percent. Think of it as a construction-free remodel.

But you can go much further and reap even bigger savings. Ultimately, the really motivated install equipment such as photovoltaic cells, high-efficiency boilers, and superinsulating materials so that their homes actually produce more energy than they use. Getting off the grid, though, is ambitious. If you're just getting started becoming a green citizen, you'll want to take simple steps first.

SEAL THE ENVELOPE The costs of heating and cooling your house account for 50 to 70 percent of your annual energy bill. Cutting that cost starts with an analysis of just how effectively sealed your home is. That means the doors, ceilings, windows, and floors that come in contact with the outdoors. Here's where heat radiates into your house in the summer and cold air sneaks in during the winter months. The tighter the seal—in other words, the more resistant these materials are to outdoor temperature changes—the lower your energy bill. It's difficult to tell on your own whether your home has a tight seal or not, unless of course you feel drafts in the winter or see condensation or frost on the inside of your windows.

For a quick estimate of whether you're paying too much to heat and cool your home, go to www.energystar.gov and check out their Home Energy Yardstick. Energy Star is the Environmental Protection Agency division that works to reduce Americans' energy consumption. By filling in your zip code and a few details, you can get a sense of how energy efficient your home is compared to others. A professional analysis is a more precise way to determine how energy efficient your house is. A common test, the blower door test, measures door and duct leakage. The blower door is a large calibrated fan temporarily mounted into the front door. Other windows and doors are closed and the fan is turned on. The test measures the leakiness of the house by measuring both the flow of air through the fan and the pressure difference between the inside and outside. By hiring a certified energy rater, you can have your home tested. You can find a rater in your area at www.natresnet.org; click on the "Consumer" button for details. Or check out the links at Energy Star's website for the agency's Home Performance program. The most common areas for leaks are the attic and the basement. As you identify leaks, caulking, spray foam, and weatherstripping can help you seal those drafts around doors and windows.

INSULATE YOUR WALLS, FLOORS, AND ATTIC The next step is to make sure your home is effectively insulated. Leaky attics are the number one reason that homes are energy inefficient. Start by plugging air leaks in your attic

with caulk. If you already have some insulation in place, roll it back and check for leaks around lighting and plumbing fixtures. Next, analyze your existing insulation. Chances are, the older your home is the more likely it is to lack adequate insulation. An energy rater can tell you how much insulation you already have and where you need more, but working on your own, you can check the attic and any walls and floors adjacent to unheated spaces such as the garage. Look for exposed insulation, if it exists, around structural frame elements, including ceiling joists or wall framing. Check the insulation's type and its thickness. If you find wet insulation, you'll want to call in a professional to fix the water problem before tackling the insulation issue.

Insulation is sold in batts (essentially rolled blankets that can be cut to fit) or as dry or wet material that is blown into walls. Before you shop for insulation, you'll want to know the appropriate R-value for your area's climate conditions. An R-value is simply a measure of how well a material conducts heat. The higher the number, the higher the resistance. Most of the country is rated for R-38, but to find the right rating for your area go to www.energystar.gov.

The most common type of insulation is the pink fiberglass batts that act like a blanket for your house. Fiberglass is cheap and easy to install, but there are downsides. Health concerns lead the list of issues, although manufacturers have taken steps to deal with the problem of airborne fibers. Homeowners with fiberglass insulation are best off leaving it undisturbed. Installation can also pose challenges. For example, if you pack fiberglass batts too tightly between your attic rafters, you'll prevent air from circulating around your roof. That can lead to moisture buildup and mold. The same thing can happen if you lay a second layer of fiberglass with a paper side on your attic floor. While the idea is well motivated, the paper will trap water too. Another mistake commonly made by do-it-yourselfers is simply laying the fiberglass the wrong way. If you live in northern climates, you'll want to place the kraft paper or plastic that creates a water barrier to the inside; if you live farther south, you'll want to do the opposite.

If you don't want to use fiberglass, there are plenty of other options:

- *Cellulose.* A green alternative for the do-it-yourselfer, cellulose is recycled newspapers that are treated to resist fire and bugs. And it's cheap.

- *Low-density polyurethane spray foam.* This is the Cadillac of insulation—and not cheap. In fact, you'll have to have a pro blow it into your walls. However, it's an excellent insulator and is flexible, so as your walls expand and shrink as the weather changes, it does too. Plus it slows the movement of moisture.

- *Mineral wool.* This alternative doesn't burn or support mildew growth. It's made of blast-furnace slag and it's cheap.

- *Cotton batts.* This is the chic green alternative—recycled blue jeans, treated to make it nonflammable. It's expensive.

- *Heat blockers.* These thin sheets of aluminum bonded to foam board reflect heat and can be used in attics to block the summer sun. Blockers are installed shiny side up on the floor of the attic or shiny side down if attached to the rafters.

Once you've plugged the gaps creating drafts, analyzed the insulation you already have, and chosen the type of insulation you want to use, you'll want to decide whether you'll make the upgrades yourself or hire a professional to do it for you. Rolling out batts of recycled cotton or fiberglass is something you can do on your own. Blowing in polyurethane will require the services of a professional.

PAY ATTENTION TO THE DETAIL You'll also want to insulate your hot-water pipes. Wrap your pipes and hot water heater in rubber or polyethylene foam tubes. That keeps the warmth from dissipating quickly. That means if you turn on your hot water once for a bath and minutes later for hot tea, you won't have to wait for the water to reheat all over again.

Ceiling fans are a good energy-saving device as well. Pick a fan with an Energy Star rating and then raise your thermostat so that your air-conditioning isn't working so hard. The key to good energy efficiency is not running the ceiling fan constantly.

Clean your refrigerator coils. The coils located behind your refriger-

ator become coated with dust, making the refrigerator more and more
inefficient. Use a long-handled brush to clean.

INTEGRATING GREEN PRACTICES
INTO RENOVATIONS

If you are planning some work on your home, such as upgrading the
kitchen, you'll have the opportunity to replace your old appliances with
energy-efficient ones or install windows specially designed to keep heat
out in the summer but let solar energy in during the winter. Energy Star
puts a seal of approval on products from lighting to appliances that meet
their standards. The program's website, www.energystar.gov, includes a
list of products in forty categories bearing the Energy Star label. You'll
also find out how much money you can save on an annual basis by buying their top-rated products.

On the other hand, if you are doing a major renovation to your
home, it's an excellent time to consider more involved projects. Before
Michael, an energy consultant, started a major renovation of his 1930s
Craftsman-style bungalow in Vermont, he had an energy audit conducted. It showed that while the home was well built, it could use better heating and ventilation systems and better insulation to keep the
second floor as warm as the first. He replaced his heater with a high-
efficiency boiler and added a heat recovery ventilation system, which in
the winter warms the cold fresh air coming into the house with the heat
of the exhaust air leaving the house. "That means when the fresh air enters the heater, it takes less energy to warm it, so you're using what
would otherwise be wasted heat in your exhaust air," he says. With these
changes, his home cost about 10 percent more than a conventional remodel might have, but it is 30 percent more energy efficient.

Besides rehabbing the original house, Michael also added a room to
the north side and raised the roof by several feet to make the second
floor more livable. For those additions, he decided to use advanced framing techniques. Though it sounds high-tech, advanced framing is simply
a method of keeping walls structurally sound while reducing the amount
of wood used in a construction project. "You have a lot of opportunities

to reduce the costs because you're not using as much lumber for the walls," says Michael. And because advanced framing uses fewer (albeit larger) studs, it leaves room for more insulation in the wall cavities—so a better-insulated home is yet another benefit.

Kira and Brian took a different route to build extra-insulated walls when they renovated their 1920s Atlanta mill house in 2001. The two rooms they added on to the home were built with structural insulated panels (SIPs). SIPs are simply preassembled walls—modular panels with six-inch insulation at the center sandwiched between two pieces of plywood for maximum efficiency. And they applied spray-on polyurethane foam insulation in the crawl space and attic. Spray-foam insulation is usually less expensive than foam boards, and also expands to fill gaps better and reduces air leaks.

Still, they figured, insulation can only accomplish so much when you have an inefficient heating and cooling system. Like many homeowners who decide to replace their boiler or furnace when they are remodeling and increasing their home's energy efficiency, Kira and Brian decided to go this route too. They were also motivated to do this because Georgia was planning to deregulate its natural gas industry. "I thought it was a bad situation, after everything that went on in California with deregulation," says Brian. Nervous about the future of gas prices in their state, they decided to install a geothermal heat pump as their heating and cooling system.

Geothermal pumps are completely combustion-free—there's no firebox or need for oil. Instead, the pumps collect heat that already exists in the dirt underneath your house. About three feet below ground level, the earth remains a relatively constant temperature year-round. Using a loop of antifreeze-filled pipes, the pumps bring that heat up from the ground into the home in the winter. In the summer, the system takes heat from the house and pumps it into the ground. Though the couple's system was expensive up front—about $20,000 to buy and install—they were vindicated when they saw gas prices nearly quadruple. Their total energy bill averages about $89 per month, compared to as much as $500 for their neighbors. "We figured the system would pay

for itself in seven years . . . and it's actually been shorter now because of the price hike," says Kira.

A typical geothermal unit to heat and cool a typical-sized home would cost about $7,500, much more expensive than a conventional heat pump system, which runs $4,000. Of course, your conventional pump won't save you money over the long run.

CREATING ENERGY: SOLAR POWER

Solar power is another major way to reduce your energy bills. Mention solar to many homeowners and they'll dismiss it out of hand—too granola-y, too impractical, too much maintenance. But keep in mind that solar power is more than just panels on the roof. There are two types of solar power: passive and active. Passive solar designs take into account how placement of windows, patios, trees, and other features will affect heat loss and gain. The idea is to maximize heat gain in the colder months and minimize it in the summer. Some of the strategies are pretty simple, such as planting trees near windows on the east and west sides of the house; in the summer they shade the house, and in the winter, when leaves drop, they allow the house to gain heat. New technologies are yielding window glazings that perform the same task, maximizing or minimizing heat absorption. Passive solar design won't heat your home, but it can reduce your heating bills by as much as 50 percent. Of course, you have to plan ahead, and you can't add trees to every house.

Over the eighteen years she's lived in her Hollywood, Florida, one-story home, Ann, a freelance graphic artist, has maximized the passive solar energy potential available to her. The house was ideally situated with a large, screened-in patio on its south side. In the winter, the patio's Mexican tile floors absorb the sun's heat during the day; at night, she closes the windows on the patio to keep it from losing the heat. On the north and east sides of the house, she planted fruit trees, which provide shade in the summer and keep heat from building up in the house.

Active solar systems include solar water heaters, solar space heaters, and photovoltaic (PV) systems, which convert solar energy to electricity. This is what most people think of when they think solar energy. Panels

of solar cells, usually installed on a south-facing roof, collect energy from the sun and turn it into heat or electricity. But these new solar cells don't look like ping-pong tables mounted on your roof, as the old ones did. Newer grid-connected photovoltaic systems funnel extra unused electricity back into the power grid and are much less expensive than the older-style off-grid systems, which use batteries to store excess electricity to use at nighttime or on cloudy days. Because these systems don't require batteries, they take up less room and are less expensive. In fact, they're now called solar shingles because of their narrow profile. They work like this: combining the solar cell with slate, metal, or even asphalt roofing, they generate electricity when the sun strikes a semiconductor layer on the shingle's surface. One shingle can run a window fan, but if you get lots of them together, you can fuel a house.

Going solar in this way, though, doesn't mean cutting your ties to the local energy utility. Working with the local utility, you use their juice at night or when it's rainy, and your own when it's sunny. The benefit is clear: on some days, your electric meter spins in reverse. The systems are best used in western and southern states that receive a lot of sun. If you live in Nevada, for example, you'll get 50 percent more out of your solar panels than if you live in Washington or Maine.

A photovoltaic system starts at around $6,000 and usually has a payback period of several years. But many local utilities are beginning to offer rebates (see "Paying for It" on page 121) for grid-connected systems, which can shorten the payback period considerably. Check out www.dsireusa.org to find programs in your area.

Be sure to check out the warranty on your solar panels. Most are under warranty for performance only. If storms damage your cells, you'll be on your own to pay for damage. Also, the warranty is typically voided if they are installed incorrectly, which is a good argument for getting professional help when you have them put in.

If you want to make a gradual shift to solar energy, it may be worth your while to invest in a solar water heater after your conventional water heater conks out. The payback for solar water heaters, which cost about $4,000 to $5,000 to install, is five to six years. The heaters fill 80 percent

of your water-heating needs and can cut your utility bills by 50 to 80 percent.

A HEALTHY HOME: REDUCING VOCs

Energy costs may be attracting a lot of homeowners to green building lately, but another big draw has been the need to improve indoor air quality. Since homes today are more tightly insulated, we're more likely to be breathing in volatile organic compounds (VOCs) released by paints, finishes, carpets, vinyl flooring, and other furniture and home products. Studies increasingly link growing rates of autism and asthma in children to the chemical-laden air they breathe at school and at home. So it's no surprise that a big buzzword in green building is the "healthy home"—one that is properly ventilated and minimizes the number of products that release VOCs into the air for years after they're built. While this field of green building may not see the same kind of financial payback as energy reduction, "there are lots of ways to quantify value," argues David Johnston, principal of What's Working, a green-building consulting company and coauthor of *Green Remodeling: Changing the World One Room at a Time.* "One of the benefits is improved air quality of the home. What's the value of preventing your kids from developing autism? It's like the MasterCard commercial—priceless."

That's the reason Kira and Brian prioritized air quality as highly as energy savings when they renovated their Atlanta home. "We had a baby on the way when we started, and we didn't want the baby to be crawling around on the floor with construction debris or to be eating the moldings," says Kira. They used low-VOC paints and finishes throughout the house and a natural linoleum floor in the kitchen (natural linoleum, made of linseed oil and wood flour, is often confused with synthetic vinyl, which emits lots of VOCs). "The sky was not the limit when we did this house," says Kira. "Since we spent so much on the heating system, I did most of the painting myself." Using low-VOC paints meant that she didn't have to worry about her son (or herself) breathing too many fumes. "It made it practical for us to live there while we were still working on it." Low-VOC paints are surprisingly common

on the market these days and available in any color that you could get in a conventional paint. The couple used Eco-Spec paints, a line from Benjamin Moore. Sherwin-Williams also has both low- and no-VOC lines. The cost for these green paints is roughly equal to the major brands' top-of-the line paints.

Aaron and Vickie also decided to use as many low-VOC products as possible when they renovated their Brookfield, Wisconsin, home in 2005, because they were going to be living in the house throughout the project. Since Aaron is a distributor of environmentally friendly building materials, he had a good idea of what he wanted to use. For insulation, they chose a combination of recycled cotton batting, "which we could install ourselves without the Tyvek suits and masks," plus a no-VOC spray foam for the smaller gaps. They also pulled out all the existing carpeting and replaced it with hard-surface floors, including natural linoleum, cork, and hardwood. Healthy-building experts usually advise against carpets, which not only emit VOCs but also trap chemicals off-gassed from other furniture or finishes in the room and can harbor dust, mold, or bacteria as well. And now that their house is finished, the couple uses only nontoxic products for keeping it clean. "For as much money as people put into their houses, they often forget about maintenance," says Aaron. "If you do all this and then use bleach and insecticides and grocery store cleaners, it's the equivalent of going to the health club and then lighting up a cigarette after you work out."

GREEN MATERIALS:
THE CHIC FACE OF CONSERVATION

Once they've taken care of the basics—superior insulation, efficient heating and cooling, and good ventilation—many green builders and remodelers choose to finish their homes with flooring, furniture, and fixtures that also conserve resources. This can mean anything from tiles and countertops made from recycled material to flooring made from cork or bamboo, which are considered sustainable because they regrow faster than hardwoods. Salvaged materials—anything from old stained-glass windows to floorboards in hard-to-find hardwoods—can also give your

home a unique look. Think of it as the more visible side of green remodeling: if you choose well, your finishing touches can be both beautiful and an advertisement of the sustainable bones that the home is built on. And in most cases, the price is roughly comparable to a high-end conventional product—which makes sense, because a major tenet of green building is using durable, long-lived products to reduce waste. "People always ask if these green materials cost more," says Aaron. "My response is: only if you'd normally use lousy products."

Architectural salvage can even be free. Finding salvage materials for your home requires a lot of local research and legwork, but the thrill of the hunt, so to speak, gives many renovators a certain pride in the salvaged components of their home. Bob, a landscape designer who lives near Boulder, Colorado, made extensive use of salvaged woods when he remodeled his home. His ceiling is made of boards and logs harvested from a stand of local pine trees that had to be cut down because of a pine beetle infestation. From a friend who runs a tree-care business, Melvin bought a large slab of Siberian elm for his kitchen counter. "People cut down the trees for whatever reason, and he saves and mills the nicer woods that he harvests. A lot of the time those trees just end up being firewood, which is such a shame if it's a beautiful wood like black walnut."

Ann, a Florida graphic artist, discovered architectural salvage almost by accident when she renovated her home. The neighborhood of small, 1950s-era "tropical bungalows," situated around a canal near the shore, has been a hotbed of teardowns in recent years. One day, Ann noticed that the new owners of a nearby house were bringing in the bulldozers. "I knew that the previous owners had installed brand-new, energy-efficient hurricane-resistant windows before they sold the house. So I called up the new owner and asked what she planned to do with them, and she said, 'I guess just throw them away.' So I asked if she would mind if I took some." She took three windows from the teardown, worth $750 each, and spent $6,000 to replace her remaining windows with Energy Star models—effectively cutting the cost of her window replacement project by a quarter.

If you don't have the time or the local resources to find salvaged materials, there are plenty of other options. When Bill and his wife built their 1,500-square-foot Seattle, Washington, home as a model for "sensible" green building, he used a combination of salvaged wood and certified-sustainable hardwood for the floors and other wood components. Certified-sustainable wood is akin to organic food: a third-party certifier, accredited by the nonprofit Forest Stewardship Council (FSC), inspects the timber company's forests to make sure they are managed and harvested in a sustainable manner. Then it puts its stamp of approval on the lumber the company sells. This FSC-certified wood is widely available—even at superstores such as Lowe's and Home Depot. And "unless you're dead set on a particular type of wood, you shouldn't have to pay more for certified wood than for conventional," says Sandy Campbell, a Seattle-based designer who specializes in green design. In theory, you can get any common type of wood—cherry, teak, oak, and so on—as an FSC-certified wood, but in practice, availability of certain woods can vary greatly. That's why Bill decided to compromise and mix FSC woods with conventional woods. "In many cases if we could wait longer, we could have done all FSC woods, but we wanted to keep things in perspective and not drag the whole process out, so we sometimes opted for the conventional product," he says.

PAYING FOR IT . . . AND MARKETING IT

There's no getting around the fact that green renovations can be expensive, but then so can conventional renovation, and the well-kept secret is that homeowners can often find subsidies for the green changes they make. Energy-efficient mortgages, tax credits, and rebates from local utilities are all available to homeowners who make certain changes that reduce energy consumption.

Conventional energy-efficient mortgages (EEMs), backed by Fannie Mae, are in essence an incentive that allows you to add the costs of your green upgrades into your total mortgage, whether you are buying a new home or refinancing an old one. First, the home is inspected by a certified energy rater and given a score for its overall efficiency (known as a

HERS score). The rater also makes recommendations as to how much you could save in energy bills by making certain improvements. Then the cost of those improvements is rolled into the total amount of the loan—anything from new windows to insulation to a new heating system. You can finance any cost-effective energy improvements worth up to 15 percent of the value of an existing home. Monthly payments are higher, but the cost is balanced out by lower monthly energy bills. There are also EEMs backed by the Federal Housing Administration and the Veterans Administration, but those are, respectively, subject to income caps and available only to veterans.

Ann also used local utility rebates to help pay for improvements. When she replaced her roof in 2002, she noticed that the insulation under the roof looked skimpy. She commissioned an energy audit of her home from Florida Power and Light, which determined that the house could indeed use more insulation—and the utility gave a rebate that paid for all but $35 of the upgrade. On top of that, she now pays about $79 per month for air-conditioning, down from an average of $150 before the work was done.

When it comes to analyzing how much of your green investment you'll get back at resale, the picture is less clear. Some of these strategies are so new that there is little consensus in the real estate industry on the degree to which they add to your bottom line when you sell your house. Appraisers, for example, have just one line on their appraisal forms for noting green investments. But the tide is changing. Some experts are already maintaining that home sellers should add $20 to their sales price for every dollar in annual energy savings reaped by improvements. It may be that by the time you sell your house, calculating your green investment will be an accepted way of doing business. Until then, you're best off evaluating your green improvements by how long they take to pay for themselves. For example, if the insulation you install cuts your energy costs in half and pays for itself over the course of one winter, then it's added to your home's efficiency and been a solid investment for you.

If you want to promote your green upgrades when it comes time to

sell, one option is to design your home to qualify for your local or state green building program, if one exists. Examples include Atlanta's Earth-Craft House program, Austin's Green Building program, and Earth Advantage in Portland, Oregon. These certification programs are usually sponsored either by a local builders' association or by a nonprofit; in some areas they may apply to new construction only, while in others there will also be a program for remodelers. Usually, they consist of a checklist of green attributes a house can achieve in several categories, such as insulation, efficient appliances, green materials, healthy air, and so on. Score a certain number of points in each category and the house qualifies for the organization's green rating (many organizations have tiered ratings—from one to five stars, for instance). Getting a house certified has a nominal fee, usually a few hundred dollars. Most of these programs are too young to say with certainty whether they directly impact the home's value, but they provide a third-party seal, in effect making the home's green attributes a tangible fact.

Many green homeowners find that they need to be a bit more proactive in making sure that their changes get factored into the resale value, but they do ultimately see a payoff. Kira and Brian, the Atlanta homeowners, got their house appraised after they overhauled it, and Brian provided the appraiser with a list of every green feature they added, from the geothermal system to the no-VOC paints. The appraiser determined that the green changes alone added 5 to 7 percent to the home's value. As Michael, the Vermont energy consultant, puts his house up for sale, he intends to take a hands-on approach. "I haven't found a Realtor who can really intelligently explain the benefits of better air quality and so on to a prospective buyer. So I'll do it myself by meeting with prospective buyers or with an informational sheet."

When Aaron, the Wisconsin green-building materials distributor, was designing his remodel, he and his wife planned to sell the house in about five years, so he paid a lot of attention to what would sell. "A lot of people get caught up in this notion that in order to build green it has to look alternative: burlap walls, a straw bale home, or an ultra-sterile look. But if you put your money in the rooms that matter most—bath-

rooms and kitchens—and have a house that looks like the kind of house people want to buy, people will pay a premium."

GUIDANCE ON GOING GREEN

The Forest Stewardship Council can help you find vendors of products that observe sustainable forestry practices. Check out www.fscus.org. If you want some hands-on advice about building green, consider hiring a green designer, architect, or builder, many of whom are listed at the website for the U.S. Green Building Council at www.usgbc.org. The organization's Leadership in Energy and Environmental Design program has developed a national standard for green building that its members practice. Certified members have to pass a written exam designed to ensure that the designer you're working with is up on the latest techniques and technologies. At www.buildingconcerns.com, you'll also find sources for green building materials and names of architects, interior designers, and landscape designers.

14

Curb Appeal:
Your Yard and Garden

DEVELOPING A YARD AND GARDEN THAT WILL PAY DIVIDENDS ISN'T difficult, but it is easy to get sidetracked by beautiful blooms at your neighborhood nursery. Your nursery salesperson is happy to see you walking away with armloads of blossoms, but the flowers should be the finishing touches on your landscaping, not the starting point. If you've recently bought a house or never seriously considered your yard before, develop an overall plan for the space. That means reevaluating everything from the walkways and driveways to the trees and shrubs. What does your family like to do in the backyard? Do you barbecue? Play badminton? Swim? What is the view from the curb—do visitors get a good first impression? Does the landscaping match the house? Depending on your space and your tastes, you'll want to develop a terrace or deck that can accommodate an eating area, a plant display that lasts all four seasons, and a place to play. If you have enough room, consider such things as a water feature (a pool, a fountain, or maybe just a zoned irrigation system), a winding garden path, an arbor, and seating away from the deck. With the myriad of options available, you'll want to carefully analyze

your situation before coming up with a plan that will have staying power and appeal.

According to a study conducted at Clemson University, attractive landscaping can add 6 to 7 percent to the value of your home. Others say the benefits can be as high as 15 percent. Energy savings can also help foot the bill for landscaping. By correctly shielding your windows and walls with plants, you can reduce your air-conditioning costs by half, according to the American Public Power Association. And the benefits aren't just financial: trees fight pollution and erosion, as well as control storm water.

The trick is applying some discipline. You'll still want to scale your investment to your home and the neighborhood. If no one else has invested in a pool and outdoor kitchen, you might not want to either. If you're spending more than 20 percent of the value of your house on outdoor upgrades, you're not likely to get the investment returned when it comes time to sell. Aim to be one of the best-designed and most attractive homes on the block, not just the most expensive.

But buying trees, shrubs, and flowers isn't the same as buying furniture for your living room. That's because the plants change over time. Setting them too close together means they crowd each other; too far apart and your garden feels thin. Being able to predict whether the bougainvillea will go with the weeping willow is part of the charm and the challenge of getting landscaping right. When it comes to planning your landscaping, it pays to think long term—or as long as you expect to stay in a house.

One shortcut that can help organize your thoughts and keep you from staring dreamily into gardening books without accomplishing anything is to break up your decision making into three categories. Pay attention to the basics of the yard, the frame of trees and shrubs that communicates much to your neighbors as well as potential buyers. Next, consider the hardscape elements of your yard—sidewalks, walkways, lighting, and driveway—that will define boundaries. Finally, there are the large investments that will transform your yard into an oasis, such as pools, spas, outdoor kitchens, and the like. All of these improvements can add value to your home.

Ultimately, upgrading your yard and landscaping is an investment, and you'll want to plan ahead before investing.

THE STARTING POINT

No matter whether your home sits on an acre of rolling countryside, a tiny divot of urban earth, or a conventional suburban quarter acre, you'll want to get started by evaluating the space and plantings you already have. Get a fresh vision of your yard. Mow the lawn, trim back the shrubs, and sod those parts of the lawn that need some help. Now that you've got an unobstructed view of your paradise, you can start asking yourself some serious questions. Is the front yard welcoming? Remember, the entry more than any other part of your house will attract visitors and, ultimately, buyers. The driveway should be well surfaced and easy to find and navigate. Does your house have enough privacy? The days of the half-acre unobstructed lawn are over. Nowadays, you'll get rewarded by developing fencing or screens that enclose your space, providing a haven from the prying eyes of neighbors. Evaluate your backyard and side yards. Do they provide adequate space for your family's needs, whether it's a play area for the children or a lap pool for Dad?

Once you've got the lay of the land, you'll want to come up with a plan. That's where most of us come up short. Instead, we buy plants and trees piecemeal. Developing a plan is as simple as getting some graph paper and drawing the dimensions of your yard, as well as the plants and other features that dominate your landscape. Your paper plan is a simple way of envisioning the changes you want. As you put together this vision of your garden, you'll want to ease the hard rectangular and horizontal lines that most yards inevitably have. This can be accomplished by designing the beds for your flowers and shrubs with a curving line. Create focal points at the edges of small yards to give visitors a sense of space. A rock garden or bench at the edge of the yard can emphasize the diagonal space and make your yard feel larger. Other limitations, such as a dramatic slope or drainage problems, will also have to be considered.

Not many of us are prepared to lay interlocking brick pavers to make the perfect front-yard walkway. Nor are we prepared to design it. If your project is large or simply intimidating, consider hiring a certified

dock

pool

lawn

garage
court

residence

cutting
garden

overlook

guest
house

entrance
court

vegetable
garden

allee

entrance
gate

naturalized
planting

A.mckay
©APSLA2007

Rural—Sprawling rural properties
can cost a fortune to landscape. Cut
costs by focusing your investment
on trees, picking specimens that
frame the house, not block it. Ornamental grasses can fill larger areas
and open views.
Ann P. Stokes Landscape Architects

landscape professional or technician, as well as a contractor. Choose one who has passed tests administered by the Professional Landcare Network (www.landcarenetwork.org). If your project is more complicated, consider hiring a landscape architect, who can not only pen your design, but also plan the grading and propose fixes for drainage. These professionals are members of the American Society of Landscape Architects (www.asla.org), have a degree in landscape architecture, three years of experience, or a license from the state where they work. Some states require landscape contractors to be licensed as well. If you're using a garden store that also provides design services, you'll sometimes find that a portion of the design costs are rebated against the price of the plants you buy. The average cost of hiring professional landscape, lawn, and tree care services is $1,170, while landscape installation and construction is the most expensive option at $3,502 on average. Designs cost $1,465 on average. If that is too much for you, consider asking an architect or technician to review your plans for $50 or $100. A thoughtful review of your plans can cut your DIY costs.

CHOOSING THE RIGHT FRAME

Choosing the right trees and placing them appropriately will provide the correct frame for your home. More than any other planting, trees are critical to selling your home and getting the right price for it. Buyers respond to homes set among mature trees. While saplings aren't a selling point, neither are trees that are so mature that they block the natural sunlight from your yard. For that reason, it pays to think about just how long you intend to be in your house when considering whether to keep the trees in your yard or buy new ones. Keep in mind, though, that the return on the money you spend on a tree—prices can range from $10 for a sapling to $10,000 or more for a mature specimen—is difficult to quantify. Trees typically aren't appraised and their value added to your home the way a kitchen or bath renovation might be. While sick or diseased trees might cost you money at the closing table, real estate agents don't put a price tag on every dogwood and elm when calculating an asking price for your house. But the overall effect can be critical to selling your home quickly.

The most important purchase to get right is the shade trees. As any arborist or landscape designer will tell you, the most valuable shade trees are the ones that take the longest to grow, such as stately oaks and elms. Unfortunately, it takes 50 years for a white oak to achieve its regal 100 feet of mature height. Buying a decent-sized specimen is expensive, as much as $10,000. Paying attention to the variety of species that you buy allows you to circumvent those problems. You can find a tree that is both a reliable, disease-resistant hardwood and one that will be enjoyed by you, not just your grandchildren. Sunny Scully, a Washington, D.C.–based landscape architect, suggests buying a tree with a four-inch caliper (that's trunk diameter) if you're planning to sell in five years. That's big enough to make a statement but not so big that you'll have to take out a second mortgage to pay for it. Of the many oak varieties, the chinkapin oak rewards midwesterners with growth rates of three feet a year; the swamp white oak pushes out about a foot a year. On the West Coast, scrub oaks and live oaks are good choices. The willow oak provides attractive, dappled shade that doesn't block grass growth. And you don't have to stick with oaks. Scully also likes the Heritage river birch, which grows quickly and is free of the bore problems that plague many birch varieties. Other favorites of the pros: linden trees, which have a uniform shape if you want to create an allée of trees in your garden, and red maples, which grow fast and give a large shade canopy in a short period of time. Check with a local arborist to find species that are native to your area or well suited for your climate. The charts that follow can guide you to trees, shrubs, and flowery plants appropriate for your region. Consult the American Horiculture Society's website at www.ahs.org to determine what hardiness zone you live in.

AMERICAN HORICULTURE SOCIETY *SMARTGARDEN* REGIONAL GUIDES
Plant Choices to Add Value to Landscapes

Common Name	Botanical Name	USDA Zones	AHS Zones
Trees and Shrubs			
Japanese maple	*Acer palmatum*	5–8	8–2
Downy serviceberry	*Amelanchier x grandiflora*	4–9	9–1
Yellow birch	*Betula nigra* "Heritage"	4–9	9–1
Katsura tree	*Cercidiphyllum japonicum*	4–8	8–1
Kousa dogwood	*Cornus kousa*	5–8	8–4
Japanese cedar	*Cryptomeria japonica*	6–9	9–4
European beech	*Fagus sylvatica*	4–7	8–4
White oak	*Quercus alba*	5–9	8–1
Persian ironwood	*Parrotia persica*	4–7	7–1
Japanese red pine	*Pinus densiflora*	4–7	7–1
Gray alder	*Alnus incana* "Aurea"	2–6	6–1
Honeylocust	*Gleditsia triancanthos*	3–7	7–1
American linden	*Tilia americana*	3–8	8–1
Japanese zelkova	*Zelkova serrata*	5–9	9–5
Bottlebrush buckeye	*Aesculus parviflora*	5–9	9–4
Common boxwood	*Buxus sempervirens*	6–8	8–6
Blue mist shrub	*Caryopteris x clandonensis*	6–9	9–5
Oakleaf hydrangea	*Hydrangea quercifolia*	5–9	9–5
Winterberry holly	*Ilex verticillata*	3–9	9–4
Ninebark	*Physocarpus opulifolius*	3–7	7–1
Perennials and Vines			
New England aster	*Aster novae-angliae*	4–8	8–1
Cranesbills	*Geranium* varieties	Vary	Vary
Purple coneflower	*Echinacea purpurea*	3–9	9–1
Fragrant Solomon's seal	*Polygonatum odoratum*	3–8	9–1
Foamflower	*Tiarella cordifolia*	3–8	7–1
Stonecrop	*Sedum* "Autumn Joy"	4–9	9–3
Longleaf pulmonaria	*Pulmonaria longifolia*	3–8	8–4
Ostrich fern	*Matteuccia struthiopteris*	2–8	8–1
Trees and Shrubs			
Fringe tree	*Chionanthus virginicus*	4–9	9–1
Blue Atlas cedar	*Cedrus atlantica* "Glauca"	6–9	9–6
Eastern redbud	*Cercis canadensis*	4–9	9–2
Flowering dogwood	*Cornus florida*	5–8	8–3

NORTHEAST

SOUTHEAST

Common Name	Botanical Name	USDA Zones	AHS Zones
Trees and Shrubs			
American beech	*Fagus grandifolia*	3–9	9–1
Kentucky coffee tree	*Gymnocladus dioicus*	5–9	9–5
Two-winged silverbell	*Halesia diptera*	4–8	8–4
American holly	*Ilex opaca*	5–9	9–5
Crape myrtle	*Lagerstroemia indica*	6–9	9–6
Southern magnolia	*Magnolia grandiflora*	7–9	9–1
Sour gum (tupelo)	*Nyssa sylvatica*	5–9	9–7
Yoshino cherry	*Prunus x yedoensis*	5–8	8–5
Southern red oak	*Quercus falcata*	6–9	9–5
Cabbage palm	*Sabal palmetto*	8–10	10–7
Japanese stewartia	*Stewartia pseudocamellia*	5–8	8–5
Bald cypress	*Taxodium distichum*	5–11	12–5
Japanese plum yew	*Cephalotaxus harringtonia*	6–9	9–5
Rhododendrons, Azaleas	*Rhododendron* varieties	Vary	Vary
Hydrangeas	*Hydrangea* varieties	Vary	Vary
Glossy abelia	*Abelia x grandiflora*	6–9	9–6
Viburnums	*Viburnum* varieties	Vary	Vary
Perennials and Vines			
Purple coneflower	*Echinacea purpurea*	4–9	9–1
Carolina yellow jessamine	*Gelsemium sempervirens*	7–9	9–6
Lenten rose	*Helleborus orientalis*	4–9	9–4
Heucheras	*Heuchera* varieties	4–9	9–1
Cinnamon fern	*Osmunda cinnamomea*	4–8	8–1
Trees and Shrubs			
Paperbark maple	*Acer griseum*	4–8	8–1
Full-moon maple	*Acer japonicum*	5–8	8–1
Paper birch	*Betula papyrifera*	2–7	7–1
Deodar cedar	*Cedrus deodara*	6–9	9–6
Lavelle hawthorn	*Crataegus x lavallei*	5–7	7–4
Maidenhair tree	*Ginkgo biloba*	5–9	9–3
Meserve holly	*Ilex x meserveae*	5–9	9–5
Crabapples	*Malus* cultivars	Vary	Vary
Dawn redwood	*Metasequoia glyptostroboides*	5–10	12–5
Colorado spruce	*Picea pungens*	2–8	8–1
Black cottonwood	*Populus trichocarpa*	4–9	9–1

SOUTHEAST

NORTHWEST

Common Name	Botanical Name	USDA Zones	AHS Zones
Trees and Shrubs			
Chinese pistachio	*Pistacia chinensis*	6–9	9–6
Chinese evergreen oak	*Quercus myrsinifolia*	7–9	9–6
Black locust	*Robinia pseudoacacia* "Frisia"	4–9	9–4
Umbrella pine	*Sciadopitys verticillata*	5–9	9–4
Fragrant snowbell	*Styrax obassia*	6–8	8–6
Windmill palm	*Trachycarpus fortunei*	8–11	12–8
Winter daphne	*Daphne odora*	7–9	9–7
Dwarf fothergilla	*Fothergilla gardenii*	4–8	8–1
Oregon grapeholly	*Mahonia aquifolium*	6–9	9–6
Perennials and Vines			
Barrenwort	*Epimedium x versicolor*	5–9	9–4
Evergreen clematis	*Clematis armandii*	7–9	9–7
Showy stonecrop	*Sedum spectabile*	4–9	9–1
Daylilies	*Hemerocallis* "Stella D'Oro"	3–9	12–1
Variegated kiwi vine	*Actinidia kolomikta* "Arctic Beauty"	5–8	8–5
Japanese painted fern	*Athyrium niponicum* var. *pictum*	5–8	8–1
Trees and Shrubs			
Norfolk Island pine	*Araucaria heterophylla*	9–11	12–9
River birch	*Betula nigra*	4–9	9–1
Flame tree	*Brachychiton acerifolius*	10–11	12–8
Palo verde	*Cercidium* "Desert Museum"	8–11	12–8
Lemon	*Citrus limon*	9–11	12–1
Smoke tree (Smoke bush)	*Cotinus coggygria*	5–10	9–3
Loquat	*Eribotrya japonica*	8–11	12–8
Cabbage gum	*Eucalyptus pauciflora*	9–11	12–10
Toyon, California holly	*Heteromeles arbutifolia*	8–10	10–7
Ocotillo	*Fouquieria splendens*	8–10	10–8
Gambel oak	*Quercus gambelii*	5–8	8–4
Valley oak	*Quercus lobata*	7–9	9–7
Silverleaf, Texas sage	*Leucophyllum frutescens*	7–9	9–7
Cottonwood	*Populus fremontii*	3–10	10–1
Oleander, Rose bay	*Nerium oleander*	9–11	12–10

NORTHWEST

SOUTHWEST

	Common Name	Botanical Name	USDA Zones	AHS Zones
S O U T H W E S T	**Trees and Shrubs**			
	Stone pine, Umbrella pine	*Pinus pinea*	9–10	12–9
	Pomegranate	*Punica granatum*	8–11	12–1
	Texas mountain laurel	*Sophora secundiflora*	8–10	12–7
	Silver linden	*Tilia tomentosa*	6–9	9–6
	Thread palm	*Washingtonia robusta*	9–11	12–10
	Perennials and Vines			
	Agave	*Agave victoriae-reginae*	9–11	12–5
	Side oats grama	*Bouteloua curtipendula*	6–9	9–6
	Penstemon	*Penstemon* varieties	Vary	Vary
	Red-hot poker	*Kniphofia* varieties	6–9	9–6
	Prairie poppy, mallow	*Callirhoe involucrata*	4–6	7–1
	Fringed lavender	*Lavandula dentata*	5–9	9–4
	Sages	*Salvia* varieties (e.g., *Salvia greggii,* autumn sage)	Vary	Vary

Don't bargain-shop when it comes to purchasing trees. If you're wandering the nursery one Saturday morning, you may find yourself drawn to the Bradford pear tree. But Texas-based landscape architect W. Gary Smith warns against buying one. The vase-shaped trees with branches that angle upward tend to self-destruct. One ice storm can bring down your tree. You'll also want to watch out for silver and Norway maples. Dean Hill, a landscape architect in Indiana, says the two rely on a root system that grows close to the surface of the ground and can make it difficult to tend the lawn below. The roots are so aggressive they can damage concrete sidewalks or even the walls of your house as they expand. Keep in mind, too, that while maples are valued for their beautiful foliage in the fall, those leaves are so dense that it can be difficult for anything to grow below the branches, including grass.

Trees can be a perfect solution for creating a line in a large yard, creating areas of visual interest, or simply directing foot traffic. Planting an allée of trees sounds like a good idea, but you'll need to choose your species with care. Remember Dutch elm disease of the 1960s and 1970s?

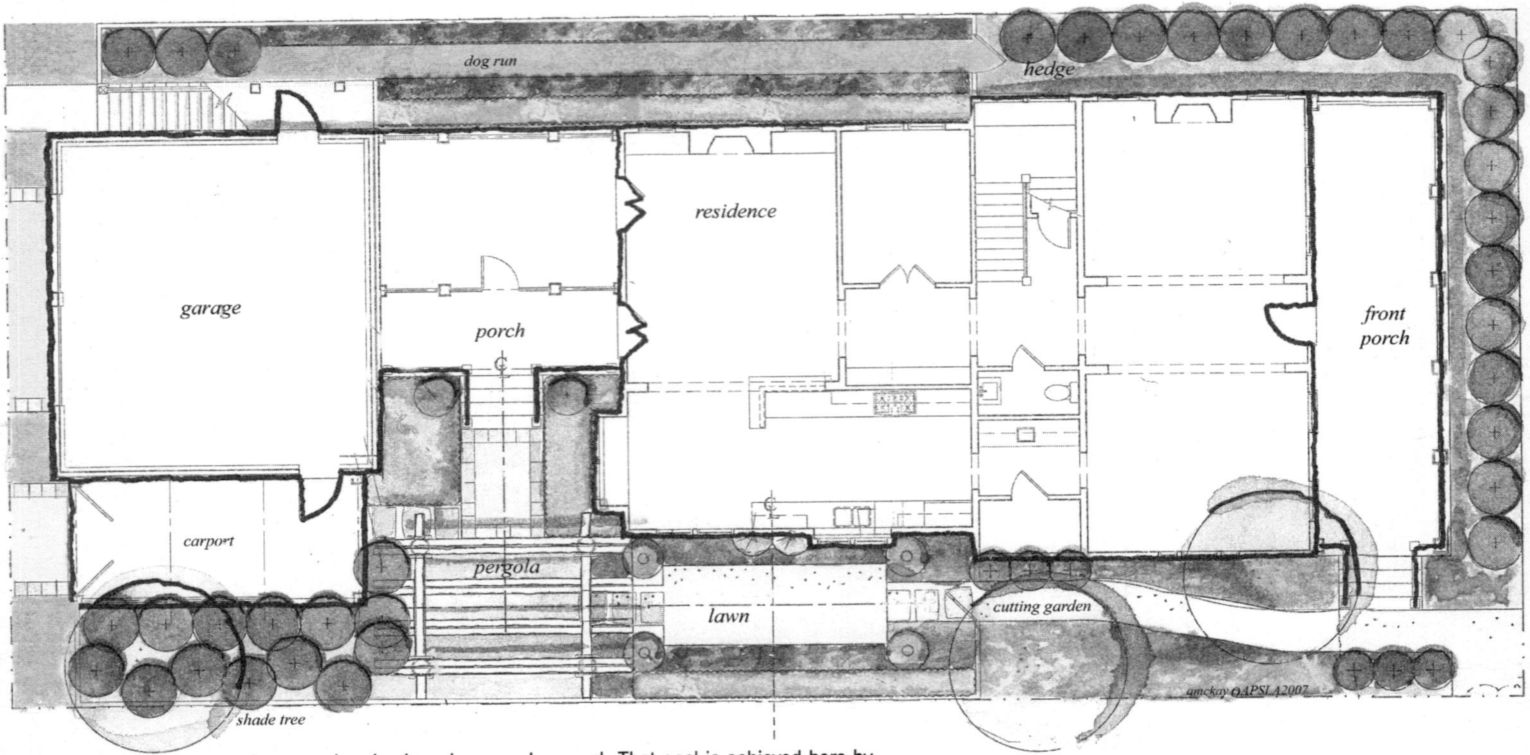
dog run
hedge
garage
porch
residence
front
porch
carport
pergola
lawn
cutting garden
shade tree
amckay ©APSLA2007

Urban—Make the most of limited space when landscaping an urban yard. That goal is achieved here by maximizing slivers of yard at the front and back of the property. Small side yards add visual interest.

Ann P. Stokes Landscape Architects

The nasty fungus carried by beetles destroyed urban landscapes where elms had been a favorite of city planners because of their graceful boughs and tolerance of air pollution. Today's landscape designers have taken a lesson from that experience. The way to promote ecological health (and the health of your wallet) is to have as diverse a population of trees as possible to prevent disease from wasting your landscaping, says Smith. For that reason, once you've picked a couple of different types of shade trees, you'll want to diversify even more by sprinkling in ornamentals and evergreens. Ornamentals are the trendsetters of the nursery. This is where designers have their fun, choosing colors or shapes that complement the landscape and the house. Designers favor fringe trees (that's right, their white springtime blooms look like fringe), the redbud, the serviceberry, and even the old-fashioned crabapple (try the fruitless varieties bred for busy suburbanites).

Another use: screening. Both trees and shrubs can block views you'd rather avoid, such as the neighbor's messy backyard or a busy street. Good choices for screens (who wants to see the neighbor's pool anyway?) are the amur maple, which is dense and grows to ten to fifteen feet with dramatic red foliage; the willowwood viburnum, a large foliage shrub; and the ever-popular and fast-growing Leyland cypress. For something different, Scully suggests a Japanese cedar, also called cryptomeria, which is charmingly puffy in appearance.

As you watch your trees grow, keep an eye out for problems. Warning signs can include trees that lean, heave up out of the ground, or grow oversized mushrooms at their base. A tree with any of those problems could fall, endangering your home, your neighbors, and your family.

When it comes to landscaping—especially planting the trees and shrubs that will fill out your yard—it can be easy to overdo it. Just as you can spend too much money upgrading the interior of your home, so too can you overdo landscaping. Frank Gregoire, a St. Petersburg, Florida, appraiser, cites the case of one homeowner whose 2,200-square-foot ranch failed to attract buyers even though it was across the street from the ocean. That's because the $50,000 worth of trees, shrubs, and winding walkways she carefully installed around her backyard pool made it feel like the set of *Dark Shadows*. "I talked to a number of buyers who

thought the landscaping made it dark and gloomy," says Gregoire. To make sure you're not overimproving, consider what all your trees will look like once they reach adulthood. Remember, oaks will typically reach eighty to one hundred feet, while ornamental trees can grow to twenty to twenty-five feet tall. Imagine what the trees you'd like to buy will look like fully grown. Will they crowd the existing plants you have? Can they all coexist? And, of course, you'll want to take into consideration the style of your home. Geraniums and pansies are more suited for the grounds of a Tudor than a contemporary-style home. One shortcut to finding species guaranteed to work in your area is to check out the plantings used by your city or village. Municipalities typically don't want to waste their money, so they make sure their choices are hardy, unlikely to become diseased, and don't drop branches. Be sure to choose low-maintenance plants; their appeal to buyers is far higher. For the same reason, you'll want to consider installing perennials rather than annuals in your flowerbeds. Buying and replanting flowers each year is expensive and time-consuming. Perennials not only save you money but will also allow you to plan out a garden with a fairly consistent look. One easy and fun way to try new species: swap with the neighbors. Self-propagating plants, such as daylilies, can grow beyond their intended borders.

Of course, simply buying and installing trees, shrubs, and flowers isn't all there is to having an attractive yard. Even if you do a great job of choosing native species and situating them correctly so that they thrive, you'll need to pay particular attention to seasonal changes that can harm your investment. Homeowners in the Northeast should pay particular attention to damage that can be caused by winter winds, which can dry out plants. Water your garden extensively in the fall—after Labor Day, water all perennials, trees, and shrubs once a week for six weeks to give them a head start for the winter. Spray-on weather shields called anti-dessicants can act as a seal for tender young shrubs to keep them from losing moisture. Another solution is to build a windbreak of burlap and board. Heavy snows can pose a threat to plants by burdening limbs and breaking branches. Sweep off heavy snows from shrubs with a broom to prevent breakage.

Also keep out an eye for plants that are exposed to the heavy salting

of roads during the winter. And if the thermometer is constantly swing-ing between balmy and frigid temperatures, watch for a process known as "heaving," when the ground can actually shove a root ball out of the ground, with the frozen ground making it nearly impossible to replant. One solution: mulching in the fall to keep the temperature as constant as possible.

WALKWAYS AND DRIVEWAYS

Once you have the frame right, you'll also want to consider what the pros call the "hardscape" of the yard. That's the pathways, driveway, and front steps—anything, in short, that's not a plant. One trend that will have staying power is the winding paths from front door to street lined with brick pavers and attractive plantings. Squared-off T-shaped walk-ways look old-fashioned. Any walkway you build should be wide enough to accommodate two people walking side by side, and make sure that its style matches that of the house. While you're at it, you'll want to brighten the front door with plantings and color to draw attention to it. Framing the walk to the front door with a wooden pergola can also be a nice touch. Upgrading the driveway is critical to homeowners con-cerned about their home as an investment because it is often one of the first things that visitors see. Make sure that its surface is unbroken and the edges well maintained.

THE BACKYARD

In the backyard, your true creativity can come through. Here is the area where your family and friends will gather, where you'll unwind after a long workday and enjoy the outdoors and even your own garden hand-iwork. In order to develop the most satisfying backyard, you'll want to consider whether you've adequately provided privacy to your family.

A brick, wooden, or stone wall or fence is one (often expensive) so-lution. Another way of providing privacy is to establish a hedge or screen of bushes or trees. The beauty of a living screen is that it can grow far taller than a fence to obscure imposing homes or ugly views. A hedge is a line of a single species, often an evergreen; a screen is often multiple layers of plants staggered along a line. Screens work best when growing

conditions are different across the lawn; keep in mind, though, they take up more space than hedges. The trick to creating a successful screen or hedge is to understand how high the plants will ultimately grow to be and what that will mean for the look of the rest of your yard. Consider, too, the view not just from the patio but also from the second floor of your home. Does the screen or hedge block the view from different vantages? At Montpelier, the home of James and Dolley Madison, the front yard offered vistas of the Shenandoah Valley and the mountains beyond. But at this grand property, which boasts some 2,700 acres, the owners sought to create some outdoor space with privacy. A two-acre formal garden set behind the house allows visitors to linger outdoors hidden behind a brick wall and multiple hedges.

DEVELOPING GATHERING ZONES

Once you've established your privacy, you'll want to think about the gathering spots in your backyard. Is the outdoor patio just the place where the family gathers for a quick Saturday dinner, or is it the neighborhood stomping ground, an informal spot that routinely attracts up to twenty people? Measure out the amount of terrace you think is appropriate and demarcate it with masking tape or garden hose. Then figure out if the outdoor table and chairs you intend to buy fit comfortably there. Typically, bigger is better when it comes to outdoor space. And while you may have an aversion to paving your entire backyard, remember that between container gardening and your outdoor furniture (don't forget the table and chairs, grill, and chaise), you'll be using a lot of space. It's the lawn that should be downsized; activity areas and areas that are planted with perennials should dominate.

Another design element to consider is walkways. Concentrate on designing walkways that allow your backyard to unveil itself slowly. As we suggested earlier, right-angled walkways are old-fashioned. Bulk up the number of plants you use so that the entire space doesn't immediately reveal itself. A walkway—whether it's just stepping-stones or a paved path—should wind through the space, so that you can see your plants up close and not just at a distance.

A terrace makes the most sense if your backyard is flat; go for the

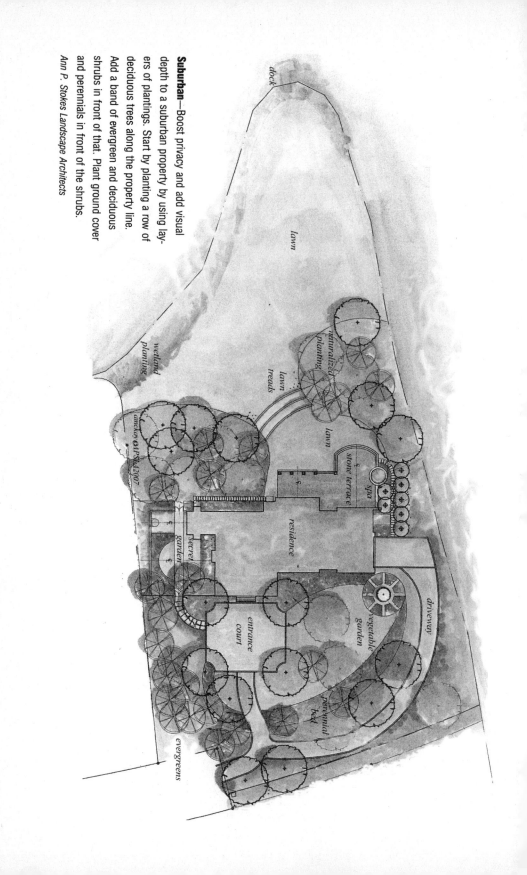

Suburban—Boost privacy and add visual depth to a suburban property by using layers of plantings. Start by planting a row of deciduous trees along the property line. Add a band of evergreen and deciduous shrubs in front of that. Plant ground cover and perennials in front of the shrubs.

Ann P. Stokes Landscape Architects

dock

lawn

wetland planting

naturalized planting

lawn treads

lawn

stone terrace

spa

residence

secret garden

driveway

vegetable garden

entrance court

perennial bed

evergreens

deck if your yard slopes away from the house. With a terrace, the critical choice you'll make (besides shape and size) will be materials. And while you'd never want to choose a cheap material for the floor of your living room, plenty of people skimp on their terraces. The two most popular materials for terraces, bluestone and brick pavers, are expensive. For that reason, you'll want to plan before the terrace is laid. Stones and bricks can't be laid directly onto the dirt; they need to have a sand base to be sufficiently set in place. And you'll want to make sure the area is graded so that you don't have big puddles when it rains. Match your material to your house. Once again, consistency in design will pay off.

Decks are typically more popular than terraces. They are the most popular DIY projects, and about a third of the new houses built in this country have one. But like building a terrace, you'll want to pay attention to materials. The most common deck material has been pressure-treated wood. While it is a less expensive alternative, it splinters and its color fades to gray as it ages. Preservatives used on pressure-treated wood can cause health problems too. Be sure to use arsenic-free lumber if you choose to go this route. Redwood and cedar are better alternatives, harder and longer-lasting, but more expensive. Plus they require annual maintenance, including power washing and resealing. You'll be surprised at the number of variations these choices are sold in. You'll be asked whether you want heartwood or sapwood—choose the former, it's hardier. Ipe, a Brazilian hardwood, is similar to teak and resistant to insects and decay, but you'll have to deal with the burden of denuding the rainforest. Wood-plastic composites, such as Trex, are another possible choice—and a good one for homeowners with hectic schedules, since maintenance is minimal. As long as you keep one of these composite decks swept clear of dirt and debris, you don't have to worry about warping, discoloration, or splinters, as you would with a real wood deck. Some people object to composite materials because they can look so perfect that you know it's not real wood.

Another critical consideration with decks is safety. Pay close attention to how your deck is attached to your home. In recent years, there have been some frightening news stories about decks that have pulled away from the buildings to which they were attached. Experienced

engineers say many decks have serious design flaws. To make sure yours doesn't, be sure it is bolted to your house, not nailed to it. Nails can easily pull away from siding or even brick, but bolts can't. And even if they loosen up, you'll get some warning that their integrity is compromised, whereas a nail can pull out with no warning at all.

Pay attention to the wooden connectors between the deck and the house. You can keep these connections dry and free from rotting by adding flashing to drain water away, protecting the house and the deck.

Unless you choose a composite material, you'll have to maintain your deck. Annual power washing is a must. Spend one day with a rented power washer to remove any mold or mildew. Choose between a simple cleanser and a restorer. If you have heavy-duty dirt and staining, buy the restorer. Restorers get rid of tannin stains and contain oxalic acid for heavy-duty cleaning. Cleaners are better for lighter jobs. Both come in liquid or crystal versions to mix with water.

Real-wood decks will need a protective treatment called deck stains every few years. While clear treatments are widely available, you're best off using a semitransparent one, because that kind is longer-lasting and blocks most of the sun's harmful rays, yet allows some of the grain of the wood to show through. Typically, oil-based stains are the best, though they are the most difficult to clean up after. Wait several days, though, after power washing before applying your stain or sealer. If a varnish has been applied to your deck, you'll have to strip it off before applying a sealer.

BIG-TICKET INVESTMENTS

WATER FEATURES Major investments such as swimming pools and other water features such as fountains and ponds will require the help not just of a contractor but also of a designer. With a pool your choices for design will be myriad. There's inground, aboveground, the spa, or the hot tub. Unlike other choices we talked about in this chapter, pools are not a universal value booster. In fact, because of safety considerations and the cost of upkeep, some families won't buy a home with a pool no matter

how attractive it is. Of course, in some parts of the country, such as Florida and Arizona, pools are considered essential. If you've decided that a pool is for you, there are four main issues to consider. First, of course, is cost. Many homeowners make the mistake of underestimating the cost of installing a pool. Beyond the price tag for your private watering hole, there's also the cost of installation, landscaping, and any decking or walkways around the pool you'll want to install. Don't forget that most states will require fencing, if not double fencing, when you install a pool. Your total costs for the inground variety can easily range from $25,000 to $50,000, while annual maintenance costs $1,500 to $2,000. Before you buy you'll also want to understand any service agreements your installer might offer.

As you plan your pool area, you'll need to choose from a variety of size and depth options. A play pool with depths of three to five feet is perfect for the family that likes to play water games and sports. If swimming laps is the point, a rectangular pool works; divers will need a deeper pool. If everybody has a different potential usage, an L-shaped pool can provide the flexibility you'll need.

If reinvestment is part of your criteria, the aboveground pool is typically a poor choice. When it comes to inground pools, your choices are essentially threefold: fiberglass, concrete, and vinyl liner. Fiberglass is the most expensive of the three, although it saves you money over the life of the pool because it requires fewer chemicals. Installation is relatively quick because the pools are factory made and then installed in one piece in your backyard. Construction takes just two weeks after excavation. Concrete pools are a more popular alternative because they are less expensive, but they can be more expensive to maintain. And while you have to choose a preset shape for your fiberglass pool, a concrete pool can be made to virtually any dimensions. Vinyl-liner pools tend to be popular in cold-weather parts of the country because draining them and covering them can easily winterize them. The pool is essentially a rubber liner held in place by a concrete footing at the bottom and vinyl ribs. In sum, pools are compicated investments that may limit your audience for resale.

OUTDOOR KITCHENS A popular remodel for the outdoors right now is the outdoor kitchen. Being able to hang out outside with the kids, grill dinner, and enjoy the outdoors all at the same time is appealing. Pair it with a pool and you may never go inside again. For the privilege of cooking al fresco in style, you'll spend anywhere from $3,000 to $50,000 for everything from the appliances and counters to the patio itself. To get started, you'll want to think about building your outdoor kitchen near the house. That's because you'll be able to use your home's electrical, gas, and plumbing hookups. What's more, it'll be easier to tote food and other materials from inside. The good news is that you can scale your outdoor kitchen to your budget. The heart of your new kitchen will be the grill (or smoker, or both, depending on your tastes). It should sit at the center of your setup. You'll probably want to opt for a gas grill so you don't have to fuss around waiting for the charcoal to heat up, unless you're a purist and want the real grilled flavor. You can buy all kinds of expensive add-ons, such as pizza ovens and masonry fireplaces, but all you really need is a grill large enough to handle your typical-sized crowd. Look for one with a built-in thermometer and gauge. Check out the grease removal setup too; a removable foil drip pan is simple but workable. Most units now carry a side burner to handle the prep of side dishes.

Once you choose the grill, it's time to think about counter space. Six feet is considered routine (generally three feet on each side of the grill); you can buy setups that are already designed. Modular storage cabinets will keep your project in line with your budget, as will an under-counter refrigerator. As you lay out the kitchen, don't be tied to the old indoor kitchen work triangle design. Instead, sink, fridge, and storage cabinet should be close to the grill for ease of preparation. Just as you avoided buying the top-of-the-line professional-style appliances for your kitchen, do the same for your outdoor kitchen. There's no guarantee buyers will pay more for fancy outdoor appliances. Of course, you'll also need space for a table to accommodate your family and guests.

One word about style: be conservative. Over-the-top outdoor

kitchens can be overwhelming. Keep your style simple and straight-forward. Materials should be timeless and design functional. You won't want buyers going through your backyard oasis and deciding it's dated.

MAINTAINING YOUR LAWN AND GARDEN

Your hard work is less likely to get noticed if your lawn grows out of control. Left to their own devices, your hedges will become unruly and your trees will grow wobbly and ultimately dangerous. Regular trimming is essential.

When dealing with shrubs, start by trimming away all the dead limbs and broken branches. Keeping the plant's original shape in mind, cut branches that are weak or that interfere with another branch or the plant's stem. By doing this, sunlight will be able to get at more of the plant's interior, encouraging growth of new stems and leaves. If you remove more than a third of the plant's branches, you're flirting with trouble. The strategy is different with a plant you want to fill out or grow. In that case, you'll want to target those stems that aren't branching out with a 45-degree cut placed just above a healthy bud. The new shoot will grow in the direction the bud is pointed.

Prune flowering plants before they bloom. Some flowering plants, like PeeGee hydrangeas and gardenias, are best pruned in late winter and early spring, while others, such as azaleas and rhododendrons, are best pruned in the late spring and early summer, after they bloom.

There's no more competitive sport in the suburbs than maintaining the lawn. But the devil is in the details. Overfertilize and you can kill your grass. Miss the early warning signs of grubs and you'll face a summer of painstakingly patching your yard. For the best results, follow these routine lawn maintenance guidelines.

1. *Don't overcut the grass.* A lengthy blade is what protects your lawn from the searing rays of the summer sun. Cut your grass once a week and don't remove more than a third of the grass's height. About three inches is a good height.

2. *Water every third day for ten minutes.* What you're aiming for is about an inch of water. If that's tough to estimate, put down some empty tuna cans on your lawn and make sure the tins don't overflow. Overwatering is a common mistake. Don't water at night—you'll promote fungus growth.

3. *Choose a good fertilizer.* When buying a fertilizer, you'll have the option of buying synthetic or organic. Man-made versions work quickly and are easy to use; however, if they aren't properly applied, you can end up burning your lawn. Organic fertilizers act more slowly and can be difficult to apply, but fans of organic fertilizers say the results are more natural looking and can create a denser lawn.

Promoting healthy grass is the best way to keep weeds at bay, and the most noxious, fastest-growing weed is crabgrass. Allow your grass to grow tall enough so that sunlight doesn't reach the soil and allow crabgrass to take root. If you start to see crabgrass growing, act fast—it spreads rapidly. Mulch the soil after removing crabgrass. That ensures that whatever roots remain don't reemerge and ruin your lawn later. Watering the area you are weeding before pulling out the crabgrass makes removal easier. What's more, you'll be more likely to pull out the entire root. Take care applying chemicals to get rid of crabgrass. An herbicide that kills only that particular weed doesn't exist, so other plants will be vulnerable.

In sum, developing a yard and garden that pays dividends isn't difficult, but it requires planning. By investing wisely, you'll not only improve your resale value and curb appeal but also increase your family's enjoyment of your home.

15

Maintaining Your Investment

THERE'S NO BETTER INVESTMENT IN YOUR HOME THAN MAINTAINING IT properly. By applying a little elbow grease and doing the basics, things such as clearing the gutters and power washing the deck, you can give your home the kind of cared-for look that buyers will be drawn to instinctively. Plus, your home will become a welcoming and safe environment for your family as well. The value of your home rests squarely on whether it is efficient and works well, so while it's all well and good to invest in a state-of-the-art entertainment room or a master bedroom addition, the condition of your whole house matters greatly. That's because upkeep often determines whether you'll have problems down the road.

Take, for example, the beautiful 1920s farmhouse Jennifer and her husband considered buying in Bedford, New York. Beautifully remodeled, the home looked like the perfect find. Its lovely façade—white clapboard accented with black shutters with quarter-moon-shaped cutouts—was repeated in two other small structures on the property, one of which had been turned into a game room. A two-story addition to the main house expanded the family space and added a spacious master

suite with skylights. The house was decorated with expensive antiques. Jennifer and her husband eagerly put in a bid, which was accepted quickly. They both attended the inspection to get a closer look at what they hoped would be their prize, but they were disappointed. The siding on the backside of the house gave way under the pressure of a flat-head screwdriver. Clearly the owners had never cleared out their gutters and water had sheeted down the side of the house. Pipes from the furnace hung so close to the aging wooden frame of the basement that it was a fire hazard. When the well was tested, it ran out of water after twenty minutes. Many of these problems could have been corrected if the owners had spent time taking care of the house. Regular cleaning of the gutters would have been a good first step, while a furnace checkup by a professional would have revealed structural problems. Jennifer and her husband quickly backed out of the deal, using their inspection results as a reason. The moral of the story: poor upkeep can keep you from selling your house. What's more, delaying maintenance can lead to bigger, more expensive problems down the road. Fail to service your furnace regularly and you could be looking at thousands to replace it. Leaky roofs can lead to costly mold problems that can recur over and over again. You get the picture: spending a little money and time now can spare you enormous investments down the road.

If you're buying a new house or trying to come up to speed on the one you already live in, the first thing you need to do is acquaint yourself with the major systems of the house: plumbing, heating, cooling, electrical, fireplaces, roof, and windows. You can think of each of these as systems that need to be functioning well to make the whole house work properly. If you hire a good inspector to help you inspect the purchase before you buy, you'll get an education in each of these. Remember, systems can work differently from house to house depending on the age of the structure and the type of materials and equipment used. For example, your heating system can be steam or forced air and fueled by oil or gas. The good news is this: once you get in the hang of checking out the health of those systems seasonally, it will become second nature to you.

SEASONAL MAINTENANCE CHECKLIST

If you've owned a home, you know that there's always something to look after or repair. Either it's something seasonal you're always chasing like clearing the gutters or its problems related to severe weather, like flooding. Your best bet to keep your family safe and your home functioning like a charm is to have a schedule that you follow like clockwork.

FALL

- Check your roof for missing or damaged shingles, whether you have asphalt shingles, terra-cotta roof tiles, or slate shingles. This is your house's primary protection from the weather. Loss of the roof covering makes your roof more vulnerable to water infiltration. Ultimately, in a storm, loose shingles will become projectiles. So make sure it's in good shape before winter begins. Cut back any overhanging tree limbs that could become heavy with winter snow and ice and fall on your house.

- Clear the gutters of leaves and other debris. Run water from your garden hose down the downspouts to make sure they are clear and dump water well away from your home's foundation. Gutter guards can reduce your workload by preventing leaves from clogging gutters, but you'll still have to check the eaves periodically—once a year or so, depending on how many trees hang over your house—for small amounts of debris that can get past the guards and accumulate over time. If your home has multiple stories, you're best off hiring a service to clear your gutters for you.

- Check the grading around your home. Your yard should slope away from the house, providing adequate drainage.

- Turn off outdoor water spigots. Drain those taps and external pipes to prevent bursting due to freezing. Check and drain your inground watering system.

- Weatherstrip windows, if needed. This is one of the most cost-effective ways to keep your winter heating bills down, and it prevents drafts inside the house.

- Have a pro come in and test your heating system to make sure everything is in working order. A professional will clean your furnace's burners and fans, lubricate parts, and change the filter. You'll reduce the chance of the heating system breaking down, plus it will run more efficiently, saving you money. Have your contractor run a carbon monoxide test while there. A malfunctioning furnace or water heater can produce carbon monoxide.

- Look for leaks under sinks and in exposed pipes that could freeze as the weather turns colder.

- Open your electrical panel and make sure there are no scorch marks. Also check outlets for scorch marks as well. As families use more and more electronic equipment, they put a greater and greater strain on their electrical system, increasing the possibility of fire.

- Have a professional chimney sweep clean and check your chimney. Creosote buildup from fires can create a fire hazard. (Every other year is okay for cleaning your chimney.)

- Check your basement sump pump before April showers flood your house.

- Look for signs of rodents and other varmints that will soon be looking for a warmer place to live—like your house. Inspect the periphery of your home and make sure there are no holes (even dime-sized openings can admit critters).

SPRING

- Clean and power-wash your deck. While you're at it, it's a good idea to apply a deck sealant.

- Check to make sure that winter ice didn't crack asphalt or concrete walkways or driveways. Look for bulges in retaining

walls. You'll want to get a professional to repair these, or reseal them on your own.

- Clear your gutters again, while you're at it watch for bird nests in your soffits and gutters.

- Replace or clean air-conditioning filters. Clean your dehumidifier.

- Pull out those window screens and make sure there are no holes in them.

- Get up to the attic and check for damp or missing insulation.

- Wash the exterior of your home to get rid of winter's grime. It's also a great way to see any damage that has occurred to your abode over the winter months.

- Clean and check the refrigerator drip pan and icemaker connections.

FINDING THE RIGHT HELP

When it comes to home repair and maintenance, many of us could use a refresher course. Dad or Uncle Joe, whom we rely on, may not live close enough to solicit advice from except occasionally. And, while you'd love to have a super for your house, the reality is you'll have to figure it out yourself. Is the bubble in the seam in your plaster wall a problem or just normal aging? What about that noise in the walls at night—is it something to worry about, or are you just being paranoid again? Develop a group of experts who can help you along the way, including a plumber, electrician, carpenter, and maybe even landscape professional. Talk to neighbors to find out whom they use and whose reputation is good. Then be loyal to them. Romance your plumber with an annual bottle of Scotch or a nice bonus; give the carpenter referrals to other neighbors. Don't overlook the people at the local hardware store or do-it-yourself chain retailer. These folks are used to dealing with homes like yours and they have heard every story imaginable. Open a tab at one store and return for all your needs, soliciting advice when it's not the busiest time of the week, Saturday morning.

As you begin to develop your Rolodex of home professionals, be on guard for scam artists. The best contractors aren't available for ad hoc work; they are too busy keeping their present clients happy. For that reason, you're best off saying thanks but no thanks to anyone who comes unannounced to your front door soliciting work.

Home buyers concerned about the condition of a house may consider a home warranty. After all, who wouldn't want a guarantee on everything in your house? Such warranties are becoming more and more common for both new construction and existing homes. Unfortunately, many warranties promise a lot but fail to deliver. Angie's List, an online community of homeowners that rates service providers, ranks warranties among the worst-performing services, rating them a D or F grade. The problems are many. First off, they don't often cover what homeowners wish they would. Second, you may be forced to choose a repair of the item that is broken rather than replacement. Third, you may have no say in which contractor is hired to do your repairs under the terms of the warranty. If you are considering a warranty, you'd do well to remember that any guarantee is only as good as the company standing behind it. Check out that company with your local Better Business Bureau.

HOME THREATS

Water is the most common threat to your home, and it can erode your home's value in many ways. There's the slow steady leak over the years that eventually results in a mold problem, or a wave of floodwater set in motion by hurricane-force winds that damage your house. But water isn't the only culprit; there are wind, hail, mudslides, and even little critters such as termites that eat away your home's value slowly but surely. Then there are the invisible toxins, such as radon, that threaten your health, and man-made problems such as burglary and fire. Smart homeowners take precautions against all of the ones they are most likely to sustain.

MONSTER STORMS Weather seems more and more extreme these days. Whether you live in the East and face the onslaught of hurricanes, in the

Midwest with its tornadoes, or in the West with its mudslides and fires, it seems as if we all have something to worry about. Experts say we are entering a period of particularly intense weather patterns, which is all the more disturbing because more and more people have moved to the coasts, where many of these problems are concentrated. Although you can't prevent nature from wreaking havoc on your property, you can take some preventative steps to lessen any damage. Before a storm hits, prepare your home, understanding how its construction can work with and against you. During a windstorm, the force of the wind pushes against the outside of your home. That force passes from your roof to your exterior walls to the foundation and then the ground. If any of those links are weak, you're apt to have damage. About 80 percent of residential hurricane damage starts with wind entering through the garage door, which tends to be constructed of lightweight materials. While that conserves weight and expense, it also makes the doors vulnerable to high winds. Once high winds pop your garage door, wind rushes into your house looking for an outlet; the resulting pressure can blow the roof off your house like a cap from a bottle of soda pop. Look for a sticker on the inside of your garage door that gives you a pressure rating. If you don't see a sticker, chances are you'll need to reinforce your doors, which can be as simple as reinforcing the inside of the door with plywood or steel.

Windows are also a point of vulnerability. If you live in a hurricane-prone zone, you may want to think of installing impact-resistant windows and permanent storm shutters designed to withstand the impact of flying debris and continuous wind. For the best protection, install windows and shutters that carry one of the following ratings: SBCCI SSTD 12; ASTM E 1886 and ASTM E 1996; or Miami-Dade Protocols PA 201, PA 202, and PA 203. These are the highest ratings a product can carry. Of course, these are not inexpensive. Shutters cost $50 to $60 per square foot of window. But the damage they can prevent—storm-force winds bursting through a picture window, allowing rain to drench your interior—make them worth it. Just as important as the strength of the glass is the strength of the window's frame. You'll need to install these windows according to the manufacturer's directions to get the best re-

sults. Remember, all these elements—frame, glass, attachment hardware, and installation method—contribute to the safety of the window.

If you don't live in an area that is routinely threatened with hurricane-force storms, it doesn't make sense to invest in storm shutters. In the event of a hurricane, though, you'll need to protect your windows by securely anchoring quarter-inch plywood sheets over the windows. Be sure to leave a generous margin of wood extending beyond the window's frame for maximum protection.

How your home is built can also determine your safety during a hurricane. Roof design is critical. A gable roof—a steep double-sloping roof with a ridge in the middle, like you might see on a Tudor—is vulnerable to heavy winds. Trussed roofs, which have a lower profile and are more commonly used now by home builders, have a better chance of surviving heavy winds if they are reinforced with truss bracing. To figure out whether your gabled roof is reinforced, go to the attic. Look for horizontally laid two-by-fours connecting the A-shaped trusses holding your roof up. If you don't have them, it's easy enough to have someone install them, or you can even do it yourself.

Another good preventive step some experts suggest is gluing down your roof—no kidding. The Federal Alliance for Home Safety recommends applying a top-grade construction adhesive with a caulking gun to the underside of your roof where it meets the support beams. This will increase the roof's resistance to uplift from the wind. Apply the glue to both sides of the intersection of the roof decking (that's the wood sheathing layer beneath your shingles) and the rafters or trusses. You'll want glue with a top strength rating, such as APA AFG-01 or ASTM D 3498.

Every year, falling trees and limbs cause hundreds of millions of dollars in damage as well as personal injuries and deaths. Look for signs of damage or disease, including cracks in the trunk or major limbs, insect infestations, and trees that look one-sided or that lean significantly. In advance of any kind of storm, make sure that your trees are free of dead limbs and that they don't hang over your house. And, of course, if branch limbs are in contact with power lines, trim those back or call the power company and get their crews to do it.

Once you get news that a hurricane or any other major storm is headed your way, bring in outdoor equipment and furniture, as well as trash cans and toys. Even a garden gnome can become a flying missile in high winds, damaging not only your house but also the neighbors'.

FLOODING You don't have to have a hurricane headed your way to suffer flood damage. Lakes, rivers, and creek beds can flood routinely. Even poor water drainage in your neighborhood can turn your yard into a swamp while everyone else is high and dry.

Maintaining gutters is essential, as Kristina and Sean's experience shows. They made an offer on a house in the spring, and, as typically happens, the closing came months later, in the late summer. By late August, not long after they moved in, hurricanes were ravaging the Eastern seaboard, and their suburban New York Tudor-style house was inundated with rain. What the couple didn't know is that the previous owners had failed to keep the gutters clean. The rush of water created such pressure along a second floor eave that it began leaking in the house and sheeting inside the walls to the dining room on the first floor. The plaster walls began to buckle. Panicked, the two borrowed a thirty-two-foot ladder and Sean nervously clambered to the top as the rain pelted him and the roof. He jammed a pair of kitchen tongs into a drainpipe located in the corner where two rooflines came together. His intuition was right: there was an obstruction there—an old bird's nest, it turned out. After plunging with the tongs repeatedly, he finally heard a satisfying whooshing sound as the nest gave way and a pool of water followed down the pipe. They were relieved to find the blockage causing the leak, but alarmed to find out weeks later that fixing the plaster and the roof would cost $4,000. Had the previous owners cleared out the gutters, the couple wouldn't have had such a dangerous and expensive problem.

Clearing the gutters isn't complicated, though it can be dangerous if your house has many levels. Grab a ladder and use a gallon plastic milk jug cut in half to scoop out leaves and branches, or hire someone to do it for you. Poor roof drainage can cause leaks almost anywhere in the house. Often those leaks occur in the basement, as roof runoff water is concentrated at your house's corners close to the foundation. This pool-

ing of water can seep through concrete or concrete-block foundation walls, causing flooding and weakening the very foundation of your house. Clear those gutters out twice a year, once in the spring and once in the fall. Also make sure your gutters are tightly secured to your home. Pay attention to your downspouts as well as your gutters. Make sure they are pointed away from your home so that they dump water from your gutter at least four feet from your home's perimeter. Check whether they function well by putting a hose in the gutters and making sure the water runs freely from your roof line to your yard. If a hose won't reach, check to be sure water is draining correctly the next time you have a solid rain shower. As a rule of thumb, you'll need one downspout for every 600 to 800 feet of roofing. Downspout extensions are cheap (about $10) and can prevent runoff from flowing too close to your foundation.

Correct grading can go a long way to preventing flooding and leaks. If you have a new home, make sure that the soil slopes away from your home. For every four feet of your home's perimeter, the ground should slope downward about six inches. If your grading needs to be bolstered, use clean fill dirt, not topsoil, to build up a slope around your house. Topsoil has too much organic matter and will hold water against your home's foundation. A landscape supplier can provide you with clean fill dirt. Depending on where you live, you can get a small truckload for about $100. Once the slope is in place, lay in some topsoil and plant grass seed to prevent erosion. Stone or mulch can also hold your slope in place.

One easy fix that can help keep your basement walls from getting repeatedly soaked: apply a specially formulated waterproof coating to the interior of the basement walls (or the exterior if you're under construction). The coating penetrates the wall surface, closing off cracks or chinks. Coatings will be clearly labeled as waterproofing paint and can be water- or oil-based; they cost about $18 a gallon.

Another, even cheaper, solution: plant your garden away from the house. Gardens retain water, and if they are flush with your foundation walls, water will seep inside. A rock border can do the trick, trapping water away from your home's foundation.

A "sell as is" philosophy for a house with any kind of water problem can be a recipe for disaster. When Mike and Susan put their suburban New York house on the market as they got ready to retire to a farm in Indiana, they quickly drew an attractive offer. But after getting a signed contract and a deposit, the new owners balked at taking the home—moisture in the basement was a serious concern. The buyers demanded their deposit back, but Mike and Susan refused. What ensued was a battle royal that went on for a year. In the end, a court agreed that the buyers didn't have to take the house because it failed to pass inspection. Mike and Susan could have fixed the problem by agreeing to spend $10,000 to seal the basement. Instead, they lost their buyers; the house became one that local Realtors referred to as a "problem." When they finally unloaded it a year later, they got $100,000 less than their original asking price.

MOLD No maintenance issue seems to draw more attention from homeowners than mold. Mold spores are everywhere, but when they flourish in your home they can create health hazards. Just ask Melinda Ballard. An infestation of *Stachybotrys chartarum* (black mold) was the last thing on her mind when she bought her twenty-two-room Georgian mansion outside Austin, Texas. Having sold her advertising business in Manhattan, she was excited about the prospect of taking the massive house—it had seven bedrooms and eight and a half baths—from a shell to a beautifully furnished home for herself, her young son, and her husband. In 1998, as she was getting her new home in order, a pipe burst in one of the bathrooms, causing water to rise on the first floor. "I immediately fixed the plumbing leak, but so much water had escaped in a two-hour period that the entire first floor was like walking in mush. The hardwood floors had a soggy feeling," she says. Ballard asked her insurance company to pay for the removal of the hardwood floors, but it declined. By early 1999, mold was crawling up her walls from the floor. The entire family began suffering from dizziness, headaches, and fatigue, then respiratory and sinus problems. Her son, then three years old, became sick, bleeding from the ears and coughing up blood. The mold

moved through the house quickly, feeding on the drywall. "Sheetrock is like a sponge," says Ballard, who has dedicated herself to organizing consumers with insurance claims from mold infestations. "If it sits in water, it soaks the water up, and it's a prime food source for mold." In April 1999, the Ballard family moved out of the house. "Everybody was sick," she says. She sued her insurer and was awarded $32 million by a jury, but that award was knocked down during a subsequent appeal. Ballard figures she lost $7 million to $8 million, including the house itself, furnishings, and other expenses. She had the house bulldozed in March 2004. While the house and property together had been valued at $6 million, she sold the property for just $975,000.

To protect your house from mold, you'll need to do more than just check your gutters and monitor your downspouts.

- Check your heating and air-conditioning systems. Systems can get moldy over time and should be inspected. Replace filters on portable air conditioners at least once a year.

- If you see bubbling or dampness on a wall's surface, have that wall opened up to check to see whether mold is lurking behind the wall.

- Ventilate your house when you can, especially bathrooms. Bathrooms and dryers should vent outside; keep carpeting and vinyl wallpapers out of the bathroom. Use a mold-proof shower curtain.

- Watch for groundwater accumulating around the periphery of your home.

- Use mold-killing bathroom cleaners and paint with mold inhibitors.

- Replace missing grout and repair or replace leaky faucets and pipes immediately.

At the first sign of mold, you can use a simple solution of water and bleach to scrub away the affected areas. It makes good sense to wear a mask when you do. If the problem is more extensive—for example, if

you've had a flood in your home that's soaked carpeting and drywall— you'll probably need to take more dramatic steps. At a minimum, you'll need to take out your carpeting and use a wet-dry vacuum to dry the flooded areas. Remove any drywall that has been soaked, as well as any upholstery or clothing. Open the windows and get some fresh air into the room. If the job is too big, too dangerous, or simply beyond your abilities, it's time to call in professional help. Unfortunately, the mold remediation industry attracts many scam artists and underqualified operators. Ask whether the company and its workers carry the "certified mold remediator" designation, which is granted by the Indoor Air Quality Association. Also check any candidates with your city or town's consumer protection division to make sure there's no backlog of complaints against them. Unless you act quickly, though, when mold strikes, you could have a problem. Mold can quickly overcome a home; many homes with severe damage have to be torn down. Remember, if you do have mold, you'll have to disclose that fact—and any fixes you made—to prospective buyers.

RADON While some threats to your home are visible, radon is not. It's an odorless and colorless radioactive gas that is the second leading cause of lung cancer. Radon is naturally emitted from the breakdown of soil, rocks, and water. It enters homes by moving up through the ground into the air and can be present in homes with or without a basement and in new or old homes, according to the Environmental Protection Agency. In fact, elevated levels of radon are present in one out of fifteen homes. If you are buying a new home or your home has never been tested, you'll want to bring in a professional. Most states require that licensed, certified, or registered personnel conduct radon tests. If your state doesn't have a list of radon pros, ask contractors if they hold a professional proficiency or certification credential. These programs provide members with a photo ID that you can check for qualifications and expiration dates. If radon testing is positive for your house, you'll need to seal cracks in the foundation and install vent pipes and fans to prevent radon from entering your home through the concrete floor. Of course, the solution

to any radon problem depends on the house and its construction. The EPA operates a radon hotline to answer questions. Call 1-800-SOS-RADON (767-7236). Costs of remediation can vary but can easily run into thousands of dollars. And be aware that if you renovate your basement into living space, you'll definitely want to test for radon, even if you already tested when you bought the house. Smokers are particularly susceptible to health problems associated with radon.

FIRE Even a small flame in your home can rage out of control in as few as thirty seconds. If a fire occurs in your home, it most likely will occur at night, when your family is sleeping. More threatening than the flames themselves are the heat, which can scorch lungs, and smoke and toxic fumes, which kill more people than flames do. You need to make sure that your home has fire alarms on every floor of the house. Test them monthly and make sure the batteries are fresh and the unit is free of dust. If you bought an older home that already has alarms, you may want to replace them. Pros recommend upgrading alarms every ten years.

If you're like many families that have multiple computers, TVs, and other electronic appliances throughout the house, you'll want to make sure you're not overloading your home's electrical system. Don't overburden circuits or extension cords. Take care not to place cords and wires under rugs, over nails, or in high-traffic areas. If an appliance overheats and emits a strange odor, shut it off. If you've bought an older home with an electrical system that hasn't been upgraded, consider having an electrician install an arc fault circuit interrupter. These devices shut off electricity when unusual arcing occurs—that is, when electricity flows to the wrong place. Arcing faults can occur when wiring has deteriorated or insulation on wiring has been punctured by nails driven to hang pictures or even the stapling of cable. Conventional circuit breakers react to overloads and short circuits but not to abnormal arcing.

If you have a fireplace in your house, you'll want to have it tested every other year. Buildup of creosote, the black tar that results from burning wood, can create conditions for a chimney fire. Of course, anyone can claim to be a chimney sweep, but you'll want to make sure that

you hire someone who is a member of the Chimney Safety Institute of America (www.csia.org). In order to get certified, members have to pass an exam and renew their certification every three years. The institute issues a photo ID to its members along with a four-digit certification number, which you should be sure to check. If any sweep offers on-the-spot replacement of a chimney liner, watch out. Chimney liners are like shoes—they aren't one size fits all. A professional will give you a written report on the inspection and give you time to investigate your options.

KEEPING YOUR HOME FREE OF PESTS Mice, termites, and other pests can ruin your property's value and create health hazards. A colony of termites can chew through a foot of wood in your home in four months. Termites alone cause $5 billion worth of damage every year; and the damage they create isn't covered by your homeowner's insurance policy. Carpenter ants infest stacks of firewood that are wet or damaged by mold. And they can attack structural wood as well. Even your dog's waste is bait for varmints.

Common sense prevails here. Keep garbage in containers that have lids on them and make sure they have no holes that mice or rats can enter. Clean up after your pets in the yard. Control clutter such as woodpiles or stacks of boxes and junk in the garage. Clean up food spills right away in your home. Store sweets such as honey and sugar in closed containers and keep the exteriors wiped down. To keep mice out of your home, seal holes as small as the diameter of a pencil in your foundation and exterior walls.

Preventing pests from invading your home is a seasonal affair. In the spring as you clean away winter's grime, clean your kitchen shelves out and pull out and dust drawers. Clear away tree branches, shrubs, and plants from the side of your home. Such vegetation can serve as a highway into your house. In the fall, you'll want to start thinking about how to keep nature's pests from finding a warm winter home in your house. The solution is a combination of baits and traps—a one-two punch that can deal with rodents. Use bait traps in the corners of the garage or an attic space or indoors. Take care to make sure that children and pets are

kept well away from these traps. To find a professional who can help you get rid of bugs or mice, check out the National Pest Management Association's website at www.pestworld.org.

PREVENTING BURGLARY A burglary occurs every thirteen seconds in the United States, and if you're in one of those families where everyone is out of the home all day, you're vulnerable. That's because more than half of those break-ins occur in broad daylight.

Your first line of defense is the locks on your doors. The best-rated deadbolts carry an ASNI Grade 1 rating. Locks carrying that grade have performed well when tested with kicking, prying, hammering, and sawing to jolt them loose. Most people know it's important to get a good lock, but few think about the door it's bolted into. Consider installing a door with security strike plate or a fiberglass door instead of a weaker wooden one.

You'll want to pay particular attention to security before going on your summer vacation. The months of June and July are some of the busiest for thieves. To trick them into thinking you're still home, make sure you're using timers on your lights; stop delivery of the mail and newspaper, or have neighbors pick up mail or any deliveries. Eliminate dark areas around your home with spotlights. A brightly lit home can dissuade many burglars.

UPGRADING

16

Financing (and Paying for) Your Renovation

FROM THE MOMENT YOU BOUGHT YOUR HOME (OR PERHAPS EVEN WHEN you toured the house for the first time with a real estate agent), you may well have thought about the upgrades or renovations that could transform the property. Perhaps you thought that all the house needed to be a true gem was an updated kitchen with professional-style appliances, or maybe you dreamed of knocking down a first-floor wall to open up the family room to the kitchen, creating a more appealing floor plan. As you consider what projects to pursue, remember, as we discussed in Chapter 12, that remodeling projects seldom pay for themselves dollar for dollar. On average, renovations return 86.6 percent of their cost at sale time, according to *Remodeling* magazine's annual Cost vs. Value survey. That doesn't mean you should not make any improvements at all—far from it. Renovations still make sense for two very important reasons. One, you can't live in your house for ten, twelve, or twenty years and not make any changes to it. If you don't maintain your home, your property will lose value. Maintenance doesn't just mean keeping your gutters cleaned. It also means recognizing the trends that are in demand by home buyers

and that make your home feel current. The average home is thirty-two years old, and its layout and design offer far less than what most families want today. A home that is kept up-to-date and well maintained will sell faster and at a higher premium than homes that appear neglected. Second, and also critically important, these investments aren't like stock certificates that you'll shove into a bank vault. You and your family will be able to enjoy the investment for years to come.

The one overriding rule when it comes to improving your house with a remodel or renovation is this: don't overdo it. It's all too easy to get caught up in home design stores with their honed granite countertops, cherrywood floors, and deep soaking tubs. But since you want your remodeling project to translate into a solid investment, you need to embark on the renovation in a smart way. Knowing your budget limits before you hire a contractor is as important as setting a budget to buy the house in the first place. The rule of thumb most commonly used is that you shouldn't spend more than 20 percent of your home's value on upgrades. That means if you live in a $350,000 home, you'll need to cap your improvement budget at $70,000.

Rules of thumb are only that: guidelines. Whatever your dream, you'll want to do some quick financial analysis to determine how much you can afford to spend given your budget and how much investment makes sense for your particular home and your neighborhood. I'll show you the financing options and how they work, and discuss one renovation cost you may not have considered: taxes.

HOW MUCH CAN YOU AFFORD?

Few questions are more important than what you can afford to pay for your renovation. This question actually has two different aspects. First off, there is the issue of how much of your monthly budget you can allocate to pay for upgrades, and second, you'll need to come to terms with how much investment in your home makes sense given its value versus others in the neighborhood. The last thing you want to do is embark on an elaborate remodeling project that pushes the value of your home beyond that of the priciest homes in the neighborhood.

It would be terrific if we could all afford to pay for our home improvements out of cash we have on hand, but the fact is that most of us will finance our renovations with a bank loan. That means you'll need to determine how much wiggle room you have in your monthly budget to make payments. To do this, we'll analyze your monthly budget just like a banker would. Lenders determine how much they will loan you by determining the proportion of debt you already have relative to your income. Typically, for the purposes of lending for home improvement, they allow you a debt-to-income ratio of 45 or perhaps 48 percent. You're best off practicing some restraint. Earmark just 40 percent of your income for debt. To calculate the maximum room in your budget for paying for renovations, fill out the following worksheet.

Step 1: Calculate your monthly pretax income as you did in Chapter 2

   1. Gross monthly salary _____

   2. Bonuses, commissions _____

   3. Divide line 2 by 12 _____

   4. Add lines 1 and 3 _____

Step 2: Calculate your monthly expenses, the fixed ones that recur every month (exclude groceries, utilities, telephone services, and other general expenses)

   1. Mortgage, for your primary home and
        for any other property _____

   2. Monthly property taxes plus homeowner's insurance _____

   3. Car loans _____

   4. Credit cards _____

   5. Child support or alimony _____

   6. College loans _____

   7. Life insurance _____

   8. Monthly payments on any other loan or note _____

   9. Total _____

Use your calculations from steps 1 and 2 to complete the following worksheet, which will determine the maximum you could spend each month for renovations.

1. Total gross monthly income from step 1, line 4 _____
2. Debt-to-income ratio (0.40) _____
3. Multiply line 1 by line 2 _____
4. Total monthly expenses from step 2, line 9 _____
5. Subtract line 4 from line 3 _____

The number in line 5 is the maximum amount you could afford to spend each month for renovations. Now you need to compare what you can afford to what your project is likely to cost. In the chart below, you'll find a list of improvements that typically add the most to your resale value and their cost. Estimates are provided by www. remodeling.net.

TOP RENOVATIONS BY REGION

NEW ENGLAND	
Midrange	**Upscale**
Siding replacement, vinyl Cost: $8,717	Siding replacement, foam-backed vinyl Cost: $10,568

MIDDLE ATLANTIC	
Midrange	**Upscale**
Window replacement, vinyl Cost: $10,682	Siding replacement, fiber cement Cost: $13,280

SOUTH ATLANTIC	
Midrange	**Upscale**
Two-story addition Cost: $96,502	Siding replacement, fiber cement Cost: $12,846

EAST NORTH CENTRAL (IN, IL, MI, OH, WI)

Midrange	Upscale
Window replacement, vinyl Cost: $10,753	Siding replacement, fiber cement Cost: $13,352

EAST SOUTH CENTRAL

Midrange	Upscale
Siding replacement, vinyl Cost: $7,933	Siding replacement, fiber cement Cost: $12,895

WEST NORTH CENTRAL

Midrange	Upscale
Siding replacement, vinyl Cost: $9,507	Siding replacement, fiber cement Cost: $13,360

WEST SOUTH CENTRAL

Midrange	Upscale
Bathroom remodel Cost: $11,585	Siding replacement, fiber cement Cost: $12,874

MOUNTAIN

Midrange	Upscale
Two-story addition Cost: $102,994	Window replacement, vinyl Cost: $12,608

PACIFIC

Midrange	Upscale
Minor kitchen remodel Cost: $19,366	Siding replacement, fiber cement Cost: $13,539

Source: 2006 Cost vs. Value survey, *Remodeling* magazine

Next, you'll need to know whether you can afford the monthly loan costs of paying for your upgrade. Check out the loan calculators at www.bankrate.com to calculate your monthly costs. Try to cap the length of your payment schedule at fifteen years, less if your improvement is small. Keeping the repayment schedule short will lower your interest costs, limiting your overall costs for the project. Prepare yourself for an interest rate higher than that for your principal mortgage, most likely something just over the prime rate plus a little bit more. The prime rate is the rate banks charge their best customers. (You can find the current prime rate also at www.bankrate.com.)

Now, compare the monthly costs from www.letsrenovate.com to how big a budget your worksheet says your budget can accommodate. If the worksheet number is lower, you may have to reconsider your plans. For example, a $47,212 upscale bathroom addition financed at a rate of 8.2 percent would cost $456.65 a month. If your worksheet estimates say you can afford $650 a month for renovation projects, then your project is a go. If you can only afford $425, it's time to scale back your project or put it on hold.

THE BIG PICTURE

Now that you know how much you can afford to spend, you'll need to consider how much it makes sense to spend. You home doesn't exist in a vacuum. You'll want to embark on renovations and upgrades that are in keeping with those of your neighbors. Overspending pushes your home out of the affordability range with people likely to buy in your area; underspending will make your house a second runner-up in any beauty contests.

While it's true that experts recommend not spending anything more than 20 percent of your home's value on upgrades, as a practical matter, you may spend somewhat more or less depending on what your market can bear. For example, if you already live in the most expensive house in town, it's a bad idea to sink even 20 percent more money into bells and whistles, since you'll only push your home's price that much further out of reach for most buyers. The opposite is true if you live in the least up-

graded home in a well-to-do neighborhood. Take the case of Moira and Charles. The couple bought a quaint but tiny carriage house in a suburban Connecticut neighborhood filled with multimillion-dollar, elaborately outfitted homes. "We always felt like the poor relations," says Charles. "The good news is we felt free to make improvements." The two spent $65,000 upgrading and expanding their kitchen and then another $115,000 expanding the second floor to create a master suite. Their $650,000 home had appreciated to $717,034 through three strong years of price gains. Their renovation expenditures of $180,000 amounted to 25 percent of their home's value. Charles didn't worry that he had overspent. "We don't have the backyard kitchen and pool like our neighbors and we probably never will, but our house is the best value in the neighborhood—and now it's very attractive and updated," he says. He notes their home's value still isn't even close to the median price of $1.7 million for their neighborhood.

To make sure you're not overspending, talk to neighbors or your real estate agent to determine the most expensive homes in your neighborhood. You can find estimated home values by address at www.zillow .com. These homes' values will set the limits for your expenditures. For example if you own a $240,000 house and the most expensive house in the neighborhood is worth $325,000, a renovation budget of 20 percent or $48,000 will easily keep you within buyers' affordability range.

Real estate, of course, is local, and to determine the popular upgrades in your area you'll need to do some research. Lee Ann wondered how her 1860s rural Maryland home might stack up against the competition. She knew that commuters to jobs in Washington, D.C., had been pushed farther and farther out to find affordable homes. Now her rural town was considered hot property. While her house was in pristine condition with many positive features—it boasted a staircase banister original to the house, four fireplaces, and a nine-hundred-square-foot master suite—she felt it still lacked some essentials. For starters, the kitchen needed updating and with just three bedrooms, the house didn't measure up to others on the market. Lee Ann knew that families drawn to the area were also considering upscale suburbs such as Chevy Chase, Mary-

land, where homes were large and four-bedroom homes predominated. She noticed more and more homeowners in her area expanding their homes. After driving around her town and adjacent towns scoping out additions, she decided to take the first step and asked her appraiser for advice. "I knew I had several options, including finishing the attic, which would be cheap," she said, adding "The appraiser told me to do a first-floor addition, no question."

She planned a five-hundred-square-foot addition that included a fourth bedroom and additional kitchen storage space. Lee Ann planned to keep costs low by handling finish work such as painting and installing fixtures herself. She figures the addition will add $50,000 in value to her home and improve its marketability given what sellers with similar homes are putting their houses on the market for.

Lee Ann's got the right idea in making sure her home offers the amenities of neighbors. You don't have to pay for the services of an appraiser to evaluate local tastes. Point your browser to the websites of local Realtors and look at homes in the price range yours would be if you spent an additional 20 percent. Do they have one more bath than yours does? Or elaborate kitchens? Is the condition of your house similar? Better or worse? Attend a few open houses in your area. Or go investigate your local housing development to find out what the competition is like. Model homes are carefully marketed properties. Little inside them is left to accident. Big home builders pour millions into researching just what home buyers are looking for.

FINANCE IT RIGHT

Best-case scenario, you'll have some cash to put into your renovation. But if you have only a small amount or none at all, there are other ways to finance your renovation. Here are the ones you're most likely to encounter.

CASH-OUT REFINANCE With a cash-out refinance, you refinance your mortgage for more than you currently owe and pocket the difference. The key here is that you are getting a brand-new mortgage loan and new

terms. This is typically popular when interest rates are low and housing prices have been rising because you'll feel like you're getting access to free money—the difference between what your home originally appraised for and it's newer, larger value.

For example, if you owed $90,000 on your 7.5 percent mortgage loan and wanted to take out $20,000 to pay for your child's first semester at Harvard or a medical bill, you might apply for a cash-out refinance. The appraiser might find the home you paid $125,000 for is now worth $160,000. You take out a new loan for $110,000 at 6 percent and pocket the $20,000. The difference to your monthly mortgage payment? You'll actually pay $6 a month less for the refinance.

But this is less benign a strategy than you might think at first. Sure, you'll be able to tap money that was previously inaccessible to you, but you'll still have to pay it back. In our example, you'll pay an additional $17,894 in interest over the course of the loan. Plus, you'll pay 2 percent to 3 percent of the loan amount in closing costs. Plus, you'll reset the terms of the loan most likely to thirty years, which means you'll be paying your home loan off longer. Make sure you understand how your monthly payments will be affected. You'll need quite a difference between your current rate and the new rate of interest to keep from paying more monthly. Finally, you're best off avoiding a cash-out refinance if your current mortgage loan carries an unusually low rate of interest—6 percent or lower.

HOME EQUITY LOAN A home equity loan is a second mortgage loan that allows you to convert equity into cash. Like your original mortgage, your property is security for the loan. When you take out a home equity loan, you borrow a lump sum of money and you pay it back over a preagreed period of time, typically fifteen years. You pay a fixed rate of interest and your monthly payments go to both interest and principal. While home equity loans don't carry the high closing costs associated with refinancing a loan, home equity loans do carry interest rates that are typically higher than home equity lines of credit.

A home equity loan is a good bet for homeowners taking out a set

amount of money for one project. For those who plan to be in a house for a short period of time—maybe your boss will reassign you to a new city in a couple of years, for example—you'll want to avoid the home equity loan because they carry longer terms, usually fifteen years. The good news is that rates on home equity loans are fixed—what you see is what you get.

Using our example above, you would borrow $20,000 at a rate of, say, 8 percent, paying $191.23 a month for fifteen years with total interest costs of $14,403.

HOME EQUITY LINE OF CREDIT (HELOC) Lines of credit work similarly to credit cards and are just as addictive. You are approved for a set amount of money to borrow, say $20,000, which you access by writing checks on your HELOC account. Let's say you borrow $8,000 using your HELOC to pay for a fancy Sub-Zero refrigerator. At that point, you still have $12,000 available to you. If you pay back $3,000, then you still owe $5,000 and have $15,000 available to you.

A typical loan might have a draw period of five years, during which, if you want, you pay only the interest you owe on the amount you've borrowed. After the draw period, you can't take out any more money and payments must expand to cover both interest and principal. Lenders will allow you to tap 100 percent of your equity if you like, but you're better off keeping a cushion of financial safety.

The good news is that HELOCs don't carry closing costs like a home equity loan or a refinance would. However, if you're borrowing money in a period of rising rates, beware. HELOC interest rates reset monthly; that means your payments can go up and up. Therefore, your debt for those new kitchen cabinets can balloon out of control. That means you'll want to avoid lines of credit for projects with indeterminate time periods for completion and payment. However, even if rates are rising, you may opt for the HELOC if you have a specific improvement project in mind you plan to pay off in short order with a bonus or other windfall that is guaranteed. A HELOC is also a great insurance policy to have if you hit a bump in the road, such as if a tree falls in your

yard and you want to fix the house while your insurer takes its time figuring out how to settle your claim.

While HELOCs don't carry closing costs, they can carry transaction fees, inactivity fees, and prepayment penalties. To find out rates for both home equity loans and lines of credit in your area, go to www.bankrate .com and www.hsh.com. The good news is that interest on up to $100,000 of home equity debt is generally tax deductible. Unless your overall mortgage debt exceeds the value of your home or you become subject to the alternative minimum tax, you'll likely be eligible for the deduction.

CONSTRUCTION LOANS A construction loan taken out at the time you buy your house can cover both the purchase price and the costs of improvements. You'll pay an additional half percent in interest over traditional mortgages. If you already own your home, you can get a construction second mortgage to cover the costs of your renovation. If you locked in a great rate for your first mortgage and don't want to refinance into a higher interest rate, a construction loan is worth considering. However, rates are about half a percentage point over rates on home equity lines as well. So you'll want to make comparisons using mortgage calculators, such as the ones at www.bankrate.com.

MAKING THE CHOICE

If you are still on the fence about what type of loan to use to finance your improvement, here are some rules of thumb. If your project costs more than $15,000, chances are you'll need to pay for it with a loan. If it will take you years to pay for the project, opt for the home equity loan, since the interest rate is fixed. Less expensive projects should be financed with a home equity line of credit, and remember, you can dip in and out of the credit line whenever you want. Construction loans really make the most sense when you are buying a new home, and cash-out refinances are logical in those instances where rates are lower than your current mortgage rate and your home's value has climbed considerably.

BUDGET FOR SURPRISES

On occasion, renovations uncover other problems in a house. "The value of your home is in its real bare bones: the skeletal systems of plumbing and electricity. If you don't take care of those things, no matter what makeup you have slapped on, it won't be okay if the ceiling is cracking," says Christine Broda, an architect who works on both commercial and residential design. She recalls meeting with a couple who wanted to enlarge their kitchen. But when she arrived at their Westchester County residence, her attention was immediately drawn to the screened-in porch. All of the screens were bowed. Turns out the screens were supporting a significant amount of the weight of the roof because a key support structure had been removed. The house also had a badly sloped floor in the master bedroom. Broda recommended that the couple make repairs on all of these rooms. "The sloping floor didn't present any imminent danger, but in terms of resale value, who is going to pay top dollar for that house?" says Broda.

While a renovation might not uncover major structural problems in a house, Broda's example points to the fact that remodeling, with tearing into walls and removing plaster, can turn up problems that you didn't even know you had. "You might find rotted pipes or electrical wires literally held together with Band-Aids. When you find these things you have to deal with them, but they will add to the cost of the project. Replacing wiring means ripping up a bunch of drywall, which can cost thousands of dollars, when all you wanted to do was retile. But in the end you can use these improvements as selling points."

Bottom line: if you're going to renovate, you'd better expect surprises. Your initial budget should include a contingency of 20 percent to begin with to cover the flubs, mess-ups, and unexpected problems along the way. When you work out the full budget, down to the cost of all the appliances and materials, decrease the contingency to about 10 percent. More often than not you'll need it. To get an accurate budget you need a very detailed layout of what you want that will help you get the most accurate bids for your project.

HIDDEN COST OF RENOVATING

Renovating seems to have many hidden costs, but one you may have forgotten to take into consideration is rising property taxes. Tax assessors typically reassess properties every year or few years, but making improvements to your house gives them a good excuse to reassess early—and raise your taxes. This may tempt you not to file the proper building permits, and contractors often encourage this kind of behavior. The best course of action: don't avoid filing the required permits when you upgrade. Your city building department can protect you if the work on your renovation is subpar. Filing permits forces your contractor to meet basic building requirements. Before you start, find out from your local building department what types of permits will be required. Determine what the assessment schedule is so you'll know when your property will be reassessed.

17

Small-Budget Improvements

ONE EASY WAY TO IMPROVE THE LOOK OF YOUR HOME WITHOUT spending a bundle: redecorating. Any real estate agent can tell you, a well-decorated home can sell at a premium compared to those that are poorly designed. Let's face it, just about everyone responds to spaces that are attractive. Judy and Don came across a tiny but beautifully decorated three-bedroom colonial in a posh New York City suburb. The house was hardly commanding—its total size was no more than 1,400 square feet. It was more of a dollhouse than a real home. But in addition to having a recently updated, well-laid-out kitchen, the entire home was tastefully decorated. The palette was warm, featuring reds and blues to match the colonial style, but color wasn't used as a substitute for good design. Furniture was scaled to the space; each room flowed easily to the next. Here and there, luxurious touches, such as an antique canopy bed in the master bedroom, made the whole house glow. In the end, the bidding on the house drove the final price above $1 million, beyond reason. Judy and Don were smart enough to stay away from the bidding war, realizing it was savvy decorating that made the house so attractive. In the hands of a decorating novice, the place could have

looked uncomfortably small and cramped. That's the power of decorating well.

Of course, bad decorating can have the opposite effect. Years ago, when a California real estate agent was asked for advice from an unmarried male client about how to prepare his house for sale, the agent said simply, "It's really all about paint and carpeting." Unfortunately, his client took him at his word. When the agent visited the house, he found one room painted royal blue with bright green shag carpeting. Another room had walls painted in a black-and-white checkerboard pattern and beige carpeting. "It was like walking into a bag of M&Ms," he remembers. Naturally, he had the client take all that out and replace it with crisp white walls and boring but inoffensive beige carpeting. The house sold quickly and for a decent price. You don't have to stray far to hear stories about homeowners who want to put homes on the market with a living room littered with dog crates for not one, not two, but three massive Rottweilers. Or the fabulous Colonial laid waste by the books, laptops, and papers of three college-age boys come home to roost.

In other words, we're not talking about finding your inner Martha Stewart. Forget for a moment *Architectural Digest*. All you need to do, really, is develop a home with a sense of order and calm. You'll want to decorate your abode in a way that is good for both you and your family as you live there and for showing when you do get ready to sell. And while a lot of professional interior decorators would like to convince you that beautifying your house requires a professional (and a professional budget), the truth is that by following a few simple principles and paying attention to detail, you can make your house more appealing without spending a fortune. That not only benefits your family right now but also will help you fetch a better price when you put your home on the market.

GETTING STARTED

The first step to creating a successful look for your house is reimagining your personal space. To do that, you'll first have to clear your space of the clutter that can ruin sightlines and make it impossible to evaluate the bones of your house.

The average family is hit with a blizzard of junk every day—mail, magazines, newspapers and the like—that can easily turn into clutter. And the more stuff that piles up, the more overwhelming it becomes. In fact, most of us have a mental block when it comes to decluttering. It's easy enough to become so confused about how to get started that you can't start at all. If the first thing you see when you walk into your home is a stack of old newspapers or the pile of electrical cords emanating from your entertainment center, it is never too early to start clearing up and cleaning out. One easy way to get started is to pretend you're moving. What is worthy of paying the movers to pack and what isn't? Grab some boxes and start filling them. Another good exercise: evaluate the use of each room and make sure that all the furnishings relate to those uses. In other words, get the treadmill out of the bedroom and the kids' toys out of the living room.

As you start to clear away the clutter, you'll start to see the rooms in your house as if for the first time. If removing the clutter doesn't allow you to start reimagining each room, think about taking everything out (lamps, the end tables, that stack of magazines) except the largest pieces of furniture. Now, imagine what you'd prefer guests to "see" first. Is it an attractive fireplace? Bay window? French doors to the patio? Don't just check out the larger features; look to small details that will register with visitors, such as cornices and trim. These are the features you'll want to play up. If you have no architectural gems to spotlight, you'll need to create interest on your own.

THE PRINCIPLES

How many times have you seen a picture in a magazine and tried to emulate the look, only to find that your version paled in comparison? Decorating successfully on your own is possible if you follow some basic principles. These work equally well whether you live in a sleek contemporary or charming Tudor.

CONSISTENCY There's nothing more unsettling than walking through a house where every room seems unconnected to the next. When the

palette, furniture style, and materials change room by room, the effect is confusing and unsettling. One way to bring consistency to a home is to pick a palette of three to six colors you can work and rework in varying shades throughout the house. While you'll be tempted to try something different in every room, narrowing your color choices will make the house feel calmer and more organized. Pick materials, too, that you'll repeat throughout the house. Possibilities for a contemporary might be glass, steel, and pine. A more traditional approach could call for cherry, brass, and leather.

Paint is one of the cheapest ways of adding consistency and freshening up a home's look. But choosing the handful of colors that will dominate in your home can be tricky. Think about pulling colors that are already at work in the house or its setting—maybe the nutty brown of wood floors paired with a light green from the garden outside, or for the beach house, the neutral beige of the sand and sky blue. One guideline: the largest areas of a room, such as the floors, walls, and ceilings, should be the most neutral, while accents carry the most saturated color. This is a rule that can be broken, but you'll want to take care in using intense wall color; some hues can't be tolerated in large doses. Remember, colors are twice as bright on the walls as they are on the paint chip.

Picking those hues, then, is key. The trick is finding colors that harmonize. Think back to high school art class and find your old color wheel so that you can start considering options that work together. One popular choice has been the monochromatic color scheme, which is exactly what it sounds like: one neutral hue dominates the room. This can be trickier than it sounds. You may choose a white sofa from one store and a white upholstered chair from another and find that when you put the two together they clash. Small differences will pop out in a color scheme based on just one color. What's more, you may find your sophisticated all-white living room feels cold in the winter when the views out the window are snow-laden landscapes. A less tricky option is to pick three colors that are next to each other on the color wheel—for example, red, russet, and orange. You may want to throw in a touch of the complementary color (that's the color opposite on the color wheel), in

this case slate blue. Other variations are possible, but you get the idea—some colors harmonize and others don't. Try to keep your house-wide color scheme in the same family, varying tonal ranges from room to room. If you keep this in mind as you decorate, when it comes time to sell you'll be ready and potential buyers will get a sense of a home that is orderly and well designed.

Of course, implementing a color scheme is easier said than done. Once you get to the hardware store, you'll be overwhelmed by the number of paint choices. Invest in small sample pots of paint, which most stores sell, as you narrow your choices so that you can actually test them on large, one- to two-foot sections of your walls. After you paint several test patches with different colors, allow yourself time to see how these different colors look at different times of day. A sunrise yellow that appears inspirational in the morning may seem overbearing at night.

Once you've decided which shades work best in your rooms for all times of day, you'll need to choose the ideal finish for your use. Flat paint should be used for the biggest surfaces—walls in the living room, dining room, and bedroom—as well as hallways. Flat finishes hide flaws in plaster and drywall but are susceptible to stains. If you're painting a high-traffic area, such as children's rooms or family rooms, choose a satin finish, also called low-luster or eggshell. The paint will have a slight sheen, which allows it to be lightly cleaned. Use semigloss finishes in baths and kitchens, where splashes and messes require frequent wipe-downs. Gloss finishes are perfect for the trim in your home because it can hold up to whatever children or pets dish out. Fingerprints are easily cleanable. Don't use gloss finishes on large surface areas, because its reflective surface will point out flaws. Don't skimp on your paint budget. The cheaper the paint you buy, the more likely it is that you'll have to add additional coats to cover your walls. You'll spend $15 to $20 a gallon for quality paint.

Part of having a consistent-looking home is good transitions. One of the most important is what you see from your front door. The view into any room from the entrance or a hallway is critical. No matter how well you plan the interiors of your rooms, it's that first impression that mat-

ters the most. For that reason, you'll want to create transitions that move visitors through the space, beckoning them into the next room. Libraries or bedrooms—rooms that are quiet—should be buffered by a linking hallway to establish the transition. A mini-hallway can do the trick. Lower the ceiling at the entrance and install bookshelves along the sides. Your transition announces you're moving to a quieter room. If you have an open floor plan, transitions become even more important. Otherwise, the space will appear undifferentiated.

SCALE AND PROPORTION It seems like there is always some issue to deal with when it comes to size. A room is too small, or perhaps too large. With the trend toward opening up the kitchen so that it flows into the family room, homeowners have struggled with how to decorate a large space where it's not at all obvious where furniture groupings should go. Few things are more disconcerting to visitors—or potential buyers—than a large space that is poorly put together.

If you have a great room, you can make sense of the muddle. First off, don't try to simply fill up the space. You'll end up with a hodgepodge of a room that has no flow. Start with the activities that will occur in your great room. What are the primary uses of the room? If your family will be watching television, create an entertainment area. Establish a clear dining area, but use chairs that can move to other parts of the room with ease. Avoid the impulse to line up the furniture along the walls. Large area rugs, lighting, and even color can distinguish your activity areas. Typically, great rooms are designed with a fireplace at one end and a kitchen at the other. Eating areas, obviously, should go near the kitchen so that food arrives hot and cleanup is easy. You may want two eating zones, maybe a breakfast bar built into your kitchen island and then a formal dining table, which can also be used as an after-school work area. Placing the table between the kitchen area and the living area often makes the most sense. To make the room feel cozy, despite its space, use natural materials and textures, as well as color to warm up the room.

One way to make a small room look bigger? Focus on the diagonal line across a small room. By placing a focal point on that long line—the

hypotenuse of the triangle—you draw the eye to the far corner, enhancing the space. The focus can be structural, like a support beam, or a small piece of furniture whose color contrasts with the rest of the room. Another strategy is to paint the ceiling the same color as the walls. The wall and ceiling are unified and the result is the feeling of bigger space. Choose furniture with low backs—high backs will emphasize the room's size. Make sure that your furniture can do double duty. For example, the coffee table may house CDs. This allows you to keep the number of furniture pieces in the room at a minimum.

Scale your furniture to match your room's proportions. The trend has been oversized furniture, but it can make small rooms look choked. Decorate your small rooms to feel more expansive than they are and your large rooms to feel intimate.

AVOID TRENDS When Sal Alfano, editorial director of *Remodeling* magazine, was first working as a contractor, a client asked him to install what was then the hottest trend—a bright purple laminate kitchen countertop. "We put it in," he recalls. "The owner was happy with it, but anyone that ever walked into that kitchen commented on that horrible choice." While it is easy to assume that today's sleek European red kitchen cabinetry is tomorrow's 1970s harvest gold refrigerator and stove, some things you take for granted as being design staples can quickly drift into obscurity. In fact, that's exactly what Mark Johnson, a fellow of the American Institute of Architects, says is happening to stainless-steel appliances. "For a period of time, people aspired to a commercial kitchen look like the chefs they see on TV," he says. "What I am seeing is more of an interest in warmth—warmer finishes in the home is a growing trend." Custom panels that dress appliances in mahogany finishes are also rising in popularity.

The point isn't that you need to go switch out your stainless-steel appliances next week, but rather that you should choose finishes and materials that will have a timeless appeal. Trends change the most quickly in kitchens and bathrooms. For that reason, you'll want to find a quality kitchen counter that won't look dated in two years. Tie your choices to the style and design of the house.

LUXURIOUS, BUT NOT EXPENSIVE FINISHES These days, it's not difficult to find cheaper substitutes for what were once luxury items. The elaborate ceiling molding that used to be made by hand by artisans is now mass-produced from plastic or urethane. It's not likely anyone will notice the difference except you and your wallet. Likewise, America's love affair with hardwood floors has spawned lots of imitators that now look increasingly like the real thing. Laminates are available that look and feel like the real thing but cost far less. Faux mink throws have been all the rage, and knockoffs of expensive home décor items are almost as common as runway knockoffs.

Too much of a good thing, though, can be too much. For example, one Westchester County, New York, family's brick home sat on one and a half acres, a generous lot size by suburban New York standards. The house boasted an indoor pool and six thousand square feet of space. But buyers shied away from some of the excess design features, such as the black Jacuzzi and black marble sinks inlaid with gold leaf faucets in the master bath, as well as the mirrors and crystal chandeliers that lit the home's interior from the entryway to the upstairs bedrooms. Show some restraint when it comes to choosing design elements.

As a model, look to hotel rooms—no kidding. Ian Schrager and other well-known hotel designers are setting the standard for mixing opulent fabrics, rich colors, and materials into design. You don't want to overdo it, but a touch of luxury here and there can add visual interest that draws buyers like bees to honey. But it's not just the occasional cashmere throw that makes a room feel expensive; careful attention to molding and lighting can also yield a feeling of luxury.

Home buyers have grown accustomed to buying houses that are stripped down, with little in the way of trim or molding on walls, doors, and windows. Adding in these finishing touches is a great and inexpensive way to bolster your home's appeal, giving your rooms a finished look without breaking the bank. For example, adding ceiling molding to a fifteen-by-fifteen-foot room will run you around $3 a linear foot or about $200 for the whole room. Of course, picking out the molding can be difficult. Go to any home improvement store and you'll find a myriad of molding choices. The trick is to make sure you choose a design

that fits with the architectural style of your home. For example, you wouldn't want to use a Doric molding style in a contemporary house because its Greek origins and classical style would clash with the modern elements of your home. That said, if your house doesn't have a distinct style, you have more options. Just make sure you choose one general style for the entire house, using the most intricate and detailed for the public rooms of the house, including the living room, family room, or dining room. If you're installing the molding yourself, buy it a week before installation and let it sit inside the house to acclimate to your home's temperature and humidity levels. If you don't, you risk having the molding shrink and bow.

Trim around a window can be a way to add a dramatic finish to a room. Wainscoting in a kitchen or bath is another way to add detail and interest at a low cost. It can be used at varying heights from 36 to 54 inches from the floor. You may also want to upgrade interior doors. Many homes have cheap doors made of a single panel of wood. Buying a door with four panels makes the home feel better built and you'll spend just $60 to $100 for the upgrade.

PAY ATTENTION TO LIGHTING You can have the most beautiful home in the world, but if the lighting is poor, the impact of expensive furnishings and finishes can be lost. Also true is the fact that an average room can be made to look opulent with the right lighting. Lighting can be used in several ways. You already know about task lighting—the fixture beside your chair or bed allowing you to read this book fits that bill. But there is also accent lighting used to create depth and add dimension by highlighting objects in a room. Ambient lighting is a gentle light that makes the room glow, while decorative lighting adds sparkle to a room (think chandelier). You don't need all of these lights in every room, but if you sprinkle them into the public rooms of the house, you can create a sophisticated look that sets a mood and adds to the value of your home. You can spend thousands of dollars to hire a lighting expert to evaluate your home, or you can do it yourself.

Kitchen lighting used to be an afterthought, with all the effort and

money sunk into the living room. But now that kitchens have become a major meeting place for family and guests alike, you'll want to upgrade lighting there, layering it to achieve a sophisticated look. Start with the task lighting above the countertops where you prepare food, the sink, and the stove. Be sure to install task lighting so that your body doesn't cast a shadow over the work area as you stand there. Task lighting in food preparation areas can be installed underneath cabinets. Don't overdo ambient lighting in a kitchen. In fact, your decorative lighting—placed on top of a wall cabinet and illuminating the ceiling—can serve as ambient lighting. Just how much light you need will depend, in part, on the color scheme you're using. A kitchen with all-white cabinets will need 50 percent less light than one with cherry cabinets or any dark color.

In the bath, you'll want light above the sink and on both sides of the mirror, creating cross lumination. A common mistake homeowners make is mounting the light above the mirror. Unfortunately, that will light your forehead and not much else. Lighting is important here, because it's where you'll apply makeup or shave. Shower lighting should be recessed and lighting units waterproof.

As you think about installing lighting, especially recessed fixtures in living areas, make sure they are adjustable so that if you rearrange the furniture in the room, you're lighting can still work with the new design. Your lighting should be as flexible as your floor plan.

To keep the costs of your lighting from spiraling out of control, think about using low-voltage fixtures with energy-efficient 50-watt halogens for accent lighting. And don't turn your nose up at fluorescent lights. While they used to cast a ghostly green color, newer versions have a far warmer light that is also easy on the pocketbook. And you don't have to buy the four-foot-long bulbs anymore; fluorescents are available in bulbs and fit into regular fixtures. Don't forget the practical either. Light switches should be located on the unhinged side of a door. Otherwise, you'll have to reach around the back of the door to flip on the switch.

As with any project, you'll need to know about state and local building codes regarding any improvements you make. These rules govern an

incredible number of aspects of construction, from safety issues, such as whether your front stoop is high enough to require a railing, to small details, such as what kinds of light bulbs you can use in your kitchen's new lighting design. Ignoring the rules can be expensive. If your renovation or remodel isn't up to code, you may have to tear it down and rebuild. A poorly constructed upgrade that breaks the rules can also stop the sale of your home in its tracks. No buyer will want to purchase a house that isn't in compliance with building codes. Good designers, contractors, and architects will help you understand the rules and make sure that every project you undertake meets or exceeds guidelines.

18

Choosing and Managing a Contractor

AMERICANS SPEND AN AVERAGE OF $169 BILLION EACH YEAR REMODEL-ing their homes. With so much money on the line, you'll want to be sure you are spending your cash wisely. Few decisions are more important for a renovation project than which professionals you bring in to design and build your project. At a minimum, you'll need to choose a designer and a general contractor if your project is anything more than the simplest bathroom upgrade.

Before you bring in the pros, it makes sense to think through the project as you envision it. Work through these questions suggested by the American Institute of Architects to prepare yourself for the many decisions you'll need to make:

1. *What activities will go on in new space that is being designed?* (The answer may be straightforward if your project is a bathroom or kitchen upgrade, less obvious if you're knocking down walls to create a great room.)

2. *What are your expectations for the project?* (For example, you might answer that a second-story addition should provide privacy and comfort for your now teenage children. Or that a new first-floor master bedroom will expand the living space for you and your spouse.)

3. *What sorts of design aspirations do you have?* (You might answer that your goal is to create an addition with features that knit it seamlessly into your existing Colonial. Or maybe you want to re-design your house's first floor to create a space that seems open and expansive.)

4. *What is your budget?*

5. *Is there a fixed deadline for completion?*

6. *How will you make decisions? Will one spouse sign off on everything or will both of you?*

GETTING A DESIGN

Once you've decided how much you can spend and talked about your expectations for the project, the next step is getting a plan—a drawing or design—that will detail your renovation. These days there are a myriad of professionals willing to do this sort of work for you. Many contractors, in fact, are prepared to design simple projects, such as a basement office. Using your contractor as your designer can cut your design costs in half. However, if your project is more elaborate, especially if it requires moving walls or changing the layout of your existing house, you'll want to hire an architect.

HIRING AN ARCHITECT

Architects are the best educated, most respected, and ultimately most expensive of the design professionals. They should be licensed and their services will account for 8 to 15 percent of the costs of your project. Before choosing an architect, you'll want to see examples of their work firsthand. Remember, you're hiring your designer for his or her aesthetic

sensibility, so you'll want to make sure your tastes are similar. Your best bet for finding someone you like is to ask friends and neighbors who have done renovations that you find attractive. Make your initial contact by telephone or in person; the point is to get a sense of the architect's personality. Check references and examine the architect's work first-hand. It pays to contact clients whose work was completed four or five years ago, because homeowners have the benefit of hindsight and can tell you how well the renovation has aged. Be sure that your architect is comfortable working within your budget parameters. Bringing in an architect to design a $20,000 kitchen upgrade is a mistake if he or she typically designs $100,000 renovations.

Check with the National Council of Architecture Registration Boards to make sure your professional is licensed. Go to www.aia.org to find out if your architect is a member of the American Institute of Architects, which requires members to meet ongoing educational requirements. The website will also give you contact information for the local AIA chapter, which will assist you in choosing an architect for free.

Personality, too, will play a role. Choose someone you can get along with, because you will spend a lot of time together, and the architect may ask a lot of questions about your personal habits in order to render a design that works best for you. Getting the most from an architect requires leveling with him or her about what you want. When one Austin entrepreneur decided to build a home, he wanted one that would impress visitors from the minute they pulled into the driveway. But he was too embarrassed to tell his architect his goal. Instead, the entrepreneur rejected plan after plan until the architect finally figured out what he was looking for. Had the homeowner leveled with his architect, the process could have been faster and more efficient.

Once you choose one architect from your list of potential candidates, you'll be asked to pay a retainer for his or her services. Your architect will present you with at least two design concepts, which will address the big picture of your renovation. You'll choose one of these; then, the design team will come up with rough plans and cost estimates. After you approve those, the architect will draw construction plans, the

detailed drawings that will explain to the contractor or builder how to build your project, and lay out the specifications.

You can pay your architect only to do everything up to this point, or you can pay an additional sum for the architect to hold your hand through the entire project. Architects can charge you a percentage of the total project cost, or they may charge you a fee per square foot. The advantage to paying on the basis of square footage is that your budget won't jump into the stratosphere if you decide to go with the granite countertops. If you want your architect to continue working with you throughout the project and to do walk-throughs checking the progress of construction, that service alone will represent 20 percent to 30 percent of the fee.

OTHER DESIGN PROFESSIONALS

Architects, of course, aren't the only design professionals. There are lots of other professionals who are well suited to projects with a smaller scale, such as upgrading a bath or redesigning your kitchen. Here are the ones you are most likely to encounter:

1. *Designers* are typically not regulated or licensed, so you'll want to know their background before hiring them. Be sure your designer has a degree from an accredited university and membership in organizations that require they adhere to professional standards, such as the American Institute of Building Design, National Council of Building Design Certification, the National Association of the Remodeling Industry, or the American Society of Interior Designers.

2. *Structural engineers* can help you make changes to the existing layout or structure of your home. They develop the plans that will go to your local building department for approvals.

3. *Kitchen and bathroom designers* are best at guiding homeowners engaged in high-end renovations through the maze of products offered in their area of specialization.

4. *Home center design teams* are a good choice for projects that need to be done quickly and on a tight budget. The downside is that their design skills can vary widely. Expect them to recommend products sold by their employer.

5. *Design/build contractors* carry a job from start to finish, handling both the architectural design and construction. Because one firm is responsible for all elements of the job, it can be more efficient.

Good designers are busy; when you contact them, ask for references and check them out with care just as you would an architect. Ask former clients what the designer was like to work with, whether he or she listened to their opinions, and whether they were satisfied with the design. Home center design teams should be limited to jobs where cost is the major priority—for example, if you're making an upgrade just before putting the house on the market. You'll have to vet kitchen and bath designers based on their experience and previous jobs. Were their clients satisfied? Was the design a good one in the end?

Once you have a design, your next step is deciding whether to hire a general contractor or do the work yourself. The general contractor is the person who hires the team of tradespeople that will work on your project, everyone from the plumber to the crew that hangs the Sheetrock. The general contractor orders materials, manages the work, and oversees the budget, making sure that everything gets done for the appropriate cost and at the right time.

ZONING

It's nearly impossible to make changes to your house without telling city hall. Cities require a permit (sometimes more than one) whenever a project involves any structural, electrical, plumbing, or mechanical systems. The rules vary by municipality, so you'll need to check locally to find out what your general contractor will need to provide. Your plans will be scrutinized by the building department to make sure they meet local code, then your project will be inspected several times, and finally

a certificate of occupancy will be issued once all the work has been done correctly. For all this work, you'll pay for your permits, with the cost assessed on the basis of your expenditures. And on top of that, the information is passed on to the city's tax assessors, who may decide to raise your property taxes if the home's value has increased because of your improvements.

It's all too tempting to decide not to file permits because of the cost involved. But that would be a mistake. The city's building department will keep your general contractor on the up and up, making sure he or she meets local codes. That means when you sell your home, an inspector won't find a problem with the changes that prevents you from selling. Even worse, a bungled renovation might have to be torn down.

If the building department doesn't like your plan and refuses to give you a permit, you can fight back by asking for a variance. You'll have to defend your request for a variance at a public hearing and pay a fee to get what you want. It's far easier and less expensive to change your plans. Zoning laws are written with the broader community in mind. Some rules restrict the proportion of the lot that can be used for construction, for example, to prevent the construction of McMansions. Other laws limit modifications of homes in historic districts to preserve the look and feel of centuries-old neighborhoods.

CHOOSING THE GENERAL CONTRACTOR

The general contractor is a critical player in any renovation project. Whether you do it yourself or hire someone to do it for you, the role of picking subcontractors and managing them will determine the quality of your renovation. He or she has to have knowledge in many areas, as well as an extensive Rolodex of able subcontractors. Some homeowners opt to do the general contractor work themselves, hiring individual tradespeople and monitoring their progress. The payoff can be thousands of dollars in savings—up to 20 percent of your budget—because you avoid markups on labor and materials and add-ons for profit that a general contractor usually charges. But you should take on this responsibility only if you can afford to be called away from your day job at any time

to respond to a problem or difficulty. If you want to be your own general contractor, be prepared to find work crews for demolition and construction, schedule inspections, handle the delivery of materials and appliances, and oversee progress. As a rule of thumb, you may want to avoid taking on general contractor responsibilities if your project requires that you file permits with the local building department or if the job will take more than a few weeks to complete.

Heather and David learned firsthand not to overestimate what they could pull off themselves. The two were searching for a Los Angeles home but found themselves priced out of the skyrocketing southern California market. They decided their best bet was buying a fixer-upper. "We didn't realize what we were getting ourselves into," says Heather. The house needed a full makeover, inside and out. They started out doing all the work themselves but quickly realized that some things were beyond their capabilities. "One time we were working on the electrical wiring for the dining room. My husband decided that he couldn't fit into the crawlspace, so I went down there. At the time, we didn't have a washer or dryer hooked up, so I was down there literally in my underwear because I didn't want my clothes to get dirty, which would necessitate yet another trip to the Laundromat. We were running cords, it was ten o'clock at night, and I was down there with a flashlight when I thought, 'Forget this, we are hiring someone.'"

Homeowner complaints about general contractors and their work regularly top state attorney generals' consumer complaint lists. One of the most common scams is soliciting deposits for work from unsuspecting homeowners and then running off with the money. For that reason, you'll want to make sure you're hiring one of the industry's good guys. Start by getting recommendations from neighbors, friends, your architect, and people you work with. Then you need to interview each prospective general contractor. Here are interview questions that will help you get a handle on each candidate:

1. *How many projects like yours has the contractor done before?* An experienced contractor will be familiar with the housing stock in

your area, and know the building codes and processes. Choose a contractor with five years of experience or more.

2. *When is he or she available? What other projects does the contractor have going on and when would he or she be available to do yours?* Describe your project in detail so that the contractor can understand its size and scope. Try to get a sense of whether this job will stretch his or her resources, and force him or her to use unfamiliar subcontractors, which could take longer and leave you with subpar work.

3. *How long will your project take to complete?* Experienced contractors will have a good sense of how long he or she is likely to be on the job.

4. *Will the contractor be on-site every day, overseeing all the work?* If not, who will be? You want to make sure someone will be on hand to fix problems or make corrections as they happen.

5. *How do we make changes to the plan as we go?* Invariably, you'll want to change some things as you go, whether it's something as simple as a doorknob or as big as the location of a door. Make sure your contractor has a formalized process for taking into account changes. Typically, he or she writes up a change order, which describes the change plus any additional anticipated costs, and both you and the contractor sign the document.

6. *Will the contractor handle getting the appropriate permits for the work?* It's best if your contractor deals with getting permits for construction, rather than you; some municipalities require it.

After asking these questions, you should have a pretty solid idea of your candidates' seriousness and capabilities. Then ask for references. Call each reference and ask specific questions: What was the general contractor like to deal with? How accommodating was the crew? Did he or she bring the job in on time and under budget? Was the quality of the work satisfactory? How did the renovation work out over time?

Would you hire this general contractor again? By now, you should have a sense of whether this is someone you'd like to work with and whether he or she has enough experience to get the job done.

Next, ask the candidates you like to visit your home to show them what you're planning. This is where you'll want to see a display of interest in the job by the contractor. If your project is sizeable, contact your insurance agent to increase the amount you are covered for to include the cost of your renovations, and if you don't already have a $1 million in liability coverage, sign up for it now.

You're not yet done with your due diligence. Every contractor you consider should have the following:

1. *A valid license,* if required by your state. Go to www.contractors-license.org for your state's rules. Verify license numbers with the appropriate state department. Unfortunately, only about half of the states in the country require contractors to be licensed. If your project is large, ask for a surety bond, a guarantee that the work will be completed. It protects you if your contractor fails to finish the project.

2. *Insurance.* If Aunt Martha's sideboard is damaged during your renovation, you'll want just compensation. Liability insurance is what protects you. Workers compensation insurance protects you if someone is injured while working on your property. Ask for certificates of insurance to prove the general contractor has coverage or contact the insurer directly. Stay away from any candidate who refuses to give you a copy of his or her license and certificate of insurance. That probably means he or she doesn't have one.

3. *A clean bill of health* from the local consumer advocacy group. Contact the local Better Business Bureau and any town or country consumer department to find out whether your contractor has had trouble with consumers in the past.

Next, ask the two to three candidates you like to come up with a written bid for the work that includes estimates of the cost for materials

and labor. Be as specific as you can about the details you want and the materials you expect. Your choices will make a big difference in price estimates. If you are planning on buying fixtures or appliances yourself to save money, now is the time to tell the contractor.

As you conduct the interviews, you'll want to be wary of predators out there who want to take the money and run. Avoid contractors who ask you to pay for work that has yet to be accomplished or for materials that haven't yet arrived. You'll want to pay on a preset schedule set up in your contract. To get things done as you want them, you'll need to dole out your money a little at a time. Plan on putting 10 percent down. That initial down payment is only an assurance to the contractor that you won't give the job to someone else. Many states set limits on how much you can be asked to put down, so check with your state attorney general's office if you're asked to put down more than 10 percent. You'll stagger the remaining payments, linking them to completion of major portions of the renovation. It's typical to put another 25 percent down when electrical and plumbing are done, another 25 percent after cabinets and windows, and 25 percent when the flooring and painting is done. Hang on to the final 15 percent until you've had ample time to test everything and make sure it works, about thirty days. Pay by check and get a receipt. Avoid contractors who only want cash for their services. Another warning signal: contractors who ask you to write checks directly to them for products, or use high-pressure sales techniques, such as offering a lowball price that's only available for a limited time.

ASSESSING BIDS

As you begin assessing bids, first toss out any clear lowball bidders. Contractors face similar costs for labor and materials, any offer that is dramatically lower than the others, could signal a problem contractor. Examine the quotes in detail and be on the lookout for terms such as *equivalent*— this means your contractor can replace materials you may have specified for cheaper materials you don't want. Finally, don't choose the general contractor who can start first. Good contractors are busy; you may have to wait to get the work started. Here are elements you should expect to see in bids for your work:

1. Materials, including lumber, flooring, cabinets, insulation

2. Labor costs and total hours required

3. Tools and construction equipment

4. Cleanup, including the cost of rental bins and dumping fees

5. Subcontractor fees from specialty contractors like plumbers

6. Finishing elements like light fixtures

GET A GOOD CONTRACT

Don't agree to pay for any work without a contract. And, it needs to be highly detailed; right down to the number of coats of paint you want on the wall. You're best off using your own contract, instead of relying on your contractor to supply one for you. Go to the American Institute of Architects' website at www.aia.org to see sample agreements which you can purchase for less than ten dollars. Any contract should specify key parts of the plan, including an estimated timeline (when work should begin and when it should end); precisely the work to be done (adding a stairwell to the first floor, for example, isn't detailed enough); payment schedule; a process for resolving disputes; who should handle the trash disposal; specifics on materials used, including specific brand names and models for appliances; and a requirement for a change order if any alterations are made to your plan.

MANAGE YOUR CONTRACTOR

Face it, if your home is being renovated, your personal space is going to be not so personal for a while. Routines will be interrupted. Take-out meals may become your mainstay. If you are redoing a kitchen, you'll need to move some basic items, such as a microwave and coffeemaker, to a different room. Think of your home as a construction work site, because that's what it is, albeit one where you have to live.

When Alan renovated the kitchen in his suburban Denver, Colorado, home, the entire project, which involved knocking down several walls, took ten months, three months longer than expected. Because the construction was right next to the master bedroom, Alan and his wife

moved into the finished basement. "We set up a little microwave and mini-refrigerator, but I felt like I was living in a Holiday Inn for months," he says.

The key to making your project go as smoothly as possible lies in how you manage the contractor. Architects, designers, and homeowners who have been through renovations will tell you that managing the contractor is a delicate dance. You want to have regular meetings and an open line of communication without being too overbearing.

You want to express your vision and concerns about the project, but within reason. Have a preconstruction meeting. At this meeting the contractor will outline how the project will proceed. This is your opportunity to figure out how all the workers will be entering the home. Where will the trucks park? How will you ensure they won't trample over your flowerbeds and track mud on your off-white carpeting? Decide where the workers will enter and what area of the home will be off limits (i.e., the upstairs bathroom). Establish hours that you expect workers to be on the job. Also find out where the construction materials will be stored, how trash will be disposed of, and how the work site will be cleaned.

As Dennis Kyte, who has renovated several houses in Connecticut's Litchfield County, puts it, "It is like having any houseguest—there are the house rules. Ask questions. Find out when they work. Will they be there five days a week or three days a week? Can they use the phone? Can they play the radio?" Finally, he says, figure out how often you will get an update, and then stay out of their way. It's best to designate one person in the family to communicate with the general contractor (not the site supervisor) on a regular basis, say, once a week. That way you won't have several different points of contact and confused communication. If you're working with an architect, he or she can also sit in on the weekly meetings.

Don't be overbearing. Remember, time is money for these people. One Stamford, Connecticut, contractor walked off the job because of an overly inquisitive homeowner. Half-hour meetings became four-hour meetings because the owner was asking so many questions. The owner was simply fascinated with the process of construction, but he drove the contractor nuts. The contractor abandoned the job because of the delays.

Make sure the contractor's time is productive. Homeowners often complain about their inability to get the contractor to come back to complete the final touches. Often this can be avoided by making decisions about what you want in terms of materials as early as possible and then sticking with those decisions. Ordering materials early makes it more likely they will arrive in a timely fashion and keep crews on-site until the job is done.

To keep up with what's going on, create a file system for bills, photos, notes from meetings, and of course permits. Make sure someone from your general contractor's team has a presence on the work site to coordinate subcontractors' work. Managing a project from an office across town is a recipe for disaster. Stay in touch with that person, meeting with them on a weekly basis to determine progress, understand the next steps they are about to undertake, and resolve any difficulties.

19

Remodeling Projects
That Pay Off for Any Budget

JOANNA AND TOM AND THEIR NEIGHBORS, ALLISON AND HENRY, HAD lived next to each other in the same suburb north of Cincinnati, Ohio, for a couple of years when both decided to upgrade their kitchens. The two had nearly identical ranch-style homes, whose kitchens hadn't been upgraded since the homes were built forty years ago. The couples made very different choices. Joanna and Tom were younger, had owned their house fewer years, and had less equity built up in their home. They replaced their cabinets with stock cherry cabinets from their local home improvement store. Joanna chose a glazed ceramic tile in a dark green for the countertops. For additional touches such as light fixtures and curtains, she sought out sales. They chose and purchased new appliances with good but not glamorous names. Tom painted the kitchen. When they were finished, the two were impressed at how much better the place looked.

Allison and Henry, two empty nesters, were determined to get the kitchen of their dreams. They ordered custom cherry cabinets with built-in sliding shelves and two appliance garages for either side of their

new professional-grade range. They ordered a top-of-the-line, ultra-quiet dishwasher and a pricey refrigerator. (They had to upgrade the home's electrical wiring to accommodate the additional energy load.) Allison found a beautiful piece of granite with the help of her kitchen designer, who also suggested upgrading the kitchen's lighting. They ripped up the old Congoleum and installed a new wood floor. The results were beautiful. But the costs were very different. Joanna and Tom spent just under $23,000, while Allison and Henry paid nearly $65,000. Ultimately, the two kitchens didn't look all that different, but the price tags were miles apart. Making the tough choices that will keep your kitchen affordable for both you and the next buyers is your responsibility. In this chapter, we'll look at the options you're most likely to encounter as you upgrade the two most important rooms in your house when it comes to resale: the kitchen and the bath.

THE KITCHEN

The kitchen is the center of the home, a gathering place for kids after school and parents after work. This is where guests will gravitate. Ideally, it is situated at the center of the house with access to other rooms, but no major traffic lanes right through it. It should have at least one window to let in natural light and high quality finishes to withstand frequent use. You'll need to have it organized for efficient usage by the cook and areas where guests can lounge.

DESIGN PRINCIPLES Not only do you want a kitchen that stands out, but you want one that works for your family and will make sense to the next buyer down the road. Think about how you use the kitchen. Are you a hobbyist chef who enjoys entertaining, or do you expect that your kitchen will get far less use? Are you a couple that cooks just a few nights a week, or do you have a family where the kitchen is very much the hub of the house?

Answering these questions not only will help you determine which appliances and amenities you need but will start you thinking about traffic patterns. Most kitchen design is based on a triangle, which refers to a

work area bounded by the sink, stove, and refrigerator, an area that for all practical purposes serves as the work hub of the kitchen. You want these three areas near each other, so that you aren't walking across a room to drain a boiling pot of pasta. The so-called legs of this triangle (i.e., the distance between, say, the sink and the refrigerator) should be between four and eight feet. The trend toward larger and larger kitchens has compromised this principle—expansive kitchens means you have to walk additional steps to grab food for prep and for cleaning. In this case, less truly is more—shorter triangle legs means less walking for you and more efficiency. You'll also want to ensure that this triangle isn't in the center of any other traffic areas. For instance, if your kids will be running through the kitchen to reach the living room from the dining area, you want to ensure that your work triangle isn't in that path.

There are other design basics to be aware of. If you are eyeing a kitchen with an island, make sure that there is enough walking space (generally forty-two to forty-eight inches) between the island and other countertops. Refrigerator and oven doors will still need room to swing open with the cook standing in front of them. Scale is critical to making the island useful and pleasing to the eye. If it's too big, it overwhelms the space; too small, it's not useful. Ideally, the island should bring the cook into the center of the room to face family and guests. That typically means bringing electrical and plumbing service to the island so that it contains a cooktop and/or a sink. It's a good idea to build your island with work surfaces at multiple heights, so that one part of the island is for eating, another for food preparation, and still another for stashing hot pots.

Getting the right counter heights, too, is critical. Most kitchens are based on designs that are three decades old. That means counter heights were designed to fit primarily women who were shorter than the average kitchen user is today, who is far more likely to be taller and possibly male. Determine the best counter height for you by standing in front of your kitchen counter and placing your palms on the horizontal work surface. If your elbows are slightly bent, then the height is right for you. Measure the distance from the surface to the floor to determine your ideal countertop height.

Today's kitchens often have more than one countertop height. Standard countertop heights are thirty-six inches, but designers should add another two inches or more for a food bar or serving area. Food preparation areas should be three to four inches lower to allow easy chopping. Cooktops should be just five to six inches lower than standard countertop heights to allow the cook to look into pots, and tabletops should typically be eight inches lower. Getting the right countertop heights will subtly increase your comfort and use of the kitchen.

Storage is critical, but unfortunately many designers overdo it, adding cabinets from ceiling to floor along every inch of horizontal space. If you've ever struggled with reaching high cabinets or wondered what was at the back of your pantry because you can't see into it, you know firsthand about the overzealousness of some kitchen designers. You'll be better off inventorying your storage needs to get a real sense of how much cabinet space you need. It's a good idea to have clear front or open cabinets in some areas, such as the ones that hold your glasses, so that visitors can easily navigate your kitchen. Another area where designers often overdo it: countertops. If you opt for stone, you can spend a fortune covering every square inch of exposed space with granite. You can save money and make your kitchen more efficient by choosing materials best suited for their function by location. For example, butcher block is a good choice for the food prep area; bakers will want a stone dough counter.

Design details matter greatly. A poorly designed cabinet over a range can block usage of back burners. Water faucets placed too close to the sink's backsplash prevents water spigots from being fully turned on.

There are also more general mistakes you can make that have less to do with the "furniture" of the kitchen and more to do with the overall design. Leah Lenney, a designer in Larchmont, New York, met with a couple that wanted to renovate a kitchen that had last been updated in 1968. "The kitchen is a series of rooms. There is a butler's pantry, two maid's rooms, and an old bathroom," says Lenney. "They are interested in updating the cabinets and the appliances, but I also suggested that they take down these walls and expand the kitchen into the other rooms, but they won't do it. They want to keep this maze of pocket-sized rooms.

They are willing to spend fifty thousand dollars on their kitchen but they're not really addressing the situation. It's sort of like my old, favorite tennis racket that I keep restringing. They can keep the walls, but I think the kitchen will end up looking like an old lady wearing a red wig." Kitchens these days are open rooms with floor plans that flow into the rest of the house. A great kitchen is typically the heart of the house, where the family and friends meet.

The last thing you want to do is pour $50,000 into a kitchen that still won't appeal to today's buyers. Once you have a grasp on these basic design principles you can start to look at specific amenities that will fit the room and your budget. We'll look at renovations you can make across three budget levels: the starter kitchen, the up-and-coming kitchen, and the boomer dream kitchen.

THE STARTER KITCHEN Most starter kitchens are galley kitchens, and that is good, since your budget probably won't allow you to change the footprint of the room. If you don't have the budget to completely replace the cabinets, you can simply refinish them, which gets rid of built-up oils and grease. You might replace just the cabinet doors and drawers or even dress up older cabinets with new hardware. An attractive chrome handle can make a cabinet look more expensive than it actually is. If you are investing in new cabinets, remember that storage space in a galley kitchen is key. For counters, granite will likely be out of your budget, so stick with a neutral-colored laminate material. Repaint walls for a clean look. Your appliances will obviously be less expensive but with the standard sizes these days you can always upgrade to a higher-end model down the road.

While you can save money on cabinets and appliances, invest in a good-quality sink because sinks get a lot of use. Considering that a galley kitchen may have minimal natural lighting, be sure that there is overhead ambient lighting, such as track lighting, as well as task lighting that highlights the work surfaces. As you are installing lighting, spend the money to ensure that the wiring is upgraded. Older and smaller homes typically haven't had their electrical system upgraded. Fixing it now will save you problems down the road.

Erika and Michael upgraded the galley kitchen in their Minneapolis townhouse for just $14,000, replacing the fronts of their existing cabinets with new doors and new drawers. They bought Energy Star appliances and a laminate countertop. Erika painted the room a cheery yellow. The changes weren't expensive, but it dressed up their whole house. And the fact that they typically enter their home through the kitchen from the garage means the upgrades greet them every time they come home. "It's got us thinking about other things we can improve," says Erika.

MATERIALS FOR THE STARTER KITCHEN

Countertops. Laminate is the single most popular choice for countertops, and it's easy to see why: costs are low, at $2 to $5 per square foot. But this isn't your grandma's Formica. Today's laminates are more attractive, resembling more expensive materials such as wood or stone. Laminate stands up well to everyday use but can be damaged by high heat.

Cabinets. Face frame cabinets can be purchased in standard sizes from large home retail chain stores for under $150 per unit. Like the name suggests, drawers and doors are bordered by a frame of solid wood that is attached to a particleboard box. One step up is a frameless melamine cabinet, for $200 or less a unit. A frameless cabinet is one in which doors and drawers are even with the edges of the unit. The melamine veneer makes it more durable than the stock cabinets. Avoid cabinets with drawer fronts that are stapled or glued to the drawer box.

Flooring. Linoleum, vinyl, and laminates will fit your budget. The least expensive, vinyl, runs just $2 to $5 per square foot and is available in a myriad of patterns and colors. It holds up well under normal use but requires mopping and sweeping to keep dirt from lodging into the surface. Linoleum is a green product, made from renewable resources. It is also inexpensive at $2 to $6 per square foot. It's durable and easy to take care of. Wood laminates allow you to get the look of wood floors without the price. The cost is $3 to $7 per square foot. Installation is easy.

THE UP-AND-COMING KITCHEN

This kitchen is larger than a starter kitchen and even has room for an island. At this level, the materials and the appliances are higher-end. In short, your options expand exponentially. At this point it's easy to go over budget. You may easily be seduced by granite countertops and forty-eight-inch-wide stainless-steel refrigerators. The key to staying on budget here is to add bits of luxury touches without going overboard. Cabinets can account for up to half of your budget, with woods varying from oak to maple to pine, and can be stained or coated with a lacquer for a shiny finish. Quality cabinets will have drawer slides fitted on the side or underneath the drawers. The box that makes up the cabinets should consist of panels that are at least a half inch thick on the side and bottom, while shelves should be at least three-quarters of an inch thick. Remember, cabinet fronts don't have to be solid wood. Glass fronts not only are attractive but have that user-friendly bonus of allowing guests to easily track down a glass. In this kitchen, you may position appliances to fit traffic patterns. The island will be a work surface with plenty of storage space. A gooseneck faucet on a deep sink will allow for stockpots to be easily filled with water.

When Regina was remodeling her rural Kentucky kitchen, she was eager to install an island that could be used for food preparation; however, she knew that buying the island would preclude getting the high-end appliances she had dreamed of. "It's a trade-off," she says. "You have to choose the things you really want and forget the extras." Even without the fancy appliances, she finds the kitchen has become the hangout room for most of the family. "We eat here, listen to the news, and trade our stories from the day."

MATERIALS FOR THE UP-AND-COMING KITCHEN

Countertops. Corian and other solid-surface products boast durability and a wide range of colors and patterns. Installed costs are $45 per square foot and higher. Advantages include the fact that marks can be sanded out. Butcher block is $30 to $35 per square foot and attractive to the eye,

but it's best used away from sinks because constant water exposure can damage it.

Cabinets. You can opt for either the frameless cabinet or move up to semicustom cabinets. Semicustom cabinets are, as the name suggests, prefabricated at the factory but can be customized. They are typically heavier and more durable than frame or frameless cabinets and can boast dovetailed joints, the kind that fit together like a puzzle. Look for drawers that pull out all the way for ease of use.

Flooring. At this level you'll have several different types of wood floors to choose from, including solid wood, prefinished, and engineered. Solid wood is just as it sounds, floorboard that is three-quarters of an inch thick; it requires extensive sanding and finishing after installation. Most common types are red and white oak. With prefinished wood, the sanding and finishing is done at the factory. Engineered floors have five to six layers of wood laminated together. It can be installed quickly. Wood flooring costs $4 to $12 a square foot. Bamboo and cork flooring are popular greener alternatives that run about $4 a square foot. Tile is also a cost-effective choice.

THE DREAM KITCHEN

Midrange and high-end kitchens have a lot in common: great lighting, luxury touches such as a deep farmhouse sink, nice hardware, quality cabinets, and touches of natural materials such as wood floors. So what really adds to the budget of the highest-end kitchen? "The difference between a $40,000 kitchen and a $100,000 or even $200,000 kitchen are the appliances, the finishes, and all of the custom touches that require specialized labor," says Lori Carroll, a designer in Tucson, Arizona.

The high-end trend has been granite, granite, granite, which is expensive, expensive, expensive. But even the most luxurious kitchen doesn't have to be paved in wall-to-wall granite. Just as we recommended in the midrange kitchen, mix up materials. If you are a baker, go with a section of marble, which maintains a cool surface temperature. Some of the other amenities in a high-end kitchen: commercial-level

appliances, a range with a double oven, two dishwashers, an island with a built-in sink, refrigerated drawers ideal for storing beverages, induction cooktops, a walk-in pantry, and a built-in wine refrigerator. Cabinets may have decorative moldings and counters may be of varying heights to accommodate different tasks (i.e., higher counters around the sink make doing dishes easier on the back.). Think storage drawers for plates. Cabinets in this kitchen mask trash bins and pull-out shelves. Appliances such as a stand mixer or food processor can be stored on pop-up shelves. Entertainment has arrived in the kitchen in the form of flat-screen televisions.

Like many homeowners, Alan and his family found a not-so-ideal home in their ideal neighborhood in a Denver, Colorado, suburb. "We instantly knew that we would have to renovate. We hated the kitchen. It was dark and was in the middle of the house. The space on the main floor was all broken up," Alan says. With the help of an architect, he knocked down walls to expand the kitchen and open up the floor plan, removing all the interior walls so that the kitchen flowed into the living room. A custom-built island houses plenty of nooks and crannies to store pots, pans, baking sheets, and even cookbooks. He put in new hardwood floors and installed cast concrete countertops. Finally, he installed three enormous four-by-four-foot windows to further open up the kitchen. "We've managed to make it impossible not to spend time in the kitchen. We like to cook and entertain, and now it is easy for us," he says.

MATERIALS FOR THE DREAM KITCHEN

Countertops. Granite is the most popular material for countertops and one of the most expensive, ranging from $50 to $100 per square foot. Other stone choices include soapstone and slate. All are durable and can take heat from pots and pans, but even granite can stain. Stainless steel and concrete are two other trendy options for dream kitchens. Concrete is expensive at $65 a square foot (even more if it needs to be shipped) and stains if not maintained, but colors and textures are nearly limitless. Stainless steel is $80 per square foot and a good choice for a modern kitchen. It is durable but can dent.

Cabinets. Top-of-the-line custom cabinets will run you $1,500 per unit. But their superior craftsmanship will make them look like pieces of furniture in your kitchen. Drawers and slides may be rated to withstand a hundred pounds of weight. Custom cabinets are specially designed for your home.

Flooring. Most likely you'll go with wood flooring, but another alternative is stone flooring, which is (and looks) expensive at up to $16 per square foot. Stone floors work well with radiant heat, a heating system that uses tubes under the floor to transfer heat from warm water across the floor. Soapstone and granite are popular choices for high-end kitchens.

BATHROOM DESIGN BASICS

An attractive bathroom will be spacious enough—or give enough of a sense of spaciousness—that visitors won't feel like they are in a hallway closet. A window is essential to letting in natural light. Traditional materials—tile for walls and showers and china for toilets—are still the best. You'll personalize your space with light fixtures, medicine cabinets, and vanities.

The space in a bathroom, just like in your kitchen, should flow. An old bathroom is likely to have bad lighting and a cramped feeling. These rooms are small, but the aim of a renovation is to make them feel spacious. Frameless glass showers and big mirrors can add to the sense of space. You want to ensure that the toilet isn't sitting so close to the door that it hits it. You'll need thirty-six inches of elbow room at the toilet. Pocket doors are an alternative to swinging doors that interfere with the space. At the very least, one bathroom in the house should have a bathtub. Bathtubs are a must for the family buyer with kids. Vanity counters should be between thirty-one and thirty-four inches in height.

Keep a unified feel in the bathroom by extending tiles used in the shower to the rest of the room. A simple floor, such as slate tiles, can provide a clean look. In addition to windows and mirrors, judicious use of color and lighting makes the rooms feel more spacious. The real differ-

ence in bathroom renovation budgets lies in the amenities you choose to install.

BASIC BATH Just like in the basic kitchen, improve the look of a bathroom by refinishing cabinets, adding a fresh coat of paint, and installing new hardware such as a towel rack. If you have an older, loud flush toilet, replace it with a new, quiet, low-water-use version. Even the entry-level models these days can sport a surprisingly artistic and sleek look.

Showers these days can mimic a car wash with multiple showerheads. But even on the low end you can get a rain showerhead with multiple spray settings that won't break the bank. You'll likely be taking a serious look at tile options. Ceramic and glass tiles are durable and attractive. These tiles are made from colored clay that are layered over glass and then glazed.

MIDRANGE BATH Along with the options discussed in the basic bathroom, consider including cupboards for storing towels. Pedestal sinks have a certain cachet, but lack the storage that comes with vanities. In the shower, you can install a double showerhead: one oversized rain shower with a handheld spray attachment. Just don't go too crazy. Leah Lenney has designed countless high-end bathrooms with every amenity imaginable, but when it came to revamping a bathroom in her Chatham, New York, weekend house, she stuck with the basics. The result was a bathroom with a classic look and recycled materials. She reused beadboard and found old doors to reface cabinetry. She kept the 1930s-era tile and didn't use marble. "A lot of my clients want tumbled marble everything, but this bathroom is more my speed and has a wide appeal," says Lenney.

HIGH-END BATH Creating a high-end bathroom is like putting a spa in your house. The items that you can choose from these days are expensive and have an increasingly artistic look to them, such as a massive 155-gallon bathtub, showerheads that are flush with the ceiling, or an oversized shower that comes equipped with a dozen warm-air jets so you can dry off right in the shower. The more bells and whistles, the greater the work to be done. Hydrothermal massage tubs need both electricity and

plumbing. There are ten-inch rain showerheads and toilets with lids that open automatically as you approach them. The options are endless and, yes, over the top. One East Hampton bathroom had his-and-hers master baths complete with a steam shower with a bench that could seat several people, a deep soaking tub, and a custom-built piece of furniture with a sink set into the top. At the high end of the market, these luxury touches mean everything, but the good news is that even folks with middle-of-the-road budgets can tap some of the goodies—such as extra showerheads and claw-foot bathtubs—from a seemingly ever-expanding list of vendors.

Improving your home, of course, doesn't just include kitchens and baths. There are all sorts of other upgrades that are popular with owners and buyers. As you begin to make decisions about which improvements to pursue, consider both what will make your family more comfortable and what future buyers are likely to pay for. One thing that kitchen and bath designers and contractors never tell you is that designs are like fashion—they go in and out of style. Any choices you make should be timeless, as attractive today as they will be tomorrow. For that reason, it's best to stay away from designs that are too distinctive. They may well be a turnoff to new buyers. And the lime color that seems so au courant today may look old and tired by the time you sell your home. Let's face it, you'll only get credit for the hard work you put into improving your home if the result fits the tastes of buyers. And buyers may not be willing to pay up for some of the improvements you thought were critical. Whether you improve your kitchen or bath or both, be sure the upgrades have broad appeal and that their style will wear well over time.

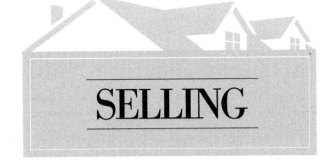

SELLING

20

Choosing a Real Estate Agent
or Going It Alone

CASHING IN ON YOUR INVESTMENT IS THE MOST NERVE-RACKING EXPE-
rience of the entire homeownership process. This is when the decisions
you made along the way get tested. Did you spend too much improving
your home? Not enough? Does your decorating style appeal to everyone or only a few? The ultimate arbiter of all these decisions will be the
market—the buyers who give your home the once-over. Not only will
you have to decide how to sell your house—whether to hire a real estate
agent or to go out on your own—but you'll also have to prepare it for
sale, market it, draw in buyers capable of paying for it, and negotiate a
solid deal.

GO IT ALONE OR HIRE AN AGENT?

Your first decision is whether you want to sell on your own or hire a real
estate agent to do the work for you. Selling on your own is far less expensive, allowing you to save the commission, which can range from 5
to 7 percent of your home's price. For example, let's say you have decided to sell your home at a price of $165,000, and you manage to ne-

gotiate a sales commission for your agent of 5 percent. His or her services will cost you $8,500 of the proceeds of your sale. If you were to sell
on your own, you'd be able to pocket that money and put it into your
next home or maybe pay tuition for a semester for your son or daughter
at a state college.

The FSBO—short for "for sale by owner"—market is the object of
much speculation but little analysis. Even so, it's clear that certain types
of FSBO owners are more likely to be successful than others. For example, if your real estate market is brisk and you live in a desirable neighborhood with few homes currently for sale, then selling on your own
will be far easier. That's because you'll be enjoying some of the best conditions available for selling. Other sellers who successfully sell on their
own are those who are highly motivated, including those with little equity in the home (and thus little cash to pay an agent), and those who
find a buyer on their own before they even start marketing the property.
For all of these people, it makes sense to sell on your own. Likewise,
some parts of the country, such as Michigan, have always been open to
FSBO selling, so selling on your own makes good sense there.

But the downsides are many. You'll have to be prepared to market
your home on your own, host open houses, and negotiate your own
deal. For many people, this simply isn't feasible. Daily schedules and responsibilities may be too onerous to accommodate these tasks. The rule
of thumb is this: if you or your partner can't drop everything at a moment's notice to attend to a home-selling issue, then you probably need
to hire an agent or maybe a discount agent who can pick up at least
some of the tasks that you'd otherwise need to accomplish on your own.

Consider hiring an agent if you are in one of the following situations:

- Your job gives you little flexibility to arrive late or leave early to
  meet potential buyers, hang For Sale signs, or write newspaper
  ads.
- The real estate market has slowed down dramatically in your
  town and prices are flat or falling.

- You're intimidated by the prospect of pricing your home for sale.

- Your spouse is starting a new job next week hundreds of miles away and the pressure is on to sell fast.

- You're not sure how to market your home to get buyers through the front door and the whole idea of hosting strangers is uncomfortable to you.

The advantages to working with an agent are many. A listing agent will be able not only to correctly price your home for the market but also vet buyers, suggest improvements you can make to speed the sale of your house, and market a home effectively both on the Internet and through old-fashioned methods such as open houses.

FINDING THE RIGHT AGENT

The key to having a successful relationship with any professional is picking the right one in the first place. Ask friends and neighbors which agents they've had a good experience with. If you've spent any time at all in the neighborhood, you may already have a sense of which agents frequently list properties and know the area well. It's important to keep in mind that it takes only fifty to sixty hours of training to become a real estate agent. The sad fact is that there are no federal standards for real estate agents as there are for, say, stockbrokers, and for most people, real estate agents control a far greater proportion of their personal wealth than stockbrokers do. State licensing requirements vary and standards can be low. Agents learn the subtleties of sales and marketing on the job. So it's important that you determine just how experienced, organized, trustworthy, and professional your agent is. Avoid the part-timers and newly minted agents. A big mistake that first-time sellers make is hiring the first agent they meet. That's what Sarah and Robert did, with disastrous consequences.

When the couple sold their condo in Sacramento, California, to move an hour north of the city, they made some mistakes. For starters, they hired an acquaintance fairly new to the business as their agent. Almost immediately, things went sour. "It was almost comical," says

Robert. "He put the For Sale sign up in front of the wrong building. My neighbor came over and told me he had eight people knocking on his door wanting to look at the condo." Things went from bad to worse. Although the property drew an attractive offer almost immediately on the strength of the local market, their agent disappeared. When it came time for the closing, the couple couldn't reach their agent and was forced to substitute an agent they had never met who was on call that day in the brokerage office. "It was a messy closing and he wasn't there to help us." Worse, the couple had agreed to pay a full commission of 6 percent and had received no help from the agent—the property wasn't marketed at all.

Choosing an agent simply on the basis of his or her years in the field isn't a solution either. When Robert got a job transfer to a suburb of Durham, North Carolina, the couple thought they were doing their due diligence in selecting a listing agent. Their relocation company limited their choice of agents, presenting them with two longtime local Realtors. Both salespeople gave them a marketing plan to sell their four-bedroom house and also an estimated sales price. They chose the president of the local Realtors association, figuring she had the experience and know-how to sell their home quickly.

"She actually told us that there was an offer coming in but she was too busy writing an offer on another house to deal with it," recalls Robert. While their agent was ignoring prospective offers on their house, the two were in limbo, paying $65 a day for temporary housing in North Carolina and delaying their plans to buy a new house until they could get a closing date for their California property. Their repeated phone calls were ignored. When they finally did get hold of her, Robert says she came up with flimsy excuses for her silence. "She claimed that she hadn't been in touch because she thought the time difference between the two coasts was five hours," says Robert. "We wanted to act pretty quickly and we were willing to come down in price if that would have helped to accelerate the process. We had a whole list of questions for her about what we could do to help the sale. She kept telling us that offers were coming, but those never materialized. We got the impression

that she had other things going on. We were not her priority. It was a pretty stressful couple of months."

While Robert and Sarah thought they had done their homework before picking an agent the second time, they didn't interview any of her former clients to find out if her credentials—her many years of experience and status as the president of the local Realtors association—matched her performance. That step could have helped them avoid such a poor communicator and unprofessional agent.

To avoid these pitfalls, call at least four agents and interview them, asking many of the same questions discussed in Chapter 4, which looked at choosing an agent from the buyer's perspective, plus a few more.

1. *How much experience do you have in my neighborhood or part of town? Is this an area you specialize in? Do you live here?* It's best to use an agent who is already familiar with the neighborhood, knows where buyers typically come from, and knows how to market to them.

2. *What price range of homes do you specialize in? High-, low-, or midpriced?* Be sure to hire an agent who is used to selling homes with the amenities and prices in your range.

3. *Are you a member of the National Association of Realtors?* Agents who are members of the National Association of Realtors are the only agents allowed to call themselves Realtors (the word is trademarked). They are bound to follow a code of ethics that requires them to pass along any pertinent information to you about a property. If a Realtor believes a buyer's credit history is spotty, he or she is obligated to alert the seller. If you have a problem with a Realtor, you can take the case to arbitration for resolution.

4. *How many clients have you worked with this year?* An agent who juggles too many customers often leaves important details to underlings who may be too junior to follow up efficiently. This may require reading between the lines. If the candidate doesn't re-

spond to your phone calls in a timely manner, that's a clue to look elsewhere.

5. *How do you communicate with clients?* If you have to move away before your home sells, this will be particularly important. An agent who is accustomed to staying in touch by e-mail may be a poor fit for the buyer who requires a daily telephone conversation.

6. *How will you market the property?* At a minimum, any real estate agent will get your home into the Multiple Listing Service (MLS), the single most important marketing tool for broadcasting your home's availability. It is especially important for alerting other real estate agents, who may in turn alert their customers to your home. Good agents just start there. Two-thirds of home buyers use the Web to shop for a home. You'll also want your agent to be technologically savvy enough to develop a Web page on the agency's website to promote your home, using 360-degree views of its best features. Be sure to check out each agent's website to determine whether it is user-friendly and intuitively designed.

7. *What is your commission and is it negotiable?* These days real estate agents are faced with new competition—both online and off-line—and many are opting to cut their commission to get business. While the average commission nationwide used to be 6 percent of the selling price of a home, today that average is 5.1 percent.

8. *Can you give me three references?* Following up with your candidate agents' clients is essential. Ask for at least three, since one is likely to be a relative or personal friend. Grill the others on the agent's effectiveness, communication skills, and marketing plan.

Compare the answers you get to these questions from all the candidates. Look for any gaps in service. Ask for details about homes in your neighborhood the agent may have sold.

SHOULD YOU HIRE A DISCOUNT BROKER?

When you're shopping for an agent, you'll pretty quickly come across brokerages that discount their services. The advantage to using a discount service is that you save money on selling costs. Discount services such as Foxtons and ZipRealty.com typically charge 2 to 5 percent of the sale price. Discounters work in a couple of different ways. Some offer their services à la carte—you pick and choose what you want them to do and pay for each separately. The actual cost will depend on which services you opt to buy, which might include a virtual tour of your home offered on the firm's website, brochures, and newspaper advertising. Many also offer access to the most important marketing tool available, the Multiple Listing Service, the most complete list available of homes for sale that is used by real estate agents and maintained by them. It's hard to overstate how important the MLS is—this database allows instant access to information on homes across the country and is sortable by key characteristics. Other discounters offer to sell your home for a flat fee, say, $2,000. Just make sure you understand the terms of the deal before you sign on with any discounter working in this way. In addition to paying the flat fee to the brokerage, they may also require you to pay a "cooperating fee" to the agent that actually lands a buyer for you. If that's the case, you might as well hire a full-service agent, because the costs are similar.

In most cases, though, the advantage to using a discount broker is that you can easily cut your selling costs in half. But to lock in those savings, you'll have to investigate the service thoroughly. Probably the most important question is this: what is the relationship between full-service brokerages and discount brokers in your area? In some areas, full-service agents have refused to show properties listed by discount brokers because they'll make less money doing so. Even if you have a listing on the MLS, it's possible that full-service agents could ignore you because their commission split might be 2.5 percent rather than 3 percent. That might sound like very little money, but it can mean a difference of thousands of dollars on payday for agents. To determine whether your home will receive fair treatment from full-service agents if you list with a discount broker, you need to talk informally with full-service agents.

Also, be sure to understand where your home will be marketed if you hire a discount agent. Many will list you on their proprietary website, but that may get little attention from buyers or agents. Will the discount agent bring potential buyers to your home for tours, or will you have to do that yourself? How much will you have to pay to get your home in the local MLS? The good news is that you'll reach more buyers than if you sell on your own. Plus you can get them to prescreen potential buyers, so you don't inadvertently end up showing your home to an enterprising burglar looking for his next score, which could happen if you're marketing your own home by placing newspaper ads.

Deciding whether to hire a full-service agent, work with a discount agent, or go it alone and sell on your own depends entirely on your own comfort and experience, the health of the market, and how open potential buyers are in your area to nontraditional methods of buying and selling. If the market is weak or going sideways, it pays to go with a full-service brokerage. This is when a full marketing push makes sense. If the local market is strong and your home is in tip-top shape, you'll preserve more of your equity as a FSBO or by using a discount brokerage firm that has been thoroughly investigated. And, of course, it never makes sense to bite off more than you can chew in terms of workload. If marketing is a foreign language to you, you're better off paying for help.

NEGOTIATING A FULL-SERVICE AGENT'S COMMISSION

It's your right to negotiate the Realtor's commission. No matter what the going rate is, you should be able to haggle; otherwise, real estate agents would be engaged in price fixing. Every percentage point of commission will likely mean thousands of dollars that will come right out of the profit you've worked so hard to build. For example, on a $300,000 home, a 6 percent commission is $18,000, but if you manage to get the commission down to 5 percent, your costs fall by $3,000.

Before you sit down with an agent to negotiate the commission, get commission requirements from each of your candidates when you inter-

view them, as suggested above. If one agent has a lower commission requirement than another, you can use that as leverage. Don't discuss commissions in your home—it's difficult for most of us to play hardball in our living room, since we've been taught to be polite to guests. Instead, negotiate at your office or even a neutral site, such as a diner or coffee shop.

If you're pressing hard to reduce commissions, you'll need to prepare a mental list of the features of your house that will make it easier to sell than the average home. If you've followed the advice of this book, you've kept up with maintenance, developed curb appeal, and updated your interior. These are factors that make the agent's job easier. He or she doesn't have to counsel you on prepping your home for sale, nor worry about whether it will show well. All these factors position your home well in the market, making it sell faster—and that will cut your agent's costs for advertising and promoting it. There's no rule that says that the commission has to be the same no matter the amount you sell your home for. Try a laddered approach. You could offer a range of commission depending on the final price. Let's say you're selling your home, which you paid $250,000 for in a fairly new suburb two years ago. Sales of homes similar to yours have recently been made for $265,000. You might offer your agent a commission of 5 percent if the house sells for $265,000, 6 percent if it sells for $275,000, and 4 percent if it sells for $250,000.

Your agent may well say that his or her office sets commissions. If that's the case, ask for a meeting with the broker who runs the agency or ask the candidate to take your proposal to that individual. Be sure the agent understands that the size of the commission is part of your decision-making process in hiring an agent.

Remember that every part of the transaction is negotiable. For example, the marketing plan isn't a given. You can bargain for everything, from the quality of the photographer to the frequency of open houses and the types of advertising you expect.

SIGNING THE LISTING AGREEMENT

If you hire a professional to represent you, either a full-service agent or a discount agent, you'll need to sign a listing agreement that will spell out the terms of your working relationship. It will set a price for your home and details about what is included in the sale and what is not. If you have fixtures, such as a family heirloom chandelier, that you intend to take with you, now is the time to spell that out. Overlooked items that can become the subject of controversy later include second refrigerators, the washer and dryer, swing sets, light fixtures, and the like. Simply take a walk through each room of your house and the yard to make sure you have included an accurate list of everything you want to take with you.

The most critical issue will be pricing your home in the agreement. Clearly, the price can change through negotiation with buyers, but in the listing agreement you set the price the home will be marketed at. If it's too high, you'll put off buyers; if it's too low, you could end up getting less out of your investment than you had hoped. We'll have more on pricing your home in Chapter 22.

The listing agreement will also specify when your agent earns his or her commission and how much it is. Be warned: your agent will earn the commission when a qualified buyer presents an offer that meets your listing price and terms. If the buyer doesn't meet your price but you decide to accept the lower offer, then your agent has earned the commission. Once you have accepted an offer, even if you change your mind and decide you want to stay in your home, the agent is still due the commission. Standard exceptions or contingencies exist in cases in which the buyer can't get financing or an inspector finds something wrong with the house that causes the buyer to rescind the offer. Be sure there is a limit to the amount of time your agent will have to sell your home. Ninety days is fairly standard. Don't agree to significantly lengthen that time. Homes on the market are like bread—the longer they sit, the more likely they are to go stale. Your priority—and your agent's priority—should be to act as quickly as possible.

The agreement will also make note of whether or not your home

will be placed on the local MLS. There is no question—you absolutely want it listed, because the MLS is the best advertising vehicle available for homeowners.

Remember, your real estate agent isn't just a salesperson, like the person who sold you your car. In most parts of the country, an agent has a responsibility—in fact, a duty—to act in your best interests. The Realtor's code of conduct establishes standards of practice:

- Realtors agree not to overprice a home in order to secure a listing from a seller.

- They agree to submit all offers and counteroffers objectively and quickly and to continue submitting them up until closing, including offers from brokerages other than their own.

- They must preserve customers' confidential information. If, for example, your move is caused by a divorce, that information isn't shared.

- They must disclose whether they obtained an offer for the house from a buyer or someone from their firm did. (Remember, keeping a deal inside the same brokerage is a financial advantage to that brokerage since both parts of the commission, for sale and for purchase, will be paid to the same company.)

- Fees for the preparation of appraisals can't be contingent on the amount of the appraisal.

RESOLVING DISPUTES WITH YOUR AGENT

There are times when buyers and their agents disagree on a critical matter. Maybe your agent failed to explain a critical part of an offer, or maybe he or she simply didn't pass along an offer. In any event, with many agents you can have the issue arbitrated instead of taking it to court. Choosing to accept binding arbitration is typically a cheaper route than utilizing the courts. Usually, matters that can be dealt with in small-claims court are excluded from having to go to binding arbitration.

GETTING THE DEAL DONE

Ultimately, if you choose the right agent (even if it's yourself as a FSBO seller), you have a far better chance of selling your home. Choosing an agent who is professional, articulate, and courteous is important. The agent is your face to the buying public. Chances are you may never even meet the buyer until you get to the closing table. A good agent will help you prepare your home, set the right price, and market your home. They'll be on hand to negotiate the offer, make suggestions for counteroffers, and tell you when it's better to walk away from a potential buyer.

21

Prepping Your Home for Sale

WHEN YOU DECIDE TO SELL YOUR HOME, YOU NEED TO RESET YOUR relationship with your house. Be objective about its strengths and weaknesses. It's not your house anymore. As an exercise, consider walking out the door and coming back in, pretending to be a buyer. What do you see from this new point of view? Is the house a little overstuffed with junk? Are the windowsills dirty? Is that a worn area on the carpet? All of these are issues you'll need to address as you get your home ready for sale.

Preparing your home for sale is a multistep process. It's not unusual for people to pay decluttering experts anywhere from $200 to $3,000 to do the work for them, but if you are disciplined, you can do it yourself for little money. You start by inspecting and repairing your home. Next, you clear out the clutter and conduct an extensive cleaning. Then you'll arrange your furniture for the most impact. This is the time to neutralize the colors in your home. Adding luxurious-looking accessories with a strong visual impact can make a difference, too. And don't forget, you'll have to repeat many of these steps outside your home. Because the changes can take time and money, you'll want to give yourself a month

to two months to get them done. This means that you should be getting your preparations under way in February in order to hit the busiest home selling time of the year, which is April, May, and June. That's when the most buyers are out and about. And don't be surprised if when you get done you decide you'd rather not sell.

THE INSPECTION

Just as you inspected the home when you bought it (at least I hope you did), you'll also want to have a professional inspector give your house a once-over before buyers cross the threshold. The reasons are twofold. First off, you're required by law to alert buyers to potential problems, and second, getting in front of real problems can keep you from having to negotiate away any profit you hope to earn on your home. Remember, serious buyers will hire their own inspector and if they find a problem that hasn't been disclosed to them, they are likely to walk away.

Your inspector will go through all of your home's major systems. That means an inspection of the home's heating and air-conditioning, plumbing, electric, roof, attic, walls, ceiling, floor, windows, doors, foundation, basement, and structural components. Keep in mind that no home—not even brand-new ones—typically emerges from an inspection with flying colors. Don't be surprised to find out some issues that you might not have known about. On the other hand, if you do get a decent inspection and you correct any problems mentioned, you can use the inspection report as a sales tool. What's more, an inspector will be able to put to rest concerns you may have had and give you answers to questions that buyers might have.

Hiring an inspector will cost you between $200 and $500. Check out the American Society of Home Inspectors at www.ashi.org to find an experienced inspector in your area, or ask friends and neighbors for recommendations.

REPAIRING YOUR HOME

One critical step in getting your home ready for sale is making sure all of its parts are in good working order. Your inspector will make certain there are no big problems, but it's the little things that belie your attentiveness (or lack of it) over the years to home buyers. One experienced handyman said the telltale signs in any home are the condition of closets, particularly the closet ceiling. He looked to see whether owners had ever bothered to paint them to match the rest of the room, and most important, where any water stains were visible. Small details matter and alert buyers to whether you've simply lived in your home while you've owned it or tried to keep it in good repair and condition.

Here is a list of items that you'll want to be sure to test because buyers may do it as well:

1. Make sure all doors open and close without getting stuck in the frame or hitting the floor or ceiling. There's nothing more annoying than doors that stick.

2. Tighten knobs, handles, and pulls on all kitchen cabinets. Knobs tend to loosen over time.

3. Be sure that windows open with ease. Children should be able to open them with one hand in case of fire.

4. Look for leaks under kitchen sinks, in bathrooms, and around basement water sources. Make sure attic windows aren't leaking either. Home buyers are well informed about mold and its dangerous properties.

5. Replace burned-out lightbulbs.

6. Fix leaky faucets.

7. Replace any cracked floor tiles.

8. If your kitchen counters are tiled, regrout the tile and replace any broken tiles.

9. Patch any holes in Sheetrock. Doorknobs slamming against walls can create dents and holes. If that has happened, repair the problem and then put a doorstop behind the door.

10. Check bathroom tubs for cracks. If caulk is discolored or peeling, remove it with a flat-head screwdriver and reapply.

11. Clear slow-running drains.

CURB APPEAL

Most home buyers know whether they will take a house seriously as a candidate for purchase from the moment they drive up to it. What they see from the curb is critical. You need to present a fresh, clean, and bright home with everything in its place, or some buyers won't even make it over the threshold. For that reason, consider these moves:

1. If your home has siding rather than brick or shingles, power wash the exterior. It removes grime or dirt and can make the exterior look new.

2. Paint the door a bright color and make sure the storm door is in good working condition. The door is the first thing in your house that visitors will touch.

3. Make sure your deck has been recently resurfaced or at least power washed. If you have a patio, repair any cracks in the concrete. Crumbling grout in stone patios should be repaired.

4. Check the automatic garage door to be sure it operates properly, especially the emergency stop.

5. Remove dirt that may have blown against casement windows in the basement. Fix lawn dents that have emerged from gutter runoff.

6. Resurface driveways with large cracks.

7. Fix broken windowpanes.

8. Remove overgrown trees that block views of the home from the street. Trim back shrubs that are higher than four feet.

9. Plant annuals that play off the color of your front door.

10. Patch dead lawn areas.

CLEAN, PAINT, AND DECLUTTER

Now that you have the major repairs done and the exterior in tip-top shape, you'll want to paint any rooms that you feel need freshening, remove any extra furniture or sentimental items, and then give the whole house a serious cleaning. The best way to get started is to begin removing the clutter that has accumulated while you've lived there. Remember, the idea is to impress strangers and encourage them to imagine all their stuff where yours is now. If you're a true packrat, you may have to rent some off-site storage to put all the extra stuff in. Here's what to remove:

Living room

1. All family pictures

2. Collections of anything

3. Awards, trophies

4. Knickknacks on end tables

5. Magazines, newspapers

Kitchen

1. Refrigerator art

2. Anything on the kitchen counters—coffeemaker, other appliances, cookbooks

3. Any plants unless in perfect condition

4. Half-empty boxes and clutter in pantry and cabinets

Bath

1. All shampoos, conditioners, and bubble bath in tub area

2. Clutter in medicine cabinets

3. Old shower curtain (replace with a new one)

Now that you've gotten rid of much of the clutter, go into each room and remove at least one piece of furniture. If you've been in the

house longer than ten years, remove two pieces of furniture. Extra end tables, TV trays, and rockers are all good things to move out, if only temporarily, while the house is on the market. Eliminating extras can be especially important in the bedrooms, which tend to be smaller anyway. Lighten up those rooms by keeping window treatments to a minimum.

PAINT

Painting a room is one of the cheapest and most efficient ways of making a room feel new. If you've painted any of your rooms a dark color or something else unusual, such as red or ochre, now is the time to neutralize those colors. Not everything has to be hospital white, but you're much better off with neutral colors such as cream and beige rather than turquoise when it comes to selling your house. Not only will it make it easier for potential buyers to really see the house, but also you won't offend people who have conservative tastes. You should also consider painting if it's been a while since you have, or if family members were heavy smokers.

CLEAN

Two weeks before the property goes on the market, conduct a serious cleaning of your home. This will take some time—perhaps two weeks, maybe more, depending on your habits—so reserve time on the calendar to get it done. Remember, your goal isn't just to get rid of dirt and grime, although that is important; you'll also want to get rid of any odors. If you have pets, now is the time to board them with other family members.

1. Remove everything from every surface—kitchen countertops, coffee tables, dining room tables, end tables, bookshelves—and clean both the surface and anything that will remain on it. Lampshades and any attractive decorative elements should be dusted.

2. If you have carpeting, have it professionally cleaned, particularly if you have pets. Be sure to get stains removed.

3. Clean out the fireplace.

4. Remove any grime from walls with a dry, clean sponge.

5. Clean out the oven and microwave.

6. Clean kitchen cabinets with a grease cutter.

7. Clean windows.

8. Organize closets and vacuum their floors. Be sure any shoes are organized neatly.

9. Bathroom fixtures should be polished.

10. Clean out light fixtures.

If all this cleaning is too much for you, or if you have to move before you can get it all done, consider hiring a cleaning service that can do it for you. You'll need to tell them up front your purpose in hiring them and that you're looking for something more than just the usual dusting and vacuuming. Try to go with a service that you've used before or that a neighbor knows well. If you can't find anyone who fits the bill, check out candidates with your local Better Business Bureau.

RESTAGE AND RENEW

Now the whole house should smell good and feel open and uncluttered and fresh. Walk through its rooms once again and consider whether the furniture is arranged in the most attractive fashion possible. One common habit is to line furniture up against the walls to make the rooms feel as big as possible. Unfortunately, it can have the opposite impact, making the rooms feel cramped and overloaded with furniture. Now that you've decluttered, bring the furniture away from the walls, particularly in the living room. Twin sofas can face each other in front of a fireplace. Dining room tables should be pulled away from walls and leaves taken out.

A final step is to put into place one or two luxurious elements that will stand out to visitors. Some homes have such elements built in, such

as a stained-glass window in the front door or wainscoting in the kitchen. If you don't have a focal point, you may want to add some touches that will be memorable to visitors. Popular extras include:

1. Wine refrigerator. It can cost a few hundred dollars, but buyers often remember homes that have them, and they are in demand.

2. A new backsplash above your kitchen countertops. Tile can be cheap and liven up a kitchen that maybe hasn't been refurbished.

3. Ceiling fans in bedrooms.

4. Lighting installed around pathways outside your home. It adds warmth to your home's look at a low cost.

Once you finish all these steps, you may feel like your home is a brand-new house, one that you don't want to part with. You may fall in love all over again. If that's the case, you'll know you have done your work well, preparing your home for sale.

22

Setting the Right Price

WHEN TOM AND ANDREA DECIDED TO MOVE FROM THEIR RURAL Connecticut bungalow to a Greenwich condo, they knew that they needed to squeeze as much money as they could out of their sale. The condo was a major upgrade with a price that reflected it. They still owed $475,000 on their home, which they had been in for only two years, and knew they'd need $28,500 to pay an agent to sell it, for a total of $503,500. With closing costs, they figured they'd be safe asking for $520,000. Unfortunately, the couple's home languished on the market for weeks. They tried everything to make it more attractive. They neutralized wall colors, kept the kids' toys put away, and even moved the dog to Andrea's mother's house. Still the house wouldn't sell. Frustrated after two months of poorly attended open houses and no credible offers, they asked their real estate agent what to do next. Simple, he said—drop your price.

When it comes to selling your home, there is no more important decision than what price to ask for it. Unfortunately, sellers like Tom and Andrea often look at this question from the wrong perspective. They ask

themselves what they need to make a profit or at least break even. And who can blame them? When you sell, there are plenty of bills to cover. The biggest one may well be the payoff figure for your present loan or loans, how much you still owe for your house. Your lender should provide you with this number. But the bills don't stop there—there is the broker's commission, any prepayment penalty on your mortgage, attorney's fees. Your agent or attorney may tell you it is customary for you to pay any of the following: title insurance premiums, transfer taxes, survey fees, inspection and repairs, recording fees, homeowner association fees, and document preparation. The sum of these is what you will owe at closing, but it isn't necessarily what you should be asking for as a sales price.

SCRUTINIZE THE COMPETITIVE
MARKET ANALYSIS

When you searched for an agent, your candidates should have provided you with a competitive market analysis (CMA). This document, more than any other, will help you figure out what price you should set for your home. A CMA is a summary of market activity for homes similar to yours. It includes homes currently on the market and homes sold within the last six months. Evaluate the listings to make sure the homes are, in fact, similar to yours. Do they have the same number of bedrooms? Baths? Is the kitchen in similar condition to yours? Are there bells and whistles such as pools that you don't have? When were the houses built? Newer homes often command a premium. Then divide the sale price of each home that has sold by the total number of square feet. This will give you a price per square foot that you can then apply to your home.

The reason you'll want to analyze brokers' CMAs is that agents sometimes try to "buy listings," that is, they engage in the unethical practice of giving sellers overly optimistic ideas of what their home is worth in order to get the business, or they may simply feel pressured by the homeowner to boost the potential price. Your agent may know all along that your home isn't worth that inflated price, but he or she may figure the price can simply be reduced later if it doesn't sell. At any rate, you'll want to be sure that the CMAs you look at are legitimate.

You should know that the agents representing buyers will be conducting the same kind of price analysis you are. They will know prices per square foot and will be attempting to find a home with a price that matches the average price per square foot or maybe is even just shy of it. For your part, deciding where to price your home is largely a function of the market dynamics itself. You'll have different strategies depending on whether the market favors buyers or sellers, is strong or weak.

In a normal market, in which neither buyers nor sellers have the advantage, price your home right in line with the average per square foot that homes in your area with similar characteristics are being sold for. If the market is weak and homes are taking two to three months to sell, you should shave your price by 10 percent or maybe more to give your home an advantage. If the market is hot and homes are selling in thirty days or less, you can boost your price to reflect the heightened competition.

KNOW YOUR BREAK POINTS

Another consideration is price break points. These are psychological limits or thresholds that a buyer may set. Break points can result in irrational behavior. For example, a buyer may have a price target of $400,000 but be willing to spend up to $499,000 on a new home. However, this same buyer may be determined not to pay $500,000 or more, despite the fact that the difference between $499,000 and $500,000 is just $1,000, hardly noticeable on a thirty-year mortgage. While buyers are notorious for expanding their budgets once they find a home they like, the reality is that they won't even come to see your home if it's priced above their psychological break point. Break points occur at every $100,000, and then at every $25,000. As a seller, you'll want to identify those break points and price just a little bit below to guarantee the widest possible audience to see your home. That means if your home is valued at $310,000, you might consider pricing it at $300,000 to get broader attention. Priced at $299,000, your listing will garner even more notice.

FSBO PRICING

If you're selling your home on your own, congratulations—you stand to save thousands of dollars. Unfortunately, buyers in the market know you are getting big savings and they expect you to offer your home for a competitive price or even an aggressive price. That means you'll do well to bring your price below the price of comparable homes. How much you underprice it is up to you. The stronger your package, meaning the better the home's condition and the more extensive its features, the less you'll need to cut its price. As a rule of thumb, consider carving 3 to 5 percent from comparable home prices.

SETTING THE RIGHT PRICE is the first and most important step in marketing your home. Remember, agents are the ones who will be vetting your price. They know the comps for your area and the average price per square foot. So if your price is way out of line, they may not even bring buyers to your house. You can't make a sale until you get potential buyers to your door. In a brisk market that may be easy, but in a slow or stalling market, it may be more difficult.

23

Marketing Your Home and Negotiating an Offer

GETTING ATTENTION FROM POTENTIAL BUYERS FOR YOUR HOME IS MORE difficult than it sounds. One of the first things your real estate agent may suggest is hosting an open house. The reality? Open houses rarely sell homes. In fact, according to the National Association of Realtors, open houses are successful as sales tools only about 2 percent of the time. The real beneficiary of an open house? Your agent. That's because most people attending an open house have simply followed signs to your front door. They have no idea whether your home is even within their price range. Worse, many people who attend often aren't even potential buyers but neighbors whom the real estate agent hopes to meet and impress as potential future clients.

Think advertising in the local newspaper is a better way to go? After all, you might assume the broad reach of local newspapers puts your home right in the hands of potential buyers. Wrong again.

The single best way to market your home is to get the attention of the people most likely to bring potential buyers to it: other real estate agents. That's right. Advertising your property to other agents has a

higher impact than direct advertising to consumers. That's because it's agents who take potential buyers on tours through neighborhoods and help them find candidates for purchase. During the first couple of weeks your home should be a flurry of activity, with buyer's agents coming to preview your home so they can sell it to their clients. Here are the kinds of events and promotions you should expect your agent to set up:

1. *The office preview.* If your agent works in a large realty office, his or her officemates will get first crack at seeing your property through an office preview. This typically happens once a week and allows your agent's office to inspect newcomers to the market first.

2. *The broker preview.* After your agent's officemates give the property the once-over, the house will be opened up for any area real estate agent interested in looking at it for a broker preview. It usually is scheduled for the first week your home is on the market. This is a critical session because most agents will quickly make a decision about whether your home is priced right and attractive enough to show to potential buyers. It doesn't hurt to have the event catered. Agents attend these events frequently and aren't above lingering longer because of the food.

3. *Marketing flyers.* In many areas, agents send around flyers about homes they have on the market to brokerage offices in the area. Yours should be professional-looking and detailed. The flyers will also be available to buyers who visit your home so that they can easily refer to the details of the house.

4. *Newspaper advertising.* Next, you'll want to focus on home buyers directly, selecting ways of reaching out that will touch many potential buyers. Typically, advertising for homes in the newspaper happens in two ways: the brokerage your agent works for may take out large ads with pictures of homes on the market, and your agent may buy a classified listing. Generally, these ads are best at

lifting awareness of the brokerage and agency. The ads, however, often help you in a roundabout way rather than directly, unless your home is located in a very hot neighborhood. Such ads should run on weekends, when buyers are most likely to be prospecting for new homes.

5. *Postcards and flyers.* When your home is placed on the market, ask your agent to send postcards to everyone in the neighborhood announcing your home is for sale with a picture of the property and details. This will lift awareness of your home. Perhaps one of your neighbors knows someone who is shopping for a home. This is a good way to spread the word. Neighbors will want you to be successful in selling your home.

6. *Internet advertising.* These days nearly every tiny mom-and-pop brokerage firm has a website that allows agents to market the homes they have for sale. This is a critical part of your effort, because more than 60 percent of buyers use the Internet as a search tool. You'll want the Web page featuring your home to have 360-degree views of your home, with pictures that make the most of its top selling points.

Of course, one of the most effective sales tools your agent will use is the local Multiple Listing Service, a directory of homes for sale accessible to all agents in your area. This is a critical part of your marketing effort, because every agent and broker in your area looking for a home for a client consults it regularly. Your home will be seen by those most likely to bring a buyer to your front door. Remember, discount brokers will often offer to get your home on the local MLS, but if a buyer's agent finds a buyer for your home after seeing it listed, you'll be obligated to pay them a 2.5 percent to 3 percent commission.

WELCOMING BUYERS

Once the word is out, your agent will start bringing through potential buyers to get a firsthand look at the place. This is your opportunity to

shine. Here are the finishing touches to add that will polish your home's appeal:

1. Buy a large, healthy plant to put in the living room or entry.

2. Set the dining room table as if you were having a big dinner party.

3. Display new color-coordinated dish towels in the kitchen. Bake cookies or boil potpourri.

4. Hang fresh matching towels and hand towels in bathrooms. Add a basket of perfumed soaps.

5. Leave and take your car with you so it is out of the driveway. Some buyers are spooked by meeting the current owners.

Selling a home is stressful. Perfect strangers will be touring your home, and if you're working with an agent, you won't be on hand to watch them. Ask your agent to vet all buyers to make sure they are qualified to purchase a home. Even so, you'll want to make sure all valuables are under lock and key. Put away jewelry and any medications you normally store in your bathroom. Staying in your home only encourages buyers to ask questions that may give them the upper hand in negotiation. Avoid conversations about the price of the house or its condition. Be sure to keep your home ultra-clean during this period. A quick vacuuming can make a big difference to buyers.

FIELDING OFFERS

Okay, now it gets exciting. After all your hard work prepping your home, at least one buyer has decided your home is worth the price—or at least *some* price. If they are working with a real estate agent, you'll get a formal offer—a sales contract that spells out their terms for purchase. They may want to pay the price you're asking, but more likely they'll be looking for some sort of discount. Remember, it's not just the price you have to think about. They may want to take all the specially built book-

cases or the refrigerator or the washer and dryer. It's important to look at the offer in detail.

When you get an offer, you have three options: you can accept the offer (and that means you have a done deal), you can write a counteroffer, or you can reject the offer on its face value. Remember, buyers have two potential ways of getting out of the deal, typically called contingencies. If they can't get a mortgage or if the house fails to pass inspection after signing a sales contract, then the deal is off. If you've already had your home inspected, you should have no trouble with the second contingency. But the first contingency can create headaches. If you're using an agent, you'll rely on the agent to vet buyers. If not, you'll have to make sure bidders have the ability to buy your home. The best way is to only accept bids from buyers who are preapproved for the loan size they'll need to buy your house. (A letter of prequalification from a lending institution isn't good enough, because they are fairly easy to get.) Ask that any buyer making an offer put down a deposit, sometimes called earnest money, because it proves the seriousness of the buyer's offer. You can ask for 1 to 3 percent of the purchase price. Ask a Realtor about what is typical in your area.

If you decide to counter the offer, focus on the issues that are a priority for you. If it's essential that you get out of the house in six weeks, then stay firm on that issue. If getting your desired price is the most important issue, counter on price, but drop yours only marginally. This signals that price is an important factor for you. It's all too common in real estate negotiations for buyers to use any reason to walk away. Don't give them that excuse. Every day you wait to sell is more money you're paying for a house that you need to move on from. Typically, the types of items that get negotiated are the following:

1. Price.

2. Occupancy date. This refers to the amount of time you'll have to complete the deal and get out of the house. Some buyers will want quick closings; others may want to schedule the close with the sale of their current home.

3. Closing costs or homeowner association dues. Some buyers in a weak market will want you to pick up some of their financing or operating costs.

4. Any appliance, such as a second refrigerator or washer and dryer.

5. Lighting fixtures, draperies, curtains, or blinds.   .

6. Outdoor maintenance or recreational equipment. You can negotiate everything from the inground pool to the ride-on lawn mower.

You may find that the buyer wants to make their offer contingent on selling their existing home. This can extend your time frame beyond what is comfortable for you. You'll want to consider an offer from such a buyer if the market is weak and this is the only offer you have on the table. You can always ask for a higher price to compensate you for the risk you're taking. However, if the market is relatively strong and you are likely to receive other offers, you may want to wait for another candidate.

It often happens that you find a buyer you like, but you wonder about how committed they are to buying your house. Maybe they complain about the inspection or balk at your timetable for selling. For that reason, you may want to obtain backup offers. The same criteria apply to vetting a second buyer as to the first. They need to be serious and capable of paying for your home. Be sure they are also preapproved for a loan.

As you go through this process, you'll face deadlines all along the way. You'll have deadlines for accepting an offer, for submitting disclosures on the house, for having it inspected. The most critical deadline is the thirty days you typically have to get through the closing or settlement process. Meeting these deadlines will require that both you and the buyer are motivated to get through the process. An agent can keep you on track. If you're selling your home on your own, an attorney or escrow agent can serve in the same role.

HANDLING MULTIPLE OFFERS

Multiple offers can be an embarrassment of riches or simply confusing. It depends on how you handle it. Most agents will try to pit buyers against each other, hoping to spark a bidding war. Have your agent tell the bidders that there is a deadline for submitting bids and all offers will be opened at the same time. This organizes the process and puts you in control. At a minimum, you'll be able to compare several offers and pick the one that best matches your needs. Remember, even if buyers offer the same price, their offers can be very different if, for example, one is planning to put 20 percent down to buy the home while another plans to use a nothing-down loan. As the seller, you are exposed to risk in every part of the deal. Your buyer could drop out because the financing doesn't come together, or maybe you can't come to terms on a settlement date. With multiple offers, you'll be able to rank potential buyers, using each as a backup.

NAVIGATING A WEAK MARKET

Instead of sitting back and collecting offers, you may have to give something to get buyers' interest. The first and most obvious action you can take is to reduce your selling price. You can also offer to pay part or all of your buyer's closing costs. Or you could opt to pay three months' worth of homeowner association dues. You can throw in appliances for buyers who appear to waffle, or agree to a repair or fix what won't set you back too much. The bottom line is that you may need to get creative to get your house sold.

If the market is really tough, you may want to offer seller financing. This is a strategy that becomes particularly popular when interest rates are high. The way this works is pretty straightforward: you collect a down payment from your buyer and require slightly higher payments than a conventional mortgage to compensate you for the extra risk you are taking. Making this move will mean more potential buyers will be eligible to buy your house. Just be careful to choose buyers who are capable of paying for the home, and don't overstretch yourself financially. If you're offering seller financing, you shouldn't be dependent on receiv-

ing the buyer's timely mortgage payment each month to make your own mortgage payment.

THE CLOSING

On the day of the closing, your buyer will likely do a final walk-through of the property to make sure that all repairs that were agreed to have been made and that it remains in the condition it was when they made their offer. If they aren't satisfied, they can put the final portion of their down payment for the home into an escrow fund until the changes they want are made.

Closing day, though, is typically a pressure cooker for the buyer. That's because the buyer will be writing the checks for the down payment and fees and taxes. Sellers attend the closing in some states, in others they may not be required to attend at all. If you do attend, the closing will take place at the office of an attorney, title company, or escrow company. At the closing, any existing loans or liens on the property will be paid; the deed will be transferred; and title insurance will be issued, ensuring a free and clear title. The seller receives the proceeds from their home one to two days after the closing.

THE TAX IMPACT

Tax benefits are a big part of why we consider buying a home in the first place. The deductibility of mortgage interest is a big allure for many tax payers. But the tax breaks don't stop when you sell your home. In fact, the home sales exclusion is a big part of the tax breaks benefiting homeowners.

The exclusion works like this: when you sell your home, your profits up to $250,000 for singles and $500,000 for couples can be excluded from capital gains taxes. For many homeowners, that means they can enjoy the proceeds of their home sale with no payment to Uncle Sam. The benefit is not without some limits. You'll have to have lived in your home for two of the last five years. Plus the home has to be your main residence.

Fortunately, there is a little wiggle room in the rules. If you have to move for a job or if you have a medical problem that requires you to

move, you may be eligible to claim a partial exclusion. For example, if you relocate for a new job (or a new business if you work for yourself), then you are entitled to a partial exclusion that is prorated to reflect the amount of time you spent in your home. The distance between your new job location and your former home must be at least fifty miles greater than the distance between your old job location and your former home. To receive a partial exclusion because of health requires that you move because you have to receive full-time care for an illness or an injury.

Also of interest to sellers is that, if you have to relocate because of your job, whether it's your first job or the same job, you may qualify for a moving deduction. This can add up if you've made a major cross-country move for a new job. You qualify if the move is at least fifty miles from where you presently live. Expenses you can deduct include your moving van rental, moving services, the cost of moving a car or pet, use of storage facilities, and any hotel room costs you incur during the move.

If you've lived in the home for a long period of time, you've probably enjoyed large capital gains. That means your profit may be more than the amount you are allowed to exclude from taxes. If you have been in your home a long time, though, no doubt you've spent a lot of money on improvements and maintenance. Uncle Sam allows you to add those improvements to the amount you paid for the home in the first place to determine your basis in the home. This is the amount you will subtract from your sales price to determine your profit. So, for example, if you paid $250,000 for your home fifteen years ago and invested another $120,000, then your basis is $370,000. Let's say you sold your home for $550,000. (Congratulations!) That means your profit is $180,000—all of which you can keep tax-free. If you hadn't made (and kept receipts for) the improvements, you would have faced a tax bill for the $50,000 over the $250,000 exclusion (if you are single).

Typical capital improvements that count include:

1. Kitchen upgrade

2. Replacing siding

3. Finishing your basement

4. Adding a bath

5. New roof

Selling your home is a nerve-racking experience that requires both patience and planning. To the degree that you can stop thinking about your house as a home and impartially evaluate its strengths and weaknesses, you'll be far more successful in selling. At this point, your house is an investment that you are cashing in on. For that reason, you'll want to pay close attention to the details, monitoring the competition and keeping your home spotless as it is being shown. Evaluate all offers quickly and thoroughly; the goal is to make the whole process move along as quickly as possible. Your success at selling this home will be a critical part of your overall wealth.

24

The Conclusion

WHEN I WAS GROWING UP, THE FOLKS DOWN THE STREET IN OUR suburban Ohio neighborhood had a house almost exactly like the one in which my family was living, a three-bedroom, two-bath ranch on a half-acre lot. They were constant upgraders—they painted, replaced doors, updated their kitchen, and worked for hours on their landscaping. The patriarch of the family divorced and remarried, but his dedication to the house never wavered. As a result, his home came to be thought of as the best in the neighborhood. It was certainly the best cared for. We all asked the couple for landscaping tips and vied to hire their contractors. Ultimately, when they sold and moved to South Carolina to retire, the house commanded a fat premium. Their $30,000 house had morphed into a $187,000 asset. I don't know that the couple ever thought of the improvements as an investment in their retirement, but it sure worked out that way.

The two had been responsible caretakers of the property, but they also had nearly 30 years of appreciation to thank for such a handsome re-turn. Today, most of us can't count on decades of appreciation to boost

our return, since we tend to move more often. We have to be smarter and more deliberate in all our choices, whether we are buying, managing, upgrading, or selling. Thinking of your home as an investment isn't a new idea, but it's not one most of us are practiced at doing well. And it doesn't require that you spend more than you might otherwise. For example, intelligent management of your property can save you from being forced to make big expenditures (such as fixing the small bathroom leak that otherwise would bloom into a mold disaster). Whenever you're making a change, whether it's buying a can of paint or refinancing your mortgage, in the back of your mind you need to be constantly asking yourself this: Will this add to the value of my home or boost my equity? Now, you've probably heard the critics of home ownership, who say that a home isn't an investment, it's just a place to live. True enough—a home is a shelter for your family. But anything that commands a minimum of a third of your household budget each and every month should also provide a return—and a solid one at that.

I count myself among those who will likely stay ten years or less in my current house, a Tudor long on charm and repair bills. In my mind, our house has a balance sheet. On one side are the investments that I know will help us in the long run—we'll upgrade our kitchen and improve the entry to the house to make it more attractive. On the other side are the liabilities—the mortgage and the constant repair bills. My bottom line is my equity—that's simply the down payment plus the value of upgrades plus any payments toward principal. When you move on, whether it's five, ten, or thirty years down the road, it's the equity that you will take with you. This is the number you should try to nurture and grow, so that after owning one home or multiple homes, you'll have a tidy nest egg.

To get the best return from your house—one that can help fund your retirement or put the kids through college—you have to get step number one right: buying. The typical misstep is overbuying—buying a home to impress parents or coworkers rather than finding the right purchase at the right price. Choose a home in a good location that is poised for solid appreciation. The quickest way to get a handle on whether a

neighborhood is a good investment is to check out the quality of the local schools.

As you narrow your focus, take particular care inspecting each candidate for potential problems. The house you choose shouldn't be the most expensive on the block or the most unusual. Spend time finding and vetting your home inspector; the single most important professional in the home-buying process is the one we often spend the least amount of time checking out. Most of us simply hire the expert our real estate agent recommends. But that is a big mistake. If there is one thing that homeowners complain to me about most during the home-buying process, it's that they didn't take the inspection seriously enough. The result? Unexpected maintenance bills for everything from repairs on slate roofs their agent said would last eighty years to leaky basements that ruin flooring as well as sentimental items stashed there.

Another step in the home-buying process that shouldn't be rushed is choosing the right mortgage loan. It used to be that getting a mortgage was a true no-brainer—your options were limited to a thirty-year fixed-rate loan. Now, though, there are literally hundreds of choices. Worse, mortgage brokers get paid bonuses to sell you the most complicated of loans. Unless you are independently wealthy or get paid in a lump sum once a year, you're best off choosing a plain vanilla product—either a thirty-year fixed-rate loan or an adjustable-rate loan in which the rate is fixed for an initial period of three to fifteen years and then resets periodically after that. An adjustable-rate loan is a decent option for people who know that they absolutely, positively will move in a specific number of years. If your choice is for the long haul, opt for the thirty-year. Avoid bells and whistles. While it may sound enticing to have the option of paying just the interest on your loan, it makes it difficult, if not impossible, to build equity.

When it comes time to close on your new home, keep your eye on the bottom line. This is when every professional in the process seems to tack on fees. A friend of mine said her real estate attorney told her it was customary to tip the title agent a hundred bucks at closing. Facing thousands in closing costs, my friend was frustrated but paid anyway, because

she was afraid the title agent would hold up the closing. Before sitting down at the closing table, you should know all the fees you'll be paying. Ask your lender for a HUD-1 form to get the details, and don't be afraid to ask questions. You aren't powerless in this situation. All the pros stand to make a tidy sum if your deal goes through. And no one will want to hold up the closing because you refuse to pay a kickback to the title agent.

The last thing you'll want to think about as you move into your home is the maintenance projects awaiting you. This is more difficult than it sounds because you'll be new to the house and won't yet have developed the sixth sense homeowners possess about their abode. One new homeowner told me how alarmed he was by the loud clanging coming from his heating system. The steam pipes banged so loudly they would wake him up at night. Only after he hired an expert in steam heat systems did he finally become comfortable with the noise. Understanding your home's systems is critical to maintaining it. Develop a seasonal checklist of maintenance projects, like that in Chapter 15. Paying attention to the little issues, such as keeping the gutters clear, can save you from a host of problems. As a new homeowner or a new-to-the-neighborhood homeowner, you'll need to develop a Rolodex of people to call when the unexpected happens. "Going green" is all the rage right now, and while it's all well and good to invest in paints with low volatile compounds, it's even better to make sure your home is energy efficient. Simple upgrades such as installing insulation or making sure that trees shade large windows pay for themselves quickly.

It's hard not to be impressed with the expensive renovation ideas you see on cable television and in glossy magazines. Designers push beautiful, but pricey, professional-grade appliances, sleek granite counters, and elaborate backsplashes. And that's just the kitchen. But I see all too many houses in which owners have opted for beautiful renovations but ignored maintenance. Like the Bedford, New York, farmhouse in which the owners had added a master suite complete with a high-end Jacuzzi but failed to keep the gutters clear enough to prevent the house's wooden clapboards from rotting. Buyers catch on when the improvements are all superficial and the home itself isn't well maintained.

When you do decide to make a major upgrade, you'll want to do more than just determine what's hot this year. Some kitchen and bath designs are like the latest in runway fashion—what you see featured this season will change by the next. You'll want to be sure to pick designs and features that will have serious long-term appeal. What's more, you'll want to scale your improvements to your neighborhood. Is your neighborhood a Wolf stove kind of place, or would Energy Star appliances with good brands be more in line with what buyers to the area could afford? Overimproving is an equity crusher. Not only do you spend too much for the upgrade, but the resulting purchase price you feel you are owed may be impossible to achieve, frustrating likely buyers.

It's all too easy to go with the path of least resistance when it comes to hiring a contractor to do your upgrades. For most people, a recommendation from a friend is reason enough to hire a professional. But you'll want to actually see their work and meet with them directly to see if you are compatible. Large-scale renovations are like a marriage—you end up spending enormous amounts of time together, much of it spent talking about money. One North Carolina couple hired a contractor who lived in their neighborhood to do their bathroom renovation. While they got along with the neighbor fine over backyard barbecues, their relationship was more contentious when it came to renovation. Costs spiraled out of control. Workmen overturned sodas on the wood floor in the entryway and left them there. Dust flew into rooms with doors left open. Ultimately, the couple realized that they should have talked to clients of the contractor before hiring him.

The final step in the cycle of home ownership is selling—and few things are more gut-wrenching. You'll have the pressure of making sure your home is in tip-top condition every day and strangers will traipse through your home, plus you may have the added anxiety of finding and closing on a new home at the same time. Fortunately, if you've followed the steps of *Home Rich,* you should be in good shape for a sale. You'll already have staged the house, making sure that the interior is neat and attractive and that the interior design is neutral and welcoming. Your lawn will be groomed and your home framed by attractive trees and shrubs.

Having done all this work, you may feel overly confident. Remember, you're best off making sure your price is in line with comparable prices achieved by homeowners with similar properties in your neighborhood. Don't base your asking price on what you need to get out of the house to satisfy the mortgage, the contractor's bill, or overinflated ideas of what your profit should be.

Becoming home rich requires plenty of planning and thinking ahead, but it's all within your grasp. Using a calculator, some hard work, and common sense, you can achieve a smart investment—one that grows over time as you and your family enjoy your property. In the end, you can have both a house you love and one that provides for the ones you love.

Acknowledgments

Home Rich was a labor of both love and passion, and would not have been possible without the talented team of producers, writers, and editors that I work with every day at CNN. My special thanks goes to Jennifer Haley, whose hard work yields insights into the field of personal finance that I am constantly amazed by.

My great thanks goes to the talented and hard working team at CNN's *Open House,* especially Mike Kane, whose long hours are legendary, and William Nunez, whose vision is critical. Kristina Guiliano, Alex Nelson, Sara Lane, Jennifer Icklan, and Ben Tinker have my appreciation and admiration, as does Walter Imparato, who continually produces compelling images to illustrate our stories.

Editors are critical, and mine at Random House is both talented and patient. Great thanks to Jane von Mehren for her steady hand at the wheel. Great thanks, too, to my team of writers who worked with me on *Home Rich,* including, first and foremost, Amy Gunderson. Great thanks to Sarah Breckenridge and Carol Dannhauser for their insights and contributions. A special thank you as well to those whose input helped re-

fine my thinking about real estate, especially Nancy Smith, Greg
McBride, and Brad Inman. I owe Ann P. Stokes a debt of gratitude for
her beautiful landscape drawings.

Working at CNN has been a rewarding experience. My thanks to
CNN President Jonathan Klein for his leadership and for creating an at-
mosphere that promotes creative thinking and fresh ideas. Thanks, too, to
Ken Jautz, executive vice president for CNN, who brought me into the
family five years ago.

Index

About the Author

GERRI WILLIS is the anchor of CNN's weekend business program *Open House,* which provides how-to essentials on all things real estate. She is also the personal finance editor for CNN Business News and offers viewers worldwide financial advice in her daily "Five Tips" segment. Prior to joining CNN, she was the senior financial correspondent for *SmartMoney* magazine and a 1992 Columbia University Knight–Bagehot fellow. She is also the author of *The SmartMoney Guide to Real Estate Investing.* She lives in Westchester County, New York, with her husband.

About the Type

This book was set in Bembo, a typeface based on an old-style Roman face that was used for Cardinal Bembo's tract *De Aetna* in 1495. Bembo was cut by Francisco Griffo in the early sixteenth century. The Lanston Monotype Company of Philadelphia brought the well-proportioned letterforms of Bembo to the United States in the 1930s.

ALSO BY GERRI WILLIS

The SmartMoney Guide to Real Estate Investing